Things Could've Been a Lot Worse

The Experiences of a German American Bellybutton Jew of Berlin Origins

Hadassa Word Press

Impressum / Imprint

Bibliografische Information der Deutschen Nationalbibliothek: Die Deutsche Nationalbibliothek verzeichnet diese Publikation in der Deutschen Nationalbibliografie; detaillierte bibliografische Daten sind im Internet über http://dnb.d-nb.de abrufbar.

Alle in diesem Buch genannten Marken und Produktnamen unterliegen warenzeichen-, marken- oder patentrechtlichem Schutz bzw. sind Warenzeichen oder eingetragene Warenzeichen der jeweiligen Inhaber. Die Wiedergabe von Marken, Produktnamen, Gebrauchsnamen, Handelsnamen, Warenbezeichnungen u.s.w. in diesem Werk berechtigt auch ohne besondere Kennzeichnung nicht zu der Annahme, dass solche Namen im Sinne der Warenzeichen- und Markenschutzgesetzgebung als frei zu betrachten wären und daher von jedermann benutzt werden dürften.

Bibliographic information published by the Deutsche Nationalbibliothek: The Deutsche Nationalbibliothek lists this publication in the Deutsche Nationalbibliografie; detailed bibliographic data are available in the Internet at http://dnb.d-nb.de.

Any brand names and product names mentioned in this book are subject to trademark, brand or patent protection and are trademarks or registered trademarks of their respective holders. The use of brand names, product names, common names, trade names, product descriptions etc. even without a particular marking in this work is in no way to be construed to mean that such names may be regarded as unrestricted in respect of trademark and brand protection legislation and could thus be used by anyone.

Coverbild / Cover image: www.ingimage.com

Verlag / Publisher:
Hadassa Word Press
ist ein Imprint der / is a trademark of
OmniScriptum GmbH & Co. KG
Bahnhofstraße 28, 66111 Saarbrücken, Deutschland / Germany
Email: info@omniscriptum.com

Herstellung: siehe letzte Seite /
Printed at: see last page
ISBN: 978-3-639-79481-6

Gerd K. Schneider

Things Could've Been a Lot Worse

Gerd K. Schneider

Things Could've Been a Lot Worse

*The Experiences of a German-American
Bellybutton Jew of Berlin Origins*

Translated from the German by
Dennis McCort

Dedicated to my mother,
my wife,
and all those who were guides along the way
in my anything-but-everyday life

CONTENTS

Translator's Note..5

Foreword: *In the Labyrinth of My Memory* 7

Part I. *My Life in Berlin*

1. The Outsider: 1931 to 1940 13
2. From School Cone to *Jungvolk*..24
3. The Horst Wessel *Gymnasium*, the Adolf Hitler School,
   and the Warthe District 30
4. Life and Destruction: The time till 1945 36
   It's War, but Life Goes On..36
   Let It Be, This Too Will Soon Pass....................................45
   April 1945: People in the Hotel 56
   The Last Days of the Third Reich 62

5. The Period from 1945 to 1951 70
   Every Beginning Is Hard — Only Never Give Up 70
   The First Turning Point: Film, Theater and Starting School 75
   Cold, Hunger, Rubble and Refugees....................................79
   Foraging Trips for Two 82
   The Black Market..87
   The Blockade, Currency Reform and Traveling
   in a Divided Germany 89
   Felicitas, Homer, Karl May and the Era of
   Mass Demonstrations 94
   The *Abitur* Exam: Analytical Geometry, Thermodynamics
   and the Ladle 101
   An Intermezzo: Relief Work 1950-51..................................107

6. Life in the Hotel am Zoo 1951-1954 111
   My Training as Ganymede...111
   Human — All Too Human..116
   Homo sum; humani nil a me alienum esse puto
   What Qualities Must a Good Waiter Have?..........................124
   Finishing Touches 127
   Dear Homeland, Adieu! 129

3

Part II. *My Life in the New World*

1. My Experiences in Canada: 1954-1962 133
   Crossing and Arrival in the New World 133
   Waiter in the New World 135
   Go North, Young Man, Go North! 143
   Legal and Illegal, Moral and Immoral
   in Edmonton, Alberta 145
   My Life Up North: Homer, Card Games and Wild Beasts 155
   My Life on Wheels and My Job
   in a Vancouver Steakhouse 167
   Flirting with Psychology 173
   A Vacation Paradise on the Gulf Islands
   and Flying Spaghetti 185

2. My Life in the United States 188
   Sex and Romantic Irony 188
   Summer Schools, Eichendorff's *Good-for-nothing*,
   and my Marriage 193
   The Vietnam War and the Students 199
   Marriage, Burial, and the Nietzsche-Symposium 200
   Magic Mountain Atmosphere in the German School
   at Middlebury College 205
   The Ambassadors' Meeting 220

On Interior Biography
   No Man Is an Island 227
   The Importance of Engagement 228
   Rejection of Stereotypes and Dogmatism 229
   Double Vision 233
   The Identity Question 233

Instead of an *Afterword* 235

Notes 238

Translator's Note

For me there are now two Gerd Schneiders: the one I've known for forty years as friend and colleague, a man with a flourishing career and family, living "the good life" of an academic and intellectual in a university town in upstate New York; and the one who came of age, just barely, through decades of war, brutal ostracism and grinding poverty. Though I'd had hints and glints of this latter Gerd through all the years of our association in innumerable casual conversations, it took the process of this translation to bring the child and younger man to vivid, enthralling life for me. And I cannot express how grateful I am to him for this rarest of experiences, that of having one's comfortable, time-tested sense of a person suddenly deepen into a rich reality fusing both past and present into something mysterious, something beyond the constraints of knowledge acquired over time. Gerd suggests something of this experience himself in his conclusion to this book where he writes of "das doppelte Sehen" or "double vision," a moment wherein early memory and current scene are suddenly superimposed on each other, catalyzed by some event that often seems inconsequential in and of itself.

Gerd Schneider could certainly have translated his own autobiography, as he has native fluency in English and has published his scholarship in both languages, favoring neither (or rather, *both*). That he has instead chosen me to render his most personal story for him has made me feel humble and privileged at once, as if I were in the truest sense entrusted with his life, and hence with the strongest obligation to "get it right." I hope to have come at least close to doing so. Certainly I've been helped enormously by Gerd's own watchful editorial eye, particularly with regard to the German lexicon of World War II weaponry. He scrutinized what I wrote as I wrote it and repeatedly kept me from translational errors of fact, style and tone. How often does the translator of an autobiography enjoy the advantages of having personally known his subject for most of his life and of having that subject almost literally by his side during the entire process?

Finally, I would mention here two matters of strategic import for this translation. First, there are one or two scenes in the narrative, primarily the one unfolding in the neighborhood bakery in Part I, in which I faced the problem of rendering the coarse and earthy big-city dialect of Berlin German. New Yorkese American struck me as an almost ideal parallel, especially since this is the English I grew up speaking and still occasionally revert to when very tired. Its "dem's," "dese's" and dose's" beautifully mirror the low-dialectal "aba's," "ooch's" and "nich's" of standard *Berlinerisch*. The second matter concerns editorial changes in the translation from Gerd's original text published by Praesens. These are very few and of minor importance, a sentence dropped here and there, and here and there one added, in each case for the English reader's convenience. A bi-lingual reader will have no trouble reading both in parallel. This edition also includes some ten additional photographs.

Dennis Mccort

* * *

Once in the late 1920's Groucho Marx, the famous American comedian, showed up at a golf club in New York City. It was very hot and he wanted to cool off in the swimming pool. He was told that this was not permitted to Jews. Whereupon Groucho replied, "I'm married to a gentile, and my son is with me. Since he's only a half-Jew, he should at least be allowed to go into the water up to his belly button." I too am just such a bellybutton Jew, and this is my story. I am one of the roughly 71,000 half-Jews who, according to a census of May 17, 1939, were then living in the German Reich.

I said to my soul, Be still, and watch the small trickling beginnings ease towards flood. Let the story declare itself, and the characters and events take me down among them and draw the words out of me. I have tried to possess my soul in patience, I have gathered all the hungers of my past in readiness, to spell out all the syllables of my life. In the morning watch I shall wait, and the quick, brown, wordy fox will come out of his hole, sniff the air, and begin his narration. It is only natural. Sooner or later, if I watch, it is bound to happen. Then I shall fill my book with profitable wonders. [1]

* * *

Foreword

In the Labyrinth of My Memory

When you write about yourself, many questions come to mind. For example, how do you judge whether your life is sufficiently interesting to others to make it worthwhile writing down? Then too, what can you remember and how true are the events you report? Is the narrative in accord with reality? A book must also have continuity, all the individual parts coordinated with one another, and that in turn raises the question as to the material to be included in the text out of aesthetic considerations and necessities and, by the same token, the material to be left out. In the same vein you ask who it is you're really writing for, since someone who has it in mind to publish his experiences writes quite differently than someone who merely intends to share them with his family.

The question of a given book's readership had already been put by Persius Flaccus in the first century of the Christian era — and in good Latin: "Quis leget haec?" I believe that my life might just have something to say to others, for it has not unfolded in an historical or political vacuum. I was born in the year 1931 in the waning days of the Weimar Republic. I spent my first years in the period of National Socialism, and yet for me the era of the last empire ran parallel to this, for my (step)father, born in 1866, told me a great deal about his life. Then came the Second World War and, at its conclusion, total collapse. There followed the period of reconstruction which I was able to observe from two divergent political sides at once, since I lived in the French sector of Berlin under the control of the four victorious powers, yet went to school until 1950 in the Russian-dominated east sector.

In my youth I came into contact with many political convictions, not only in the abstract but in the concrete sense as well. My progenitor was a Jew, but not my mother, which marked me as a half-Jew, or, in the classification of the later Nuremberg Laws, a first-degree *Mischling*. Moreover, I grew up in the cosmopolitan city of Berlin, and in the north end of the city to boot, in a so-called *Kiez*² in which lower-class workers and petty clerks lived together peacefully, or maybe not so peacefully. My experiences reflect the views and political attitudes of the residents of that time. In that sense the first part of the book at hand is also a *Kiez* story in which much is related that would've turned out quite differently for someone in my situation living in another part of Berlin, for I believe that a first-degree *Mischling* living in the "finer districts" of Dahlem or Zehlendorf would doubtless have been treated differently and regarded more favorably than I was.

The question whether one can recollect the details of decades past is a good deal harder to answer. Anyone who writes about his own life must endeavor to summon up both the good and the bad, for, as Erich Kästner has expressed it in his poem, "In Memoriam Memoriae,"

> *Memory is a power mysterious,*
> *A force that changes one to the quick.*
> *If you forget what was fine you grow bilious.*
> *If you forget what was bad you grow thick.*[3]

Forgetting" is, of course, a *vis activa,* as Freud has emphasized, a defense mechanism that consigns much to the underworld lest life above be jeopardized. Stefan Zweig gives a masterful description of the struggle built into the process of remembering in his novella, "Bookmendel," where he says that memory ships experience down into the darkness of the underworld and refuses to bring it back up without force. However, one need only conjure up a few bits and pieces of memory "and at once the forgotten material flashes up and out of the darkly streaming surface anew, brimming with quivering life, like a fish on the line."[4] You climb down into the labyrinth of the past, and in coming to grips with your own experiences you sometimes confront gaps, such that you find yourself tempted to invent memory in order to bridge those gaps. This is especially the case when you're reporting on early childhood. Here you must rely on second-hand reports to keep yourself objective. This is certainly true in my own case, and there is material here that I have reproduced from the perspective of my mother, of whose experiences I learned from conversations that I recorded, in large part, on tape. Memory begins to crystallize for me as of my fifth year, so that I can consciously reach back about that far to my own experiences. Some of these are not of the kind that would fall into the category of "the sunny past," but they are perhaps all the more accessible for that, for it is precisely the disruptive experiences one can more easily recall than those in a so-called normal life.

There is, among my aids to memory, also a diary that has been of use, one that I began soon after my arrival in Canada. For my life in the States there was, moreover, the very helpful report that I requested from

Washington under the Freedom of Information Act. This eighty-one page report contains copies of every official document concerning me since my arrival in the States, among them even precise information as to my residences and workplaces. One reason for such a thick dossier was that I was suspected of having illegally brought a car from Canada into the USA. The name of the suspected perpetrator, later arrested, was Gustav Schneider, in short form "G. Schneider." Another reason for the documentation may be that materials on the life of many immigrants were collected by the government, and this without the knowledge of the persons concerned.

The journey recorded here is, in its temporal aspect, easy to describe since one can proceed chronologically, or horizontally, as it were. More problematic is the vertical approach required when you go into yourself and probe your own interior life. It is astonishing how much lies within us, and I agree here with Novalis when he writes that we all dream of journeys through the cosmos, entirely forgetting that the universe with all its stars and galaxies also lies within us. One might add here: the "black holes" too, which have hermetically sealed their depths and throw off nothing to the outer world, lie within. These experiences and events remain locked in the mind's deepest dungeons, perhaps for existential reasons, for if they were to rise to consciousness *de profundis* uncensored, one would be hard-pressed indeed even to live with, much less deal with them. How much truth can a man bear? Sten Nadolny makes this point when he writes, "Memory is capable of forgetting what tortures it." But then he continues, to the effect that there are certain chimaeras "that punch holes in memory and, along with it, when things go wrong, ultimately overcome the whole person, *imagines necantes.*" [5] These chimaeras lie beyond memory, rising to the surface only occasionally as nightmares when consciousness sleeps.

In addition to this inner, unconscious truth, which bars all access to itself, there is the problem of conscious or recoverable truth. Since an autobiography is not only about yourself but also about people with whom you've come into contact and with whom you've shared common experiences, you cannot stray far from these facts. Yet, in this area you must decide how much not to mention, either because it might harm others or because you don't cut a particularly good figure yourself. How much is diminished, edited or euphemized by your own super-ego so that you can continue to look in the mirror and tell yourself, "There I am, and I'm not nearly so bad as I or others sometimes believe." Nietzsche once expressed this fissure in man in a nutshell: "'I did it,' says my memory. 'I couldn't have done it'-says my pride, rock-like in its implacability. In the end, it is memory that yields."[6] One must, in confronting the earlier ego, guard against embellishing oneself, and thus engaging in the kind of inner duplicity of which Danton accuses his antagonist Robespierre: "Conscience is a mirror before which an ape tortures itself; each of us primps as best he can and each of us in his own way has his fun in doing so" (I, 6). Remembering can be is problematic, as Lukas B. Suter attests:

> *If it's so that true life only presses memory into the light of day when I am not so much what I do or feel in the moment but rather much more what I later remember of it, the question arises, who am I when memory is deceiving me — myself? Another? Also, who am I when I allow myself to be seduced into intentionally falsifying my own memories; who am I when I must convict myself of suppressing memory; and finally, who am I when I decorate my memories with alien feathers?*[7]

There are no simple answers to such questions. In any given moment of action we consist of memories that determine our behavior, and if these somehow get falsified, then our ego is likewise falsified, and we end up changing our "defective" past into a better one, into a celebration of self.[8] And then we live with this new showcase-ego.[9]

Certainly, like the German philosopher Arthur Schopenhauer, you can better judge your earlier life from a temporal distance to see what you did right and what wrong. You live, better yet: experience, then journey backwards in order to evaluate a given person or issue. Writing too is meaningful in this way, or at least it can be. You carry on a kind of hermeneutics-for-life to figure out whether the individual parts of experience fit together into a relatively harmonious whole, or not. Or, put another way, whether life had a sense or was senseless.

Finally, one writes out of a feeling of solidarity with the generation to come after us. Slowly my life is now ebbing towards its end, and more and more I've come to feel myself a kindred spirit to Kleist's Prince of Homburg, who, upon spying his own excavated grave, is moved to reflect on his end: "The dervish says that life is but a journey, / And so it is, a short one, of two spans/ Atop the earth and then two underneath. / I'd like to settle down about halfway!" (IV, 3). And I am already well past the halfway mark of my own span.

The book at hand is divided into two major sections: my life in Berlin and my life in the New World. In the first part I take up the period from 1931 to 1954, the year of my emigration to Canada. The second part is devoted to my experiences in the New World, first those in Canada, then in the United States. The book closes with a brief section on my inner biography. The subdivisions are intended to make it easier for the reader to follow me on my paths and their detours.

Here I would also like to thank all those who have helped me along my way. First and foremost I must mention my mother, and not only for biological reasons, as will later become evident:

My mother: Ella Marie Auguste Schneider, nee Thieß, 1894-1973
Occupation: housewife

This book bears the following pronouncement of hers as its title:

"My boy, the whole business was, for long stretches, difficult and terrible. For my own part, I would not care to go through it again. Still — things could've been a lot worse."

In addition, there are many others who deserve mention. I agree with Goethe who has the princess say in *Tasso:* "And what one is one owes to others" (I, 1). In the same vein the poet also says in his *Wilhelm Meister* that all our experiences leave behind traces, yet contribute imperceptibly to our inner formation. That goes as well for the interpolation of the many literary quotations and references in the present autobiography, for I have had the great good fortune of studying with teachers who imparted literature to me and my fellow students as *itself* a mode of experience. This contributed, not only to my education, but to a better understanding of self as well. My hope in recording my life is that it will find favor with some readers, in the spirit of Goethe's words, "Though you page by page may snicker, / Still you're drawn in by the whole."[10]

Part I

My Life in Berlin

1. The Outsider: 1931 - 1940

As my mother would later tell me, it all began more or less normally. She reported to me the remarks of the gynecologist who was treating her: "Should we have him circumcised or not? The father is a Jew, it says so right here: legal father Leopold Ritter, occupation merchant, of the Mosaic confession, residing at Berlin No. 65, Müllerstraße 1a." My obstetrician waited a moment for an answer, which my mother was slow to give, until she finally said to him in a firm voice: "I don't think so. You see, this little one has been born out of wedlock. His father is married and has a furniture business — actually several. He never showed any concern for me, even though he knew I was pregnant. I cleaned house for him, and once he gave me a few glasses of wine, which I didn't handle well since I'd never drunk anything like that before. And then he slept with me. Apart from that, he's never had anything at all to do with my boy. The little one belongs to me, he is mine alone, and I am not a Jew." And so the procedure was waived in my case, to my good fortune, since I was thereby spared much unpleasantness to come. The doctor looked probingly at my mother; it wasn't clear whether he agreed with her. But then he looked down at me, with hair down to my shoulders, and said with a grin, "Well, then I wish you much luck on this earth. He looks quite passable; actually, all he needs is the doctoral cap and gown and you've got yourself a professor." I only wish I could tell him now how prophetic his words were.

As for the hoped-for "luck on this earth," things did not look very rosy. I could not have said with old master Goethe, "As on the day that gave you to the cosmos, / The sun shown bright in greeting to the planets." In the Berlin tenement on Müllerstraße which my mother moved into with me after my birth on April 1, 1931, it was only the upper stories that enjoyed the sun, and, having little money, my mother had to take the cheapest lodgings on the ground floor. Not a ray of sunlight found its way into this apartment. Just outside the single small window which looked onto the courtyard, there were six trash cans which were always full since the tenement complex consisted of a central building and two side wings, all so tightly constructed together in typical turn-of-the-century style that there was plenty of shade and little light. There were no playgrounds about, at least not for the children who grew up in this proletarian ghetto, but plenty for the many rats that could be seen running every which way even during the day. They were inured even to the loud shrieking of the children, a shrieking apparently imitated by their parents especially on Friday when the husband was expected to bring home his full wages, but did so only rarely. The guilty party here was the many corner taverns that infested our neighborhood like weeds and that were full to bursting especially on payday. More often than not, the women would show up around midnight and grab their men by the ear, more dragging than walking them home. The verbal musical accompaniment was anything but harmonious, and the children were eager music students; some could even reproduce the staccato of the profanity word for word. The rats had no language, but, as I later became convinced, if they'd had one, it would've been precisely the one they got to hear every weekend.

Our existence — and by that I mean my own and that of my mother — was nowhere near as grand as that of the rats, since, in contrast to these gnawing vermin, we only rarely had garbage. The little room, a kind of kitchenette, had a small stove and a shelf, but rarely was anything edible to be seen on either. Had it not been for a few sympathetic souls in the house and in the Salvation Army, this story would already be at an end. My mother was very thankful to the socially activist army of God and went around with them singing songs on the street corners of the working-class neighborhoods, songs that extolled the glories of the heavenly life, in contrast to the shabby reality of life on earth. Beyond this, they provided our only meal. She took me along, at first on her arm, and when I grew too heavy for her, one of the brothers would take his kettledrum out of its little carriage and stick me in it. And so I went along, and it's highly likely that I also sang along, though maybe not always to the same beat and in the same key as the soldiers and soldierettes of God. My mother sang with zeal; she had a beautiful voice and hoped, as did all the other brothers and sisters, to soften the hearts of repentant sinners through the power of song and lead them back to the right path, which for them led to church. Almost all the street-corner sermons began with the sentence, "Are we not all His creatures; are we not fellow human beings, and

14

does that not mean that we must live together with our fellows and not against our fellows?" He might just as well have said that we're all sitting in the same boat, but that, while this boat had a solid floor for some, for others it was full of holes, with water seeping in through them.

And water was also the only way out of her situation my mother could see, what with no money for the rent and little for groceries. And so one day she again took me on her arm, but this time not in order to march with the Salvation Army; rather she went straight to the Weidendamm Bridge, which spanned the Spree not too far from our paltry dwelling. However, her plan, to put an end, with a leap into the water, to her life and mine (mine not even having properly begun yet), was foiled. This, through the intervention of an older man who, barely five foot tall, was small of stature but big of heart. Our rescuer, a certain Mr. Friedrich Schneider, a widowed, retired pipeline foreman for the Berlin gasworks, born in 1866, was already 65 years old at that time. He was strong enough to hold my mother back, who already had one foot over the railing, and to set her back down on *terra firma* with both feet. He also gave her a not quite clean handkerchief which she used to wipe away her tears and, right afterward, blow her nose. My mother was very practical, yet another virtue I was able to verify later, and thanks to her "can-do" spirit I was able to overcome various potentially dangerous situations. I do believe this quality of my mother's promptly moved my and her lifesaver to propose marriage to her. And so the two of them were lawfully wed in the very same year.

The entry in the *Stammbuch*[11] reads as follows: "Certificate of Marriage: matrimony between Friedrich Karl Schneider, retiree, from Berlin, born April 3, 1866, in Niewitz, district of Luckau, and Ella Marie Auguste Thieß, born May 1, 1894, in Gottschimmerbruch, district of Friedeberg-Neumark." The date of the marriage was September 3, 1931. The album contained a three-page preface clearly anticipating the coming era with its penchant for ancestral research. To wit, this significant paragraph: "For your descendants you should also foster and cultivate the in no way insignificant field of family history! We are, to be sure, not only the children of our parents; we are the offspring of an entire series of generations." This would also explain, so the text continues, "why on occasion physical or mental aptitudes appear in family members that cannot be hereditarily traced back to the parents." We also influence our descendents, which entails an ethical obligation to be models for our progeny "because we are responsible with our lives to the generations that come after — far beyond the third and fourth links. For we can live 'upwards' for all of our distant progeny and become a blessing to them; but we can also live 'downwards' and be anything but a blessing to them." I don't know whether I lived upwards or downwards in those days since I never met my forebears and my knowledge of them is scanty, to say the least. The little I do know is based primarily on the tales of my mother and some acquaintances. What mattered later on was not the direction in which you lived but, quite simply, whether you lived at all.

Why didn't my mother sue my biological father and demand alimony, which would doubtless have provided her with the necessary means of subsistence? To answer this question we must consider the historical conditions prevailing then. The year was 1931 and the Nazis were already hard at work disseminating their patriotic slogans to the masses, particularly in our quarter which showed a concentration of Communists and Socialists. People were holding mass meetings, especially in the Pharus Halls at Müllerstraße 142, these "Nordic Taj Mahals" being the preferred venue of the SPD (*Sozial-Demokratische Partei Deutschlands*) in Red Wedding. These halls were well known. They had got into the political press in 1927 when Goebbels used the Brown Shirts in an effort to quash an SPD meeting and later mined the ensuing brawl for propaganda. My biological father, whom I had never personally met, owned several furniture stores, one of which was managed by a silent partner, who might well have been characterized as silent towards my father, but who must've been downright chatty towards the authorities at the time. To these he reported that my father, who had recognized the brown plague for what it was well beforehand, had transferred several large sums of money to foreign banks, acts that constituted offences against the state according to the foreign exchange laws of the day. My father was charged, found guilty and, in short order, delivered to Tegel penitentiary where he was to serve a lengthy sentence.

All of this took place before and just after my birth. Although my mother learned of my biological father's arrest, in her dire circumstances she did not let herself be deterred from suing him for alimony payments immediately after my birth. Since she had no money for a lawyer, her case was handled pro bono. The judgment fell in my mother's favor, and the venerable document handed down to her was checkered with over twenty official stamps so that there could be no doubt that the judicial authorities had announced and sealed their judgment. This document is the only evidence my mother ever received regarding the personal circumstances of the man who sired me. Consequently, the only means I had of getting to know my father lay in the contemporary bureaucratese. Through this official writ, my sire, the merchant Leopold Ritter, of the Mosaic confession, residing at Müllerstraße 1a, was sentenced to make quarterly payments to the plaintiff of 120 Deutschmarks from 1 April 1931 to 31 October, and in addition, from 1 November 1931 till the completion of his 16th year to provide a quarterly annuity of 105 imperial marks. The catch in all this was that he couldn't pay, since he was sitting behind bars. But his whereabouts later on remain uncertain. He was brought to Theresienstadt some years thereafter and subsequent requests for information proved fruitless. One response that I later received to my inquiry stated quite laconically, "Deportation to Theresienstadt 1942. Status 'missing,' i.e., there are no reliable data concerning his death." So much for my paternal forebears.

On my mother's side the genealogical research was simpler since I had in her a reliable source of testimony. And so I learned that my mother lost *her* mother in childbirth, that my grandfather van Thieß, who was of Dutch extraction, had married again, as was customary in those days in rural areas, and that her stepmother did full justice to the initial component of her title. She kept her boot on my mother's neck and beat her with a cat-o'-nine-tails[12] festooned with sharp nettles. She made her do all the extra housework, meanwhile bestowing all the love of which she was capable, just as in the fairy tale, upon her two daughters, whose father was just as much the father of my mother. Until her fourteenth year my mother went to something that passed for a grade school where she was taught only the barest fundamentals of reading and writing. It was a school that gave its teachers the authority to use corporal punishment, an authority of which they made liberal use indeed, as my mother told the tale. Once my mother completed her compulsory education, she ran away from home.

That was in the year 1908, and the city that lured so many runaways, male and female, was Berlin. The imperial capital offered work, especially in the northern part of the city where most of the workers lived. She found immediate employment as a cleaning lady, which she had learned to be from her rural upbringing. After that she took a poorly paid job at Osram, where she had to pack light bulbs in cartons, thereafter at the AEG where, again, she cleaned the workplaces and offices at the end of the work shift. Subsequently, she was employed by the post office as a letter sorter, and once a week she worked as a cleaning woman. Even though the job at the post office occasionally required night work, she could do it with peace of mind since my foster father, who was retired, could take care of me.

And that he had to, for it just didn't seem right to many in our neighborhood that someone was being brought up in their midst who, in their opinion, did not belong. That someone was me, who was later to be listed under the rubric, first-degree *Mischling* or half-Jew. In order better to understand what follows, the reader needs to know something about the Wedding section of Berlin, since Pasewalkerstraße, the street I grew up on, belongs to the district of Wedding. This was a district of workers and petty bureaucrats who, not having been blessed with wealth, had made up for it by inculcating in themselves strong, uncompromising moral and political convictions. Later I came to think that these people must have had a profound need to resuscitate their faith in *something,* and that, in the wake of the ideological rubble of the Kaiser period and the Weimar republic, they saw in the Nazi ideology a message of deliverance that filled the ideological vacuum and gave them a psychological "fix." And in this ideology people like me had no place; the so-called genotype that I introduced into our area was declared alien and a danger to the community, for, in their eyes, it was corrupt and un-German.

This belief, for many a rigid conviction, is documented in a photo in which I, just under a year old, can be seen sitting on the lap of a matronly looking woman from our neighborhood:

Anonym

This picture is of course no more than a half-length portrait, as the woman had taken pains to have her head neatly cut out of the shot. She said, so my mother told me, "Your boy looks definitely Jewish. And I'd like to spare myself the embarrassment of having had a Jew baby on my arm. What would people say if they saw such a thing?" I was not long in experiencing the answer to this clearly rhetorical question — on my own body. Meanwhile, however, my mother was careful to keep me out of the social spotlight, as best she could. My stepfather, whom I regarded as my true father and who will be characterized as such in what follows, was anything but wicked, as the appellation might lead one to believe. He had a little garden in the Wilhelmsruh district, and in my stroller I was the center of this rustic idyll. Not to mention that I was sheltered here from my fellows:

My sanctuary

The garden was situated near some fields that were fertilized with sewage. Irrigated by run-off waters from the city of Berlin, these fields sprouted handsome crops of white and savoy cabbage. One may assume that the degree of toxicity in the soil was increasing right along with the growth of industrialization, but nobody gave that a thought in those days, and we always came back from those fields with a few heads of cabbage, to which the industrial waste waters apparently made not one jot's difference — nor did they to us, since we fed for days on one cabbage head. Meals were often skimpy in our household, and my mother knew how to spice up the cabbage heads deliciously.

Sometimes my memory of those hand-to-mouth days impinges on me in a palpable, almost bodily way. Every time I return to Berlin I experience proof of this. We often went in those early days to the Paul Gerhardt *Stift,* a church-affiliated hospital, on Müllerstraße. In one of its recesses they had set up a field kitchen from which to dole out pea soup to the local populace. I myself was given a bowl of this soup, and even today, when I walk down that street, I can smell its wonderful aroma, although the field kitchen with free pea soup is long gone, and most people these days no longer need it anyway. Maybe this very olfactory association is responsible for the fact that Berlin and pea soup belong together, as Aschinger rightly understood. This canny businessman had his own bakery on Sophienstraße, which allowed him to supply his many restaurants with rolls gratis. This was a welcome state of affairs for many students, other starvelings and people like me, who would come in and order a bowl of pea soup.

I spent a lot of time in the garden, since it lay in a sparsely settled area. Of the two neighboring properties, one contained a two-family house, and the two families occupying it had no children and were always at work during the day. So it was pervaded by a serene stillness that contrasted strongly with our flat on Pasewalkerstraße where life simmered either in the street or at an open window, from which you got to hear many of the neighbors' family secrets, which in turn served as fuel for conversation among the leaners (you leaned out of the window propped up on a pillow) and listeners.

The other property, a corner parcel, belonged to a Germanized Polish family by the name of Gronzil that had a boy and a girl, both around my age. Every Saturday we would all get our baths together in a big tub, even after we had started school, and it was here that I noticed for the first time the difference between the sexes, a difference that of course made little difference to me at this stage of my development. I was more interested in games that were the rage then. One of the hottest of these was cops and robbers, soon replaced by Nazis and Commies. We drew lots to decide who was who, and sometimes I was very proud to belong to the strong "German" party, which, by the rules, always had to win and always did. The Commies mostly ended up in jail, which was a make-shift tent propped up behind our arbor and surrounded by raspberry and blackberry hedges, along with red and green gooseberry bushes. Needless to say, the inmates could sweeten their own punishment by eating the berries, and at times doubts arose in me as to whether winning was such a good thing, since there were slim pickings left over for the winner.

I remember well these politically tinged childlike, or better, childish, games. I was on our property almost every weekend, sitting in my little stroller and enjoying my rural environs. These were made up of different fruit trees, a walnut tree, many flowers and a majestic oak, which my father had planted when he bought the property, some forty years earlier. There was also an arbor that served as a hideaway for naps. Every Sunday afternoon we had my mother's homemade cake in the garden. She had honed her baking skills to such an artistic level that our neighbors, momentarily forgetting their proud Aryan social status, often came over and asked her to bake them a cake or at least give them the recipe. Sometimes the demand was so great that our little gas oven couldn't hold all the big tin cake trays; and so, early in the morning, I would have to carry them over to the baker for finishing and, returning there in the afternoon, pick them up, surrounded by the other kids. Only once were the cakes taken from me, but the empty trays showed up the very next day in front of our door, moving my mother to opine that the world was certainly a bad place, but then again, maybe not quite so bad as many people assumed. I saw it differently, believing that the evildoers just wanted more cake and returned the trays to my mother for no other reason.

This paradise of mine was temporally and spatially limited, temporally in that the good times rolled mainly on weekends, spatially in that they rolled only within the enclave of our garden. Outside our tranquil nook, reality looked quite different. When I later returned to Berlin, in 1957, I asked my mother about this period and recorded her response on tape. Here is an unedited excerpt:

> *When you were born, I was happy you were a boy. You had hair down to your shoulders. And then later when Hitler took over the government there was a lot of suffering you had to go through. They brought you upstairs covered with blood; I thought it was an accident. Somebody'd offered money to have you beaten to death. You were five at the time but it'd already begun when you were three years old. And so I'd always had to suffer a lot on your account. And Papa often cried. But God kept His merciful hand over you.*

Once it happened as I was coming down Pasewalkerstraße that three young guys between fifteen and seventeen came up to me and told me that they would be rewarded for putting you up against a wall and shooting you. Then Herr Modrow [an acquaintance] said to leave Gerd alone. So even in school you suffered a lot, but I'll say it again, those prayers always preserved you from all evil. It could've turned out worse. Friends, acquaintances who worked in the Ministry helped you but then there were always the masses. Just the way it is again now.

Papa was in the hospital and you were sick. I brought an acquaintance over to stay with you and you wanted to go out. You got up on the first day [of your illness] and the neighbor's kid who's two years older than you beat you in the gutter and boy did I let loose. When I came home from the hospital his mother was standing behind the house door and started punching me and calling me Jew sow[13] and you sow Jew. Some workers came over from work, from Osram, and they pulled her off me, that was after she bashed me in the head with a milk bottle and I bled so much over my eyes I couldn't see where to aim my punches. But even that misery passed. Then when Papa got out of the hospital again he really put it to her. Once you were supposed to pick up cigars and she hit you in the hallway too and called you "old Jew bum."

One day we were coming from the garden and I was looking for Gerd because we had to set up for the blackout and so I asked Frau Modrow: have you seen Gerd? As I turned the corner I saw the street full of people and Gerd came running up to me drenched in blood. Again they had given the kids money and told them to beat Gerd to death. When I got upstairs with him Papa thought he had been in an accident. And that kind of thing happened all the time. You had a lot to put up with. We couldn't let him out again. He always had to go with us and we mostly went to the garden, frequently on weekends and we stayed there and slept in the arbor. But things could've been worse. And God protected you over and over again and a few times He even made the Brown Shirts protect you.

This event I remember particularly well. I was about six years old on that day as I walked along the street stirring up the passions of the "leaners" with my patriotic Bleyle sailor's suit. It was on a Saturday afternoon, and since the sun was shining, there were plenty of people on the street. One of the taller youths saw me, pointed to the suit and said, "You can't wear that. Only a German can wear that, and you're no German. You're a Jew." He repeated this a few times, each time getting louder. The other kids were getting a big kick out of this, and it wasn't long before the solo voice turned into a roaring chorus: "You can't do that. You're not a German. You're a Jew." After that it wasn't long before it got physical and I wound up on the ground with the whole mob on top of me. Battered by the blows, I was liberally dripping blood and my entire beautiful sailor's suit looked like the aftermath of battle, a battle I had lost. But it could've been even worse, for the grownups who witnessed the spectacle — and that's what it was for them — with a strong rooting interest in the aggressors, egged their children on to hit even harder. And that's exactly what they did. Although I cried, it wasn't because it hurt but because my beautiful suit was done in and I was afraid to present myself thus to my mother. And then I heard a voice nearby coming from a man in a brown shirt, with shoulder straps and a waist belt, which later he then unhooked and swung over his head like a lasso as he shouted out to the presumed victors: "I will kill anyone who takes one more step forward." The kids shrank back, as did the grownups who recognized in the man the local *Blockwart*, [14] one of the earliest to join the party. This man came visiting often to warn us in case another raid was in the works. The kids and their parents and the other grownups quietly withdrew, and my mother, who was just rounding the corner, took me in her arms, brought me upstairs, washed the blood off me, took my suit off and put me to bed. The following week I saw the suit again, in my closet, freshly cleaned and pressed. After that I only wore it one more time, and that was on my first day of school, since at the time my thinking was that this suit was the actual reason I had been beaten.

The other time I was reminded of my Jewishness happened shortly thereafter. I was standing right near our house door, as my mother had forbidden me to stray any distance from it so that she would be right there in the vicinity to help me in case anything happened. Three older boys who were hanging around started roughing me up and telling me that Pasewalkerstraße was supposed to be a Jew-free street. Since this obviously wasn't the case, they were volunteering to make it so, and one after another they began hammering their fists up under my chin so that, with each blow, the back of my head banged against the wall. It didn't take long for the blood to start flowing, and had an SS-officer not happened by at that moment, the street would certainly have become Jew-free. This man drew his revolver, aimed it at the three and said in a voice steeled by command: "Whoever throws the next punch gets a bullet in the gut. As Germans you should be ashamed of yourselves for battering a defenseless boy." The three of them took off and I was able to make it upstairs where my mother at first cried but then took me in her arms. Then we went to the free clinic where the laceration on the back of my head was irrigated and stitched up. Next day, a Saturday, we headed off to the garden again where I insisted this time on playing the SS-officer who, through his intervention, had rescued me from my attackers.

2. From School Cone to *Jungvolk*

Then came my first day of school. I was given a big cone, bigger than I was, into which my mother had stuffed not only nutritious snacks but also such delights as chocolate, cookies and a self-controlled Schuco toy car:

The School Cone: the sweetening of a new stage of life

My school, Elementary School No. 14, was located at the corner of Anton- and Plantagenstraße. By virtue of the narrow angle into which the grounds receded, the school had a relatively big yard for the pupils to run around in during recess; and just across from the school stood the crematorium, surrounded by a high wall that was ideal for ball games, so that for me graveyard and playing ball somehow belonged together. I enjoyed playing ball, since this kind of game was not a contact sport, and contact was something I didn't have anyway. The reason was that I ended up sitting at the rearmost desk in class, was taken little notice of and was all but invisible to the other children. The parents were to blame for this: they didn't want their children coming into contact with a Jewish child. I was denounced several times to the director of the school, who showed two of these letters to my mother. Later she told me that the letters basically contained the same kinds of things I was used to hearing outside school.

The year 1938 was especially bad. One day I had to pick up rolls at the bakery. When I got there I saw that some store display windows had been smashed. This had happened in the night from 9 to 10 November, 1938, in a Nazi action that became known as "crystal night" or, less euphemistically, "pogrom night." We had a large jewelry store on Reinickendorferstraße that had marvelous Junker watches on display, watches I had long been fond of and had always wished to get for my birthday but never did. Now the glass pane was kaput and the object of my longing lay right before me. With so many people rummaging through the shards of glass, shoving various items into their pockets, and on top of that being encouraged in their behavior by two men in SA (i.e., *Sturmabteilung* or Storm Trooper Nazi) uniforms, the temptation to join in rose up in me. I don't know why I didn't do it; maybe it was fear of getting caught, maybe I remembered my mother's advice not to draw attention to myself, or maybe my super-ego proved stronger than my larcenous grabby-ego.

After pogrom night I became an even bigger target of hostilities. Nazi propaganda stoked hatred of the Jews and going to class became a nightmare for me. Constantly hearing that I looked like a Jew, mainly by virtue of my dark hair and long "Jewish" nose, I looked for a remedy. One day, while my mother was out shopping, I noticed a can of white paint in the storeroom. I opened it and streaked my hair with the stuff, in order to make myself "Jew-free." Alas, it did no good, and when my mother got home, a good whipping topped off my disappointment. Later in life, when I came upon Anna Mitgutsch's novel, *The Punishment,* I read that children who are often beaten by their parents beat their own children in turn. On the other hand, maybe I did deserve those whacks.

Since I occasionally had to serve the class as an object lesson for a Jew, and since I was constantly being asked if my father also had such a long nose and such dark hair, I looked into Meyers encyclopedia, a few volumes of which we had inherited, and tried to find racial characteristics that were similar to the ones tending to occur in Jews. I discovered that the Dinaric race had an appearance vaguely similar to that of the Jewish race. This delighted me since I shared with the former my long, narrow face, my round chin, my extremely thick, curly hair and, above all, my big, slightly downward-sloping, powerful nose. Inspired, I went on to invent my own family tree in which I traced my ancestors back ten generations and turned them into owners of knightly estates. But this swindle was very quickly seen through and I became once again the pedagogical illustration of a Jew.

All of this took place between my sixth and tenth years, and I must confess that, by the end of that period, I still didn't know what a Jew was, how one behaved and what made me different from the other children. All I knew was that they all avoided me since they had had it drummed into their heads by their parents not to have anything to do with the Jew boy. Moreover, my future could be said to have looked as grim as my present. Confirmation of this came to me one day on our way to the Christmas market with some acquaintances who, like my father, were retired. The market extended from Leopold Square to Seestraße on both sides of Müllerstraße. As we walked I overheard one of my mother's male acquaintances say, "Sure, Ella, your son looks very bright, but he'll never get a German woman. You know very well a first degree *Mischling* is forbidden to marry a German. That would be racial dishonor." This, of course, meant little to me at the time, since in those days I wasn't interested in women; but later on the fact of this exclusion would be brought home to me again and again, right up to the time years later when I asked my girlfriend whether she really cared for me and wanted to marry me. When she said no, it immediately occurred to me that my mother's acquaintance had already known this way back then, or had at least had an inkling. It took me a long time to get over her rejection.

Before I began my career at the *Gymnasium,* I had two experiences, one of which was appalling, the other by contrast quite beautiful. Around this time I was looking profoundly emaciated and famished, no doubt due to the fact that I had suddenly gone into a rapid growth spurt and that my flesh couldn't fill out the gaps in my body quickly enough. One day I went with my mother to the pastry shop on the corner of Plantagenstraße which had these fabulous cream puffs, but my mother had no intention of buying me my favorite confection. She only wanted a few rolls. I eyed my cream puffs, but they were behind glass, and in front of the glass stood my mother. Not one but two barriers! I got the brilliant idea to cry, since that strategy had sometimes worked for me, at first just whimpering, then ever louder and with increasing melodrama. This drew the attention of the other customers in the shop, and they began asking me what the problem was. Overcome with sobbing, I couldn't get a word out and was reduced to pointing at the object in question behind the glass. A maternal looking woman asked me if I was hungry. I nodded yes. It went on from there, she wanting to know if my mother was feeding me properly. Scenting the sympathy of the others, I squealed "no" in a voice thick with agony. Whereupon this little ad hoc community turned its outrage against my mother, and taunts rang out such as: "Hey, get a load a' dis overstuffed one here. Piggin' out'll fatten ya up awright, and ain't she duh livin' proof a' dat? And her kid she lets starve. Look what a tootpick 'e is; duh little meat he's got is just hangin' offa his bones. T'sa miracle he's still alive. He's a waste awright, a useless good-fuh-nuttin', but dat don' mean 'e should starve eeder." I understood the language these people spoke very well, but I had trouble understanding their feelings, since I had learned only too well with my own body that most people in the neighborhood, including most of those gathered here, would rather have seen me dead then alive. My mother, not wanting to inflame the uproar I had caused any further, bought me the desired creampuff, accompanied as she did so by the applause of my benefactors. She even had the lady add an extra dollop of whipped cream. Then she took me by the hand and we ran home, without her saying a word to me. Once there, she unwrapped the luscious sweet, pulled the paper back from the cream, and, before I knew it, everything was all over my face, for that's exactly where my mother had thrown both. And then she said to me with icy composure, "If you ever pull a stunt like that again, I will beat you so badly you won't be able to walk. And from now on there won't be any more cream puffs either." To my good fortune, she did not enforce this ban with absolute rigor.

Of course, the episode had a little sequel: one of the women informed the authorities, and I had to report for a medical exam. The fact is, I *was* a little undernourished, so they sent me to the Baltic-Sea island of Usedom for a bit of fattening-up, or, more accurately, to the seaside resort Ückeritz, a former picturesque fishing and farming village between the Baltic and the

Achterwasser. There I flopped for six weeks, mostly in a deckchair. I ate five square meals a day and was permitted to swim in the Baltic twice a week, and generally just loll about in the sun. In no time I made plenty of friends, since nobody had a clue there was anything wrong with my Aryan papers. It was a splendid time, and I put on a few pounds as well, so that the cure really did me a lot of good.

My first great catastrophe came in the same year. When I went to school in the spring of 1940, I saw that all my classmates were either wearing a brown shirt or passing around a Hitler Youth knife. They had both because they were now in the *Jungvolk,* and they were in the *Jungvolk* because they were almost all a year older than I was, putting them in position to be selected well ahead of me. I, on the other hand, had received no letter urging me to present myself, yet I nourished the most ardent wish to belong to the group. I went home and asked my mother for the reason. And for the first time she revealed to me the truth that my biological father was a Jew and that people tolerated me, at best, as a second-class citizen. Again and again I had heard over the years that my mother was a Jew sow and I a sow Jew, yet up to that moment it had never been clear to me why people kept saying that and accosting us over it. Now, however, what had long been an inkling suddenly became a reality. I had a nervous breakdown, cursed my mother and wanted to jump out of the window. That was my first profound disappointment because all I wanted was to be like everybody else. My mother looked at me long and hard and then snapped, "My boy, put on new pants and shirt and come with me." That signaled to me that big things were in the offing, for every time this order was issued, something unexpected happened. This time was no exception: she took me by the arm and we headed for the subway. I no longer remember what station we got out at, but my mother ran straight over to a large building and went in with me.

On arriving the doorman asked where we were going and my mother answered, "To the office of Baldur von Schirach, Reich Youth Leader." To the secretary's question whether we had an appointment, my mother responded with stony silence. Then she resolutely and forcefully shoved the three-legged rolling chair the secretary was sitting on into the corner, and, notwithstanding the latter's fierce protestations, the path to the desired office door was clear. My mother entered alone, without knocking beforehand, and came out again after a few moments — not alone but accompanied by a uniformed gentleman who then motioned me, unaccompanied, into his office. I knew from photographs that this was Baldur von Schirach, but I wasn't nervous since he didn't look threatening. On the contrary. And thus commenced my interrogation, for it was nothing less than that. He asked whether I didn't agree that the *Führer* was the greatest German of all time. I answered in the affirmative since I didn't know many great Germans; besides, it seemed advisable to avoid answering "no" to questions that already had yes-answers in them. Then he asked me whether I believed that German, or Aryan, blood was superior to Jewish blood. Since, based on my experience, I imagined Jewish blood to taste like cod liver oil, which I hated, but German blood like a bubbling fountain of lemonade, I again answered "yes." The third question was whether I was raised in the Jewish faith. This was the only question I could answer with a clear conscience. It put me on my own turf and gave me a chance to steer the conversation my way. I had no idea what it was like to be brought up in the Jewish faith, but the Christian faith was another story. And so I ran my mouth off: I told him how I had been baptized in the Church of Thanksgiving, how I had admired its baptismal font, and that, although my mother and I certainly didn't go to church on a regular basis, we always did on the feast days, i.e., the Christian feast days, and that we always had lamb on Easter, and once a week ham, and that pork tasted better to me than beef. All of Herr von Schirach's efforts to shut me up were of no avail, and this is a trait I have retained to the present day. And so he quickly rang for his secretary and told her my mother could come and fetch me. When she came in, he informed her that he was satisfied that I had been raised in a Christian household, that I had good German parents, and that he was giving me permission to join the *Jungvolk* until the completion of my 14th year, but not the Hitler Youth. He emphasized that I should never forget I was merely being tolerated in the *Jungvolk* and that I should do all within my power to prove myself an authentic German. The "doing-all-within-my power" flourish sounded just like my mother's refrain, and since I never contradicted her, I was not about to contradict this gentleman either. Later on it occurred to me that I probably would not have gotten off so easily with Arthur Axmann, his successor that same year. And so I was able to join the *Jungvolk* on 20 April 1940. [15]

This concession made me the happiest youngster in Berlin. My reward, from the little pastry shop on Reinickendorferstraße, corner of Plantagenstraße, was my favorite sweet, a cream puff with whipped cream. Then we went into the Brown Store on Plantagenstraße where we bought my summer and winter uniforms, along with a Hitler Youth knife, a waist belt and the esteemed belt buckle. At last I no longer felt excluded; on the contrary, with my acceptance into the *Jungvolk* I believed I had overcome all liabilities of my marginalization. However, the owner of the Brown Store was an evil omen: she was our neighbor, the one who had often called my mother a Jew sow and me a Jew bum. She gave me my purchases, but added with a toxic glare, "Just wait till you're fourteen years old. Then they'll come and pick you up and you'll wind up in a camp where a good-for-nothing like you belongs. And you'll never get out of there again. Use the time you've got left well, but never show your face in my store again."

One reason for this woman's hateful remarks was that her son had to continue attending the elementary school. He hadn't passed the acceptance exam for the next level. In our area it was typically the case that children graduated from elementary school and then entered upon an apprenticeship in order to learn a practical trade. In our *Kiez* environment was destiny; my mother, on the other hand, believed that I was born for something higher, and she reminded me of this on an almost weekly basis. No doubt this was also a reason she had me take violin lessons, something quite unusual in our neighborhood. My mother had no money for a full-sized violin, so she bought me a half-sized one in a junk shop and arranged instruction for me with a Herr Seidel on Reinickendorferstraße. From then on I had to go to hour-long lessons twice a week in order to get properly trained in this instrument, and, within a few years, I had progressed in it to a point where I could play certain Bach cantatas well enough to avoid inflicting serious injury on the ears of connoisseurs.

3. The Horst Wessel *Gymnasium,* the Adolf Hitler School and the Warthe District

Since my mother's faith in me as a special child remained unshakable, we went one weekend in 1940 to the local *Realschule*[16] where I was to sit for an entrance exam. Of course, it never got that far: as soon as my mother answered "no" to the question whether I was Aryan, she and I were told that there was no place there for half Jews. My mother proffered the mitigating circumstance that I had grown up in an Aryan household, but this did not assuage the administration. So home we went. My mother consoled me by buying me another cream puff with whipped cream, which I immediately devoured down to the last crumb while sitting on the shabby, patched-up leather sofa in the pastry shop. All in all, not getting accepted didn't seem so bad, and I secretly hoped there might be other schools in the area with an Aryan standard. This turned out to be the case, for in the secondary school we looked up next the same thing happened. The administration official who interviewed us was wearing a brown uniform, so I knew right upon entering that I could lay claim to yet another cream puff with whipped cream. I could now see my entire future path laid out before me paved with numberless cream puffs loaded with whipped cream, a prospect that struck me as anything but grim. My mother, however, had other ideas. She was tough and stubborn, and when she wanted something, she got her way.

And so one day we made our way to Schönhauser Avenue, in another district, where a humanistic *Gymnasium*[17] was located, paradoxically named after Horst Wessel,[18] one of its former students, whose name should never be mentioned in the same breath with humanistic education. My mother funneled a few last-minute names and dates into my head, this school representing my last chance to move on from my elementary school. So I learned that Horst Wessel was an early fighter for National Socialism, that the Communists had shot him in 1930 and that he wrote the "Horst Wessel Song" which everybody had to learn by heart since "The banners high, the columns locked together" was played at all official Nazi functions and had to be sung by all.[19] Needless to say, in the long entrance exam, which primarily tested my skill in writing essays (my forte), I was not asked about the man who had given the school its name for this period in its history.

Thus I was accepted into this *Gymnasium*. The news circulated through the neighborhood very quickly, and many thought it was a mistake that would, "please God," be exposed by my poor performance. The news was also relayed to the principal of my elementary school, a Herr Wolf, who then at once came into our class, summoned me to the blackboard and had me write the word *"Gymnasium"* thereon. I wrote it just as he had pronounced it, with an "i" instead of a "y," whereupon he instructed me that the first component of this word in Greek meant "naked," a fact that could wryly be taken to symbolize my poor command of German. He was right, for I came from a working-class neighborhood, a fact immediately apparent from my pronunciation and choice of words, which regularly featured such aberrant gems as "Doncha know," "Y'see," "Natch," and even "Ain't dat right." No doubt I leaned on these self-serving solecisms to help me get past my insecurities and my inferiority complex. Nevertheless, the principal affected a certain joviality and promised to take me back upon my dismissal from this prestigious school, which, he prophesied, was imminent. Thereupon all my classmates broke out into a "brutish laughter" (as I later learned from Homer). Once again, on this last day of elementary school, I found myself standing "Outside before the Door" and went sadly home to tell my mother I had thought it over and decided I didn't want to go to high school, since I would never make it there. My mother reacted by slapping me in the face and insisting she never wanted to hear such nonsense from me again. Worse yet, this time she passed on the cream puff.

In the Fall of 1940 I transferred to the *Gymnasium,* which was a financial burden for my parents since the school cost 20 marks per month. The beginning was difficult for me. In fact, the very first day was a catastrophe. We were having Latin class, and in our primer there was the sentence: "Gallus cantat." This sentence stymied me because it could mean two different things: "The rooster is crowing" or "the Frenchman is singing." For quite a while I mulled over the question how it was possible that one and the same word could be read in two different ways. Young as I was, I linked the singing Frenchman with the upside of life, since anybody who sings can't be bad. The senseless and dangerous aspects of life I associated with the crowing rooster, since my mother once opined that roosters who crowed too early in the morning should have their heads cut off and be dropped into the soup pot. Of course, not all of them suffered the same fate, she assured me, many were spared and got away with their lives. My mother was certainly having qualms about the simplistic logic I was using here, so she set up my first private lesson, given to me by an assistant principal for whom my mother cleaned house. This learned gentleman explained to me that a word could sometimes have two meanings and that only the context could decide which one was correct. Since the gentleman fancied himself a skilled pedagogue, he explained the situation in a way he judged commensurate with the capacity of a ten-year-old mind. In this particular case, he began, the choice was between a gaily singing Frenchman and a chicken in a chicken coop, but these days that was really a distinction without a difference, since all of France with all its decadent Frenchmen was a filthy chicken coop that would have to be cleaned out by German troops. The gay singing appealed to me more than the chicken coop, so I decided in favor of the first option. Naturally, our Latin teacher decided in favor of the crowing rooster. From this episode I learned that interpretations can certainly be quite subjective and that the stronger of two interpreters will usually decide by fiat what's correct and what's not.

The atmosphere in *Gymnasium* was better than that in elementary school. Most students came from good homes; the fathers were doctors, lawyers or professors, and occasionally I had the good fortune to be invited by one of them. Only once was I asked why I wasn't wearing a Jewish star.[20] I answered that, as a half-Jew, I wasn't required to wear one. This gave rise to a witty remark by my host, a lawyer with whose son I studied, to the effect that I should at least be made to wear a three-pointed star, since the Star of David had six. But such remarks were rare, and my mother was very proud of me, telling me over and over again that I would go far, farther than she and Papa.

My father continued to take care of me; he was home all the time during the war years while my mother went to work at the post office sorting letters. In the afternoons he would tell me about his life. First up was always "the good old days," which meant the Imperial Era, in which a glass of beer and a sausage cost no more than ten cents each and a decent suit could be had for twenty gold marks. Besides that, he made enough money to buy himself a plot of land in Wilhelmsruh, to which he would walk every weekend, only rarely using public transportation, as I recall. Other historical dates, known to him not from books but his own personal experience, included the abdication of the Kaiser on November 9, 1918, and the election of SPD chairman Friedrich Ebert as first Imperial President. I also learned about the decline of the Republic from him, the worldwide economic crisis of 1929, inflation and the number of unemployed, which topped six million in 1932. My father also taught me many practical things which were useful to me later on. Though a retiree, he maintained a disciplined work ethic: he got up every day at five-thirty and made breakfast, especially on mornings after my mother had worked the night shift. Then he would clean up and, on some weekdays, prepare lunch, usually consisting of some hearty soup. I helped out in these tasks as best I could, and still enjoy doing them today, which has proven very useful in my marriage. Above all my father insisted that I do my homework, and since I was always in danger of being ganged up on in the street, he motivated me to read, and he would read too, mostly subscription magazines. I was also given many books on holidays and birthdays, so that in time I had an entire library to call my own. Among my favorite books were Waldemar Bonsel's *The Adventures of Maja the Bee*, *Adventures in Dr. Kleinermacher's Garden* by Herbert Paatz and a leather-bound book with a title something like *The Young Fisherman from Norderney*. At this time it was especially the book by Paatz that enthralled me. It sparked in me the fervent wish to go on a journey of my own into the interior of a leaf with a tiny vehicle. Of course, my father told me that this wouldn't be possible until I had studied the natural sciences, since only then would I know in which direction to steer the vehicle, there being so many canals in any given leaf. I did intend to follow his advice, but drifted away from it, now deciding I would rather be a cook, since I very much liked to eat and my father had taught me the necessary culinary skills, or so I thought.

At that time I also began to supplement my reading with visits to the theater. The illusional space of the stage transported me to a totally different world. The first piece I ever saw was *L'il Pete's Moon Voyage* at the Theater am Schiffbauerdamm. With passionate empathy I followed the misadventures of the widowed, one-hundred-plus-year-old May bug Sumsemann, whose sixth leg had been hacked off by a thieving woodcutter, which was then saved by a fairy and brought to safety on the moon's highest mountain. L'il Pete and Anneliese, both my age, set out on the quest together with a bear, roaming the galaxies and, to the delight of the young audience, getting shot out of a canon to the moon, where they had to face a voracious man, yet happily managing in the end to get shot back down to earth with the rescued leg. I identified effortlessly with L'il Pete, but privately thought to myself that if I were in his shoes, I would be in no particular hurry to get back to earth. Another favorite piece was *Robinson Is Not to Die,* for I had already read Defoe's book with great interest, and in my mind I painted the picture of my island existence as if I were alone in my garden, with Friday as my best friend. And then I would go with him to the little restaurant not far from the Schiffbauerdamm and drink lemonade which, with the insertion of a dime, would in some mysterious way gush right out of the marble wall into the glass placed at its base. I always waited for the glass to run over, but, again mysteriously, that never happened, so that I came to believe somebody behind the wall was controlling the process.

In school I was doing well in all my subjects, even in Latin, to which I had originally taken a deep distrust. I was especially fascinated by mathematics. One question in particular interested me: what happens if you divide a number, say "one," by zero? When I asked this question in class, the teacher laughed and said that wasn't permissible, since the result would be infinity and as mortal beings we couldn't grasp that. Aha, I thought, that's forbidden, just like a locked door in a fairy tale that no one dare open because behind it are many secrets meant to remain hidden to mere mortals.

But it was in sports that I excelled above all. I was the best in sprints and distance running; I could jump farther and higher than the others; and I was always the first to the top in climbing. And why not? I'd had plenty of training in all these skills, having always to be superior to my pursuers, who often enough were right on my heels. Had I fallen into their clutches, I would never have gotten away from them in one piece. Besides this, we played sports every week in the *Jungvolk,* and since I was expected to be better than all the others, as my mother drummed into my head almost daily, I did my level best to cross the finish line first, which is usually what happened. In running I had a foolproof method for winning: I simply let myself fall forward, then having to scramble madly to avoid hitting the ground. In this way my muscles steeled themselves, becoming tougher year by year. People started noticing and I was usually the first one chosen by my classmates, especially for ball games, such as dodgeball, for instance, since I was able to throw the heavy medicine ball harder than most others.

It was probably on account of my academic and athletic accomplishments that I received an official letter summoning me to take an entrance examination for the Adolf Hitler School. My mother was quite alarmed, fearing that something ominous was behind it. But she saw no way out, other than to tell me to put on a clean shirt and behave as inconspicuously as possible. I went there on a Saturday, and the exam was quite long and anything but simple, especially since I had to identify many names. The easiest were Goering and Goebbels, but I could only guess at Ley and others. I must've guessed right, since the very next week I received notice to transfer to the Adolf Hitler School in the vicinity of Berlin. I said good-bye to my mother, who, I assumed, could now breathe a sigh of relief, since no one was ever moved out of this politically elite preparatory school into a camp for "special assignment." Of course, in two days the news broke that there was a half-Jew among them, in an institution supposed to be educating the future leaders of the party. That evening I was summarily loaded onto a truck, driven deep into the forest and then thrown down from my seat. As I hit the ground, I was told, "You're a Jew and Jews are supposed to be too intelligent to lose their lives. So do honor to your ancestors because, if you don't, the wolves will come and eat you alive!" I had no intention of letting the wolves have me for dinner and tried to orient myself. I knew from my reading of Karl May[21] that moss grows mainly on the north side of trees, and since the city was located somewhere south of me, I would have to run away from the moss side to get back to it. I ran for about two hours, finally arriving home in good shape. Next morning I was back at my old school desk, pretending I'd been ill for the past two days. My handful of Karl May books, among them *Winnetou I* and *II* and

Old Surehand I and *II,* ascended to the place of honor in my little library, right up front. It was then that I understood for the first time the maxim: *non scholae sed vitae discimus* — it is not for school but for life that we learn. The net result was that, in the wake of this brief but life-threatening episode, my performance in Latin improved significantly, a source of deep satisfaction for me and my family. Moreover, there was another reason I could count myself lucky for having fled this school, even before I had properly begun: the long-term effects of the intellectually formative subjects taught there might well have been to burden me with strong prejudices for my studies later on.

But I was denounced even at the *Gymnasium.* My Greek teacher, a Dr. Corvinus, whom I liked well enough mainly for his stories about his travels through North America, would inform me every now and then that the principal had received yet another letter, but I'm assuming there were far fewer of these than in my elementary school. Only one other time was my nose rubbed in my half-Jewishness, and that happened when one of the students, a rabid apologist for the ideology of the Third Reich and already by his 13th year a platoon leader in the *Jungvolk,* was missing the green-and-white braided cord he wore with his uniform. Someone had taken it and I was suspected because I was not an authentic German. I was extensively interrogated and threatened with expulsion. But then, thank God, the cord showed up again. It had been surreptitiously returned to its proper place, and so I was allowed to take part in the class once again. The lesson for me was that my presence there was not as assured as I had thought, and that I would always be the first to come under suspicion whenever anything happened.

4. Life and Destruction: Time till 1945

It's War, but Life Goes On

Much happened around 1939, none of it attributable to me. The war had begun in that year, but Berlin was at first spared from air raids. These did not commence until after 1940. At first the damage was minimal; when a bomb fell on the upper story of a house in the neighborhood, a complete tribal migration took place to inspect the damage. Everyone looked, laughed and went away. But the laughter was short-lived as the air attacks came with increasing frequency and the bombs fell more and more heavily on our area. Of course, at first we had no idea how much destruction such a bomb could cause. Whenever the fore-alarm sounded, we would stay in our flat; and we continued to stay upstairs even when the rising and falling howl of the sirens gave more urgent warnings. In accord with the blackout order, we had only a small lamp in the living room where we played "Man, don't get mad!", while waiting for the all-clear. But even that arrangement was soon abandoned when, in one attack, the bombs fell so close that we decided we'd better head for the air-raid shelter in the basement. We managed to push open the apartment door but couldn't take a single step outside, as the air pressure kept flinging us back. In my hand I was holding a cage with Peter, my parakeet, who was very attached to me, and I kept my body in front of the cage so as to protect my bird from the air pressure. We did finally manage to get down into to the shelter, and in the attacks that followed I was always the first to rush in with my cage. After an attack it was my job to search the attic for incendiary bombs. This was easy enough to do since the German Civil Defense or *Deutscher Luftschutzbund,* known as the DLB, had ordered the clearing-out of all attics, so that everything flammable had already been removed. The little attic safety-cages stood there empty, but for a bucket of water and a sack of sand, and it was no longer legal to secure them by lock. Only once did I ever find anything: an incendiary bomb had fallen through the skylight and started burning on impact. Boldly I picked it up by its end and hurled it back out the skylight onto the street, just as I'd been taught. And I felt like a real hero.

But there were many others who thought of themselves as heroes. People we knew would sometimes drop by and tell us of the struggles on the Eastern front, and how they were pushing ever farther to the East. It was the end of 1942, and the 6th Army under General Paulus was encamped before Stalingrad—though not for long, as Paulus capitulated at the beginning of 1943. Many soldiers were taken prisoner, and my father's nephew suffered what at that time was euphemistically called a "hero's death." It wasn't long thereafter that the reports of soldiers coming home on leave began sounding more critical and considerably more pessimistic. A few soldiers, whom we had known a long time, sat in our kitchen and opened up about the shadow side of life on the front, which bore no resemblance at all to what we had heard on the radio or seen in newsreels. It was then that I began to regard wartime life with some skepticism; some of the wives who came over broke down in tears, and the air attacks were utterly nerve-wracking.

That same year something happened that, at the time, was totally accepted and celebrated. On February 18, 1943, Reich's Propaganda Minister

Goebbels gave a rousing speech at the Berlin *Sportpalast* before 3,000 Nazi-sympathizers. He put to the crowd the seemingly rhetorical question (the real significance of which escaped everyone), "Do you want total war?" The masses cheered hysterically in agreement and sealed their approval by spontaneously breaking out into the first stanza of the national anthem. I remember this demagogic spectacle very well, since I was there. The young people had the job of forming a closed column, and, infected by the mass psychosis as we were, all of us, including me, mindlessly bleated our "Ja." This took place after the capitulation of General Paulus in Stalingrad, a battle leaving thousands of casualties on both sides. It occurred to me later on that the hysterical response to this question, which of course revealed itself in short order to be not entirely rhetorical, was the effect of a calculated appeal to the never-say-die spirit of the people, a spirit that had been shaken by the defeat at Stalingrad. People feared "Jewish Bolshevism," a plague they were convinced would sweep over the country, unless its people were ready to sacrifice all. And the sacrifices to be made included the tearing-apart of families, for there was now in place a military obligation for men and adolescent boys between 16 and 65, and even women were being drafted.

To be sure, women had long been playing a key role, for they had the "noble" mission of supplying the German Reich with cannon fodder. One time my mother took me to a ceremony in which the Mother's Cross[22] was awarded to mothers with many children. This sort of thing typically took place at solemn meetings: women with four or five children received the Mother's Cross in bronze, those with six or seven the same cross in silver, and with eight children or more the Cross was awarded in gold. The women accepted their Crosses with pride, in the belief that they had set their children on this earth for the sake of *Führer,* Reich and Fatherland, a belief that remained unshaken even upon their receiving the news that those children had left their lives on the field of honor. I asked my mother if she wished such an award for herself, and she replied with little hesitation, "My boy, a Mother's Cross wouldn't cut it. What I should get is a Knight's Cross, one with all the frills and fancy stuff on it; with all I've had to go through with you, I think I've more than earned it."[23]

In the months that followed, we witnessed the effects of total war. Not only did the air attacks increase, we also had to stand on street corners in uniform and collect money for the *Winterhilfswerk* (Winter Charity Campaign or WHW), an annual drive to help the needy. You couldn't exactly call these donations voluntary, since most were given as a way of expressing solidarity with the German people, and besides, in return you usually received handsome, artfully designed badges, items in traditional-costume or flower bouquet series, which you could pin to your lapel. On weekends we went from door to door, asking for non-ferrous metal and old paper, raw materials being in short supply. We were also regularly reminded of these shortages by the many *Kohlenklauplakate* or coal-thief posters that began to crop up everywhere, like the following one that you would find plastered on walls or all over newspapers warning against energy wastrels:

> *Again he's at it!*
> *His belly growls, his sack is limp,*
> *He snoops around, the greedy pimp.*
> *Round oven, stove, near tap and pan,*
> *At window, door and 'lectric fan*
> *He picks up every jot you spill,*
> *And robs the army of its fill.*
> *The army needs your bit as well,*
> *Which he now seeks in town and dell.*
> *Grab him!*

Among the various thrift measures was also something called "Groschengrab," literally "penny grave," the alliterative partner of Kohlenklau. The point of Groschengrab was to warn people, particularly women, against all unnecessary spending. Then there were the colorful cardboard piglets which aimed for the same result. You hung them up on the wall, especially in the kitchen.

Thrift measures were also printed on restaurant menus, or were supposed to be. Many of us observed the so-called "one-pot-Sunday," on which we ate pea or barley soup, meatless dishes, the meat then being delivered to the front for the soldiers. My mother never quite got into the spirit of this, for it had always been our way to have goulash on Sunday, which she always prepared with many spices, and with potatoes and vegetables as well. Wednesdays, of course, like so many others, she made eggs, sunny-side up, with spinach and fried potatoes, also a dish light on meat. We were told this was Hitler's favorite dish, and that he ate it on Wednesdays just like us. No one doubted this, for the consumption of this plain fare was meant to show the solidarity of the *Führer* with his people and was the culinary expression of the widespread shibboleth: *ein Reich, ein Volk, ein Führer!* Now one could add: *ein Essen.*

Since the air attacks increased along with the German readiness for total war, school attendance became quite irregular, and it wasn't long before our school was relocated to the Warthegau in the fall of 1943. This was undertaken as part of the *Kinderlandverschickung* (Child Evacuation Movement, or KLV for short), which had already been planned in 1940. Enacted on the orders of *Reichsleiter* [24] Martin Bormann, the project was turned over for execution to none other than Baldur von Schirach, a man I assumed I knew quite well by that point. The circular, which I didn't see until later, contained the following:

> *The Führer has ordered that young people be moved on a voluntary basis out of areas subject to constant nocturnal air alarms to other areas of the Reich. Priority in this matter is to be given, above all, to children from allotment areas and from those urban areas that contain no adequate air raid shelters. Accommodations are to be made, as far as possible, by school, even by class [...]. This need not entail public propaganda, particularly via the press [...]. By order of the Führer the project is not to be referred to as an evacuation, but merely as an area resettlement [Landverschickung] of urban youth.* [25]

Many students left Berlin for the Warthegau. Not all did, however, as some merely changed schools and remained in the city under constant threat of air attack. I, of course, took part in the resettlement.

Arriving at our destination, we at first holed up in an abandoned building where classes were held and living quarters assigned. That didn't last long, however, as one night about a week later the marching orders came: we were to line up in front of the school building with our "monkey" (i.e., a knapsack) packed. We had exactly fifteen minutes to gather our things together and be at the assigned spot. Knapsacks fastened to our backs, off we marched. Eleven kilometers along a bumpy country road that had huge holes in some spots over which we occasionally stumbled in the dark. Since we had to sing, you couldn't quite make out the profanity, but then maybe that was the reason for the order to sing. In a few hours we arrived at our new digs: a monastery. It was located in Altwerder, the Germanized name for the former Grabow, in the administrative district of Kempen. We were exhausted and slept, until summoned at dawn by reveille to roll call.

The reason for all this paramilitary training was that we had a Knight's Cross recipient as our camp leader. Every morning he had us fall in for inspection, and his young stooges would spit out their "Eyes right!", "Eyes left!", or "Eyes straight ahead!", depending on the direction from which he came to inspect us. If something was out of order, we'd be punished, and I hated that because often I would be singled out as an example of how not to do something, whether it was that my shoes were not spit-shined or my shirt was missing a button. I had a carbine placed on my fingertips and was then ordered to do progressive knee-bends one through ten, each time squatting about an inch further down. Usually he would slow down the count at around six, and God help you if the carbine began to tremble or, horror of horrors, fell to the ground. Then you'd usually have to double-time it upstairs to the attic to pump water into the reserve tanks, a tough job for us, or you'd be assigned KP duty, peeling potatoes or washing turnips. Still, we didn't all suffer the same fate; my friend Günter, who was somewhat older than I and very good-looking, sometimes spent the entire night in the commandant's room, both of them being, shall we say, of the homosexual persuasion. Günter was also exempt from the nightly paramilitary exercises. We, on the other hand, were not.

Every two weeks an alarm would sound in the night, and we would have to fall in barefoot in our nightshirts and pajamas. We would then march up to two kilometers in one direction, halt, do an about-face and march back the same way we'd come. Obstacles along the way were there for the sole purpose of being overcome by us, for, as the camp commandant was often heard to say, one proved one's authentic "Germanity" by spurning all detours and charging straight ahead to one's goal, although, as I saw it, there could be only one goal for this kind of exercise: home to bed, but precisely this was not permitted us. And so the marching route was selected by virtue of its obstacles. It went through the Prosna, a river in our area, across fields of stubble, which tore up the skin on your soles, and straight through stacks of hay and straw. One night it happened that we had to go through a strawstack. We climbed up the bales and slid down the other side. We all managed it, except for one kid who veered off his downward course and got himself buried half to death, almost asphyxiated. Somebody obviously made a big deal of the incident, since on the very next day an investigative commission showed up and on the day after that we had a new commandant. We found out that the commandant was not a legitimate holder of the Knight's Cross but had procured the decoration "with a little help from his friends."

The new commandant was a little milder and shared the power of command with our academic director, a teacher from our school who liked to play the organ. For this he had plenty of opportunity since we were living in a monastery, and the organ was undamaged. It had a powerful sound, resonating deeply into the huge cellar vault where my classmates played football in the afternoons. For a ball we used the skulls of the monks buried there, of which there were many, so that there was no problem replacing a damaged ball. Cemeteries and playing ball were, of course, a familiar juxtaposition to me; still, I found this particular situation a bit much. When I mentioned this to someone, he replied that we couldn't play outdoors since the Polish teenagers seized every opportunity to entangle us in fistfights, and since they had grown up in the country, they were far superior to us city-slickers in strength and stamina.

Swimming was another favored form of sport. The Prosna, which emptied into the Warthe, wasn't deep but it churned with strong currents. We used the river for distance swimming, i.e., you had to swim for 45 minutes, at the end of which you had to dive headfirst from a height of some five meters, being careful as you did so not to ram your head into the flat riverbed. This event took place in the winter in order, as they said, to harden us as Germans. After breaking up some of the ice floes and even towing a few of the larger ones away, forty of us plunged into the icy water. It wasn't long before the herd began thinning out, as one of us after another exited the river running like a blue streak. All exited but two. One was my friend Günter, who wanted to prove his courage after being forced to endure a series of hostile challenges in the wake of the uncloaked commandant's removal. The other was yours truly. I was ice-cold, though after a while I hardly felt the cold anymore. Slowly my energy was beginning to wane, when it suddenly occurred to me that you could actually run in this river, which in this particular spot was especially flat, and that if you were clever enough about it, it would look just as if you were swimming. So there I was, moving my arms in a swimming rhythm while actually running in short steps along the riverbed. The ruse worked perfectly. After 45 minutes we were pulled from the water and vigorously rubbed down. Then it was time for diving. Günter climbed up onto the guard rail and dove headfirst into the water, which had been cleared of all the little straggling ice floes by the kids who were watching. After him I climbed up to the same spot, naked as I was, since we swam sans swim trunks, looked down and froze. It's not that I was getting colder, but that I simply couldn't move. I believe the reason for this lay in the test of courage that had been forced on me the week before.

There was this one huge factory smokestack, and we had to climb up it from the inside, right up to the very top where we then had to let both legs dangle over the rim, only after that climbing back down. The problem was that some of the iron pegs inside the stack had loosened over time, so that you were in a relentless panic over prying one of them out and doing a free fall to the bottom. I had succeeded in getting to the top, also managing to let both legs hang down from the rim, but then began the descent, which was considerably trickier than the ascent. You couldn't tell where the peg was located or how intact it was. Just as I began to sweat blood and think it was all over for me, one of the pegs came loose and fell to the bottom, striking the concrete floor with a sharp crack. Luckily I was tall enough to reach the next peg with my hand, and did so, regaining my confidence that I would reach the ground. But this experience left its scar in that I suffer from acrophobia to this day. So it was impossible for me to dive from the bridge into the water, despite all the encouragement shouted at me from both sides of the bridge. After I'd been standing up there quivering for about ten minutes, they all began screaming "coward" and ran off. I climbed down from the rail, looked for my things, which they'd hidden, found them, put them on and went to my room. I did succeed in proving my courage a few weeks later when the whole region was covered with snow. The camp leaders had received skis from the occupied territories and gave them out to us. None of us had a clue about skiing, but we thought it was "cool" to glide down from a small rise into the valley in the middle of which were tracks along which trains occasionally passed. The test of courage consisted in calculating precisely when the locomotive was down below, so that you could ski-jump over the tracks just ahead of it. All you really had to know was when to dig the ski poles into the snow so as to take off with split-second timing. I did it several times to prove I was at least as good as the others. In fact, I outdid the others, as nobody managed it more than twice, whereas I, now an experienced "daredevil," jumped across in front of the charging train at least six times, each time reducing the distance between me and it. Of course, I never told a word of this to my mother. I knew it was the last thing she'd ever want to hear about.

During the Fall of 1944, after school, the whole class had to go to the manor, located in the same village, to help out with the potato harvest. I couldn't stand the Polish workers. They had found out that I was of Jewish descent and proceeded to have their fun with me. They asked me if I would like to ride, and when I enthusiastically nodded yes, they took three horses, bound them together, set me atop the middle one, and whipped all three into a meadow with a cluster of trees in it. The horses made a beeline for the trees, and I was so dumbfounded that I forgot to duck, so that the low-hanging branches clawed me in the face, which was now bleeding all over. Somehow I sensed that it wasn't only the workers but the horses too that had something against me; maybe they could smell that I wasn't racially pure, no more than they themselves. In any case, we had to work with these farmhands to get the potatoes out of the ground and drag the heavy sacks over to the wagon, to which were hitched the same horses that had taken me under the trees. One of the animals eyed me briefly. Fearing that the spectacle might repeat itself, I emptied the sack into the wagon and got out of there fast. Before leaving the area, we sat down and ate the raw potatoes lying around the field — after all, we were hungry. Later back in the camp, we usually had turnip jam and rye bread, a combination I cannot abide to this day.

No doubt eating all those raw potatoes played a part in my becoming sick. I developed upset stomach, headache, diarrhea and bouts of fever. The nurse who took care of us put me in one of the two beds in the infirmary and fed me semolina pudding. Not nearly so solicitous was the academic camp leader who came by and promptly accused me of malingering in order to escape the drudgery of potato duty. And so I dozed on and off for two weeks, threw up a few times and had feverish visions that kept me from sleeping at night. The nurse became alarmed and sent for the village doctor, who examined me and immediately ordered an ambulance to take me to the district hospital in Kempen. It was night when we took off, the ambulance moving at frightening speed along a country road full of potholes. I moaned in pain. Upon arrival I was placed in a bathtub to clean me up, and that's when I lost consciousness. Next morning I was informed that I had to be operated. I was on the operating table at 8:00 o'clock where I lay waiting for over two hours, because the surgeon had an ear appointment at the military hospital. I remember this span of time on the table very well, for, although a white cloth was suspended outstretched before my eyes, I was still able to follow the passage of time on the plainly visible wall clock behind me. When the surgeon finally arrived, I was given the anesthetic and woke up with a thick bandage around my stomach, from which a draining tube protruded. My mother was informed and came the next day. They told her the reason for my illness was a protracted appendicitis resulting in an abscess, and if they hadn't intervened when they did, the pus would've oozed into my abdominal cavity and I would've died. My mother was at my side during the whole two weeks of my hospital stay and told me she was filing a complaint with the responsible district head, since it was obvious the camp leader should've called in a doctor much sooner than he did. Then she took me back to the camp and went home, not, however, before being assured that I would be permitted to return to Berlin.

In the meantime I was quartered with the big boys, i.e., the students in the higher grades. These guys whooped it up every evening, slugging some rotgut they'd picked up in a Polish bar. There was also plenty of sexual play; in the evening the Polish servant girls would be brought to the room, voluntarily or not. They would drink it up and sooner or later let the boys undress them and make love to them. I had never seen anything like it, and since I would usually be lying on the upper bunk, I would have to bend way down to get an eyeful, which led, one evening, to the collapse of the bed frame holding the individual support slats, with me landing hard on the floor. My wound reopened and I'd bitten my lip so hard that it began to bleed. Someone fetched the nurse and I was returned to the infirmary.

My mother's complaint was successful to the extent that, from then on, they took better care of me. I had permission to return to Berlin, and they even gave me a teacher as an escort. Our first stop was Posen where we had a four-hour layover. I was allowed to go downtown by myself as long as I promised to be back at the railroad station by a particular time. The first thing I did was to take a streetcar through the city. Unfortunately I could only see very little because the window panes of the car were covered over from the inside with a thick white paint. The conductor explained the reason for this to me, that this car's route went through the Jewish ghetto. But someone had scratched just enough paint from one of the glass edges to allow you to see through. Which, of course, is what I did; I could see some people on the street wearing the yellow star. And then I spotted a boy who looked to be about my age. He was standing at the door of his house, and I was convinced he was my brother, since he looked exactly like me. He looked at the streetcar and I couldn't tell whether he could see me from out there, but the sight of him is something I'll never forget, just as I'll never forget the groups of Jews I saw being herded through the city for deportation by the SS, some of whom fell down and got trampled by the ones coming after. And I just stood there and did nothing; I was only afraid the same thing could happen to me.

Let It Go, This Too Will Soon Pass

Back in Berlin, I learned from my mother that there had been many air attacks while I was away. In my interview with her she talked about this time:

Once we were under extremely heavy attack. And a bomb fell through the cellar window and lay there several days. We weren't aware of it and just continued sleeping in our apartment. Then a man came and told us that we needed to leave the house immediately because there was a live five-hundredweight bomb lying in the cellar. We had to get out of the house, together with our visitor from Finsterwalde, and he took off right away for home, since some houses were burning that day, and as we walked down the street, there were many dead lying around, and water, water everywhere, since the water pipes had burst. Then we went into the bunker and slept there. And then it turned out that in the next cellar over, where the people from the bombed-out staircase were sitting, everything was kaput. So this bomb was just lying there. It was a dud; it had turned over on impact and was lying with the nose facing upward. There were many wounded and one dead man, an old fellow who'd had a heart attack. Then they took the bomb out and deactivated it, and finally on an afternoon we were allowed back into the house, because, you know, we were all completely frozen through and hungry as well. Yeah, that's the way it goes in war. But over and over again God has protected us from the worst.

In the first night I spent at home there were two alarms. The bombs were falling close enough to us; but the nerve-wracking thing wasn't the explosions: it was the howling crescendo of the bombs as they dropped, a howling that would finally culminate in an explosion, but only after a span of time that struck me as weirdly long. And the explosion would always cause our cellar emergency-exit-door to clatter wildly. I decided after this I'd had just about enough of my visit to Berlin and set out for Altwerder again the next day.

But I wasn't to remain there long. It was July, 1944, and the Russians were by now not that far away from our camp. So I went back to Berlin with a few others and got shoved all over the place like a chess piece, because my mother was very nervous about the roundups in our area. Sometimes we'd get the alert from Inge, a grandchild of my father's from his first marriage. She worked as a switchboard operator in the Ministry of Propaganda and could usually find out when such a roundup was scheduled to take place in our neighborhood. She would then inform my mother, who would either send me off to our property in Wilhelmsruh or have me taken in by a friendly family nearby, though never for more than two days, since there was always the fear of being denounced. That's how I got to know some sections of the city pretty well and was later able to turn this knowledge to profit by taking sightseers all around the city on tours. The situation worsened after October when my father got sick and could no longer look after the garden. Not only this, but his three daughters were pressuring him to give them their inheritance, and so, without any fuss, he sold his property with the massive oak tree to a realtor who gave him 5000 Reichsmarks in five-mark pieces for it. I took a peek into the living room where the five-mark fortune lay on the table, and I was worried that the table might sag and even collapse under the burden. Of course, nothing of the sort happened. Later on I caught my father wiping tears from his eyes. A part of his world was gone, a fact that hit him even harder when, after the sale, he went back to his property and saw the great old oak chopped down and lying across the grass. It had brought a little more than 5000 marks in the sale, as he then learned to his sorrow.

Later that same year (1944), people began making preparations for the feast of Christmas. For the past year or so of war, there had been severe food shortages, so that you sometimes had to go to bed hungry. Certainly there were *Lebensmittelkarten* (ration cards),[26] intended to obviate social disparities. But just as certainly, there were lacunae in this supply system, for it was possible to buy extra food rations on the black market. Since I was always hungry, my mother would always use up her food rations well before the next shopping date, so that by the end of every month Slim Pickins became head chef in our kitchen. So-called advance purchases of food rations, though technically not allowed, were nevertheless tolerated. Our Mom-and-Pop grocery on Adolfstraße, where my mother had shopped for decades, was particularly helpful in this regard. There you could not only catch up on the latest gossip but also shop in small quantities, such as, e.g., a quarter pound of liverwurst or a hundred grams of Tilsit cheese, but without the crust, to keep the weight down. The woman who owned the place would sometimes extend my mother credit, since my mother was very conscientious and paid her debts promptly, as soon as my father's pension check arrived. The food ration cards were every bit as important as money, and my mother kept ours in a tin can, which was the first thing anyone reached for on our way to the cellar in an air attack. In the cellar my mother would complain about this or that store or dealer who was exploiting the rationing system for his own illicit profit. Sometimes, for example, the bread was baked with an excess of moisture so that it weighed more; or, in the pro-rationing of meat, the bones, gristle and slippery fat were weighed in, raising the weight and lowering nutritional value.

Even in this period of scarcity, my mother had an idea how we might still celebrate Christmas in a festive way. She had a half-sister, Erna, who lived with her husband in Netzebruch in the district of Landsberg, where my mother was born and spent the first fourteen years of her life. The farmers there had enough to eat, she figured, and one might presume to share just a little of their abundance. Getting there, however, was anything but easy. Unless you were traveling for your job, you had to apply for a permit anytime you wanted to go more than 50 km. Unfortunately this applied to Landsberg, so a permit was my first order of business. I put on my uniform, went to the railroad station and told them at the checkpoint I wanted to visit my uncle in the military hospital. Of course, the large suitcase I was carrying aroused suspicion and I was asked what was in it. I couldn't tell these people the truth since my mother had stuffed the thing with several pieces of silverware and good tablecloths and linen bedding, fearing the Russians would confiscate everything on entering the city. So I told them it contained presents for the family. In Landsberg I rode in a horse-drawn carriage along the dyke, arriving in good shape at the station, which was not all that far from the Netze. You had to take the ferry across the river, which caused some delay since there were many carriages needing to be ferried over. My half-aunt was happy to see me and received me royally with a humongous dish of scrambled eggs and greasy pork. There was plenty of pork in the area, since most local farmers were carrying out forced slaughters to prevent meat from falling into the hands of the advancing Russians. During the night I got sick and had to throw up several times, since I was no longer used to such fatty food. Next day I buried the well-wrapped valuables in the suitcase in the vicinity of the farm, in a spot where they may still be today, assuming they didn't decay from the subsequent bursting of the dam and the resulting flood waters. The following day my aunt packed the suitcase full; I was given several pounds of *Hackepeter*[27] a big ham, three pounds of butter packed in rhubarb leaves for freshness, and a big, fat goose. Loaded up with these valuables, I headed home and arrived there in good order, just in time to pursue my new enterprise.

In an effort to bring home some extra money and food, I went over to the railroad station and offered to carry suitcases. What with various modes of transportation in the city shut down because of the air attacks, people had to make it home on foot, and since it was mostly older people, the young being away at the front, they were happy to find someone to carry their suitcases.

Now and then I got the short end, like the time an older lady had to walk from the Stettin station to Tegel, a stretch Berliners called JWD[28]. It took hours, but I was well compensated with a dozen eggs and a pound of butter, which enriched our meal plan handsomely. Often I'd be given money, which I put away for the purchase of Christmas presents. I had a lot of time, since school was closed for vacation, and my attendance at this time was, at any rate, very irregular. In the week before Christmas I worked the job of delivering Christmas trees, and that too put a little extra money in the till.

Something bad happened at Christmas. During the cold snap my mother had hung the goose I'd brought back with me from the flower boxes outside the kitchen window to keep it fresh. But then when she went to retrieve it on December 23, it was gone. Someone had cut the rope from which it was hanging. My mother was furious and suspected the party living directly above us, a woman with whom she was usually at loggerheads. The woman, of course, protested her innocence. So, on the first day of Christmas, my mother went skulking around the building, sniffing at every door in an effort to discover the whereabouts of our goose, doubtless transformed by now into a crispy roast. Soon enough, however, the alarm sounded and we all had to head for the cellar for a few hours. The goose was never located. The incident fortified my mother in her belief that man was basically bad and that, in the hierarchy of human values, eating one's fill was number one, and far below that, if indeed anywhere at all, was morality. In the case of a goose, though, it was nowhere to be found.

The following months were even more harrowing than those just past. The air raids were coming in ever shorter intervals, and we'd sit around our *Volksempfänger* (People's receiver or radio) in the evening and listen for the cuckoo, the sign that an air attack was imminent. The moment we were informed that the squadrons were flying over Hannover-Braunschweig and the howl of sirens sounded the warning, we'd be on our way to the cellar. Always I carried Peter with me in his cage, along with a small suitcase containing things useful for first aid, or so I imagined. These included band-aids, gauze bandages and a two-pound package of glucose, which, I read somewhere, was supposed to go straight into the bloodstream and give you lots of power and energy. In addition, I took along my box full of my favorite books, among which now belonged those of Karl May.

In one attack in early February, 1945, an unusual number of incendiary bombs fell on Köslinerstraße, where mainly workers lived. I went there right after the all-clear to look up my uncle. He lived in a *Myers Hof,*[29] a large apartment block with a front building and five backyards which were so narrow and close together that families would sometimes pass food dishes across the yard from one flat to its opposite number. Living conditions were nothing short of catastrophic there and called to mind the pronouncement of the sketch artist and social critic Heinrich Zilles that you could kill a man with such a flat as efficiently as with an axe. These apartment blocks were also highly dangerous in the sense that, should an incendiary or phosphorus bomb hit the front house, it would be easy for the flames to spread to the rear buildings, resulting in a flaming sea of total destruction. To be sure, the Panke, which comes from Chausseestraße and empties into the Spree both above and below ground, flowed behind the houses above ground, but it wouldn't have been of any use in putting out a fire, since, in the first place, it was frozen, and, in the second, it was too shallow to get much water from. And so many houses burned down from roof to cellar, including the one in which my uncle lived. It was an infernal spectacle, one that was often to repeat itself in the time to come.

At the end of February, 1945, the number of air blitzes increased. My attendance at school became more and more irregular because the rapid transit which I took to Schönhauser Ave. often had to shut down operations due to bomb damage to the tracks. I took to commuting by bike; at this point classes were still being held, but usually in the school basement. We slaved away at our Latin and Greek syllabus until about mid-March and were also given instruction in math. One day Volker, who was my age and lived at the corner of Gericht and Pasewalkerstraße, dropped by for a visit. When the alarm sounded, he stayed with us. My father, Volker and I headed down to the cellar to wait for the all-clear, which on this particular February day was a good long time in coming. Clearly our area had been pin-pointed for this attack; this was obvious from the howling of scores of bombs. The hits were getting closer and closer, and we placed ourselves, just as we'd been trained, on the floor with open mouths so that our lungs wouldn't burst from the explosions. Finally, after a few moments of calm, as we began to think it was over, we heard a howling that grew louder and louder and seemed to last forever. The din came ever so close and we feared the worst. Then came the explosion. The emergency exit door, joining our shelter via a break in the wall with all the others, clattered like crazy, and the air vent flap, camouflaged as a wood panel, slammed against the wall with a tremendous bang. The lime fell from the cellar's whitewashed walls, the light went out and you couldn't see your hand before your eyes. Fortunately, the cellar ceiling didn't cave in, as all shelter ceilings were required by law to be reinforced with whitewashed joists. Right after that there was a loud crash just outside the shelter window, which had wisely been plugged up with sand. It was our jalousies that we'd had installed a few years earlier, in compliance with the blackout directives. All gone with one blow. When we went back upstairs, we were stepping on glass everywhere; all window panes were blown out, and in some apartments even the window frames had fallen down into the yard. My father was white as a sheet, for he was the only one who hadn't gotten down on the floor, and the air pressure had flung the air vent flap right past his head, so that wood fragments lay about everywhere.

Volker went right home, though only in a manner of speaking, since his apartment building, including front house, side wings and rear house, had been leveled. No stone sat atop another, as it were, and one section of the front house even lay across the intersection of Paserwalker- and Gerichtstraße. My mother described this attack as follows:

I was working at the post office. When the news spread that Paserwalkerstraße had been hit, we were told to tie up our letters and go home. And as I walked home with a co-worker—we had to walk, since there was no train — we ran into another co-worker coming from Wedding, and she said, "Oh God, an aerial mine's [30] *fallen on Pasewalkerstraße and everything's kaput." When we got to the street, the steam shovels were already there digging people out of the rubble, but almost all of them were dead. I'd estimate around thirty — there were an awful lot of casualties. Later on they found lots of bones when they cleared out the mountain of debris. And the woman who owned the bakery had just that morning received five tons of coal, and many people piled into the bakery kitchen when the alarm went off, because it was warm. The air pressure had blown many people up against the hot oven. They got stuck there and scorched. Everything was destroyed. The steam shovels came right away and people tried to help the workers, but all the victims were dead. The rescue attempt was futile.*

Volker's mother was among the dead. When the steam shovel pulled her out by one leg, he shed not a single tear. He merely said, in a voice filled with hate, "I will kill the ones who've done this." Later I learned that he'd joined the *Werwölfe* (Werewolves).[31] He was killed in an attack by soldiers on patrol and buried next to his mother in the *Dankesfriedhof* (Thanksgiving Cemetery) in December, 1945. I was at his burial and laid a small fir branch on his grave.

Then at the end of February, 1945, our house too burned down. The attack came in daylight and we had set up house in the shelter as comfortably as possible. I had fixed myself a neat little sleeping nook in the corner, and my father had a plank-bed on which he could sleep, if not exactly well, at least without interruption and, in any case, better than upstairs in our room. The instant we heard a terrific impact that was *not* preceded by the howl of a falling bomb, we knew our house had been hit. The light at first flickered and then went out. When I saw our shelter floor writhe up from the hit and come to a kind of arch, I screamed in fear that we'd be overrun by mice and rats, but a woman took me on her lap, wrapped her arms around me and said simply, "Let it be, this too will soon pass." After the dust settled, we went upstairs. We had to brace ourselves against the door and push; something inside was blocking it. A man deftly removed an axe from the wall and hacked an opening in the door. Inside in front of the door lay a window frame that had been blown out by the air pressure and lodged against the door. We climbed over it and past the shards of glass lying everywhere, just happy that our house was still standing. Or more precisely, a section of the house, namely our staircase. The staircase in the adjacent section of the building was on the ground in ruins, completely leveled. Once again we believed we'd come away relatively unscathed, but our joy was short-lived.

That evening we noticed that one side of the damaged section of the apartment block began to burn. The reason for this was that the occupants with the bombed-out staircase were raking through the rubble for their belongings, eventually causing the flames smoldering under the floor stones to leap up to the gas pipe suspended above the rubble, setting it on fire. Then too, all stoves were heated, since it was very cold. The fire spread with astonishing rapidity, taking hold of the roof timbers, and the building burned down floor by floor from top to bottom. It was now almost midnight and the sirens announced yet another attack. At this point nothing fazed us, and it occurred to me that the blackout was unnecessary, since the burning houses themselves offered the bomber pilots the clearest possible targets. Since we lived only one flight up, we were able to salvage some furnishings. I took down the big wall mirror and maneuvered it down the stairs and out the door. Then I rescued my books, the number of which had increased substantially in recent months. The stairway was now full of smoke, and there was a danger of suffocation. I ran inside two more times and saved a few clothes, some bedding, some dishware and a satchel full of my collectibles. By then it was no longer possible to enter the house. My father and I went into the house across the street directly opposite ours, and since we knew the tenants on the fourth floor, we could see from their window how the flames slowly but surely made their way down and towards the sides. Our neighbor owned a beautiful, black Bechstein grand piano. At first the flames only licked at the legs, but soon they were inching higher and higher, finally engulfing the keyboard. With the intense heat the strings began to rupture, and this rupturing was something you could actually hear from behind our safe window across the street. The tempo of the bursting strings accelerated more and more until it sounded like a macabre symphony of annihilation. My father watched his apartment go up in flames, and once again I could see tears roll down his cheeks. He had lived there for over forty years.

We were now out on the street, and to top it all off, it began to rain. I tried to save my books, but it was no use. The teeming rain turned everything to mush, and pages fell from the bindings. I stood next to my father and began crying with him. I felt the whole world was conspiring against me. In that moment Frau Groggert, whom I'd seen a number of times talking with my mother, came up to us and said we could move into her basement. She was very religious, though nothing of the literalist-fundamentalist type; rather she practiced a kind of pragmatic charity. She lived close by on Gerichtstraße. We accepted her kind offer and so managed at least to get off the street.

Next morning, when we went back over to our burned-down house to secure our belongings from the street, we saw that a great deal had been stolen. Among the missing items was a collector's album it had taken me a lot of effort to put together. One series in the album showed how Germans in the colonies were civilizing the natives of Southwest Africa.[32] Among my other treasures nowhere to be found were two cigar boxes. One of these contained two collections of luminescent badges which you could wear on the lapel of your coat or jacket to avoid being jostled in the street at night. These badges were covered with a layer of phosphorus which gave off a weak, greenish glow in the darkened streets alerting others to a possible collision. The badges came in series, and I had a wonderful fairy-tale series featuring Hansel and Gretel, Snow White, Sleeping Beauty, Rumpelstilzchen and other Grimm figures. The other series consisted of ships, from the sailing ships of old right up to the modern battle ships, such as the Scharnhorst and, above all, the Tirpitz, on which the father of a former classmate of mine had served. The other cigar box was filled with grenade and bomb fragments I had collected after the air raids. Some of these with their sharp, jagged edges looked dangerous, but also beautiful nonetheless, since they sometimes emitted a green-bluish glow. These fragments were first-rate exchange currency, and the bigger they were and the more shimmering bearing rings they had, the more valuable they became for trading. I myself, for example, had traded many of them for glow-badges, especially when I was on the hunt for a badge to complete my series; I'd also traded them for those little racing cars we used for our curbside races. We would stuff the hollow undersides of the cars full of putty to make them go faster. Now it was all gone.

My mother described the burning-down of our house to me as follows:

Our house was hit a few days after they dropped the aerial mine. In February we had two heavy attacks; all of Berlin was on fire. I was at the doctor's, and a woman who also worked at the post office came by and said to me, "Oh Frau Schneider, everything's lost!" We were on our way back and I said to her, "But look, the house is still standing," but as I came around the corner, I could see the staircase next door had collapsed and everything was lying in the street. And I said to the woman, "Come on upstairs with me, I've got a meal on the stove," but that meal was now lying down below all over the yard. We had to wait till evening to get something to eat. We tried to get into different schools where there was supposed to be food, but everything was on fire, and whenever we'd come to a particular school, we'd find everything already gone. And so all of us—Papa, you and I—had to go hungry. Finally we got lucky. We went into a school that still had food and were fed pea soup from a field kitchen. They had sandwiches there too. Then we went back to pick up our things that were lying in the street, but when we got there, they'd already stolen my beautiful bedding, replacing it with their own filthy bedding. So we were only able to salvage two sets of bedding out of four, and we had to see about buying another one for Gerd. And in the meantime we just settled in as best we could. Then we got lucky. An apartment on the third floor was empty, and we moved into it after two weeks in the cellar. It looked horrible. It had no windows or doors, and the one bedroom was completely demolished by the bomb that had fallen on it. Still, it was better than life in the cellar. And besides, Gerd made his confirmation at the end of February, and we had a little celebration for him.

I still remember this confirmation very well. I had half a year of confirmation instruction, which was given in the basement of a church in Neukölln on account of the air raids. When we were told at Christmas time about the heavenly hosts that proclaimed God's glory from on high, we asked ourselves what the word "glory" really meant. We certainly had every right to ask this question, since the bomber squadrons that came in the night were very much like the heavenly hosts, except that the message they proclaimed was quite different from the Biblical one. Actually, enemy planes dropped *Leuchtraketen* and *Leuchtbomben* (flairs), dubbed *Weihnachtsbäume* (Christmas trees) by the people, even before the attacks to mark off the area that was to be bombed. If we happened to be inside the illuminated square, we knew we were in for it.

For the topic of the first essay I had to write and recite in confirmation instruction I chose King David's relationship with Bathsheba. The reasons for this seem, in retrospect, rather obvious. In the first place, I was going through puberty and sex was beginning to interest me. But added to this was the fact that, in our neighborhood, someone would often be sent to the Eastern front for quite personal reasons, especially when that person had criticized the war, which is exactly what David did to Uriah, Bathsheba's husband. In composing the essay, I let my imagination supply all the details the Bible had seen fit to omit, describing everything down to a T, just as I envisioned the couple's sexual liaison. Putting off all attempts of the priest to cut off my recital, I was staunchly following my mother's advice to assert myself; and besides, my fellow confirmees were gleefully spurring me on, applauding wildly at the end as I concluded with the sentence, "And that's the way a royal act of sexual intercourse should be." In spite of this I was allowed to make my Confirmation. Of course, I needed a suit for the ceremony, just at a time when textiles were scarce. My mother submitted an application, and I received a brand new garment, one manufactured, alas, with paper fibers. I wasn't aware of this, but sure found out about it on my day of honor: as I came out of the church, it proceeded to come down in buckets, and the suit grew smaller and smaller. The pants were, as we say in Berlin, "at half-mast," and the sleeves had shrunk right up to the elbows. Surveying the disaster, my mother could only sigh resignedly, "Oh well, that's war for you. What can you expect?" And at home she had baked a potato pie that we now all dug into with delight. To be sure, the sirens began to howl during the meal and the hostile hosts appeared from on high. We saved the end of our celebration for the shelter and didn't go back upstairs until the all-clear. We were just glad that we still had an "upstairs."

At the end of March, 1945, school closed, rendered unfeasible by what were now virtually uninterrupted attacks. Our daily rhythm was down and back up, and back down and back up. My parakeet had an anxiety reaction, since, after all, we were constantly disturbing his night's sleep; sometimes we would find him cringing down on the floor on his cage, totally freaked out. But whenever I opened the shelter door, he'd fly right over to me, regardless what time of day it was, and chatter a blue streak into my ear. Then he'd perch on my finger, stick his head under his wing and go to sleep. He has it pretty good, I would think, and then think, "Were I a little bird," things would be better. But I was no little bird, and things weren't better, not for me, and not even for him, as it later turned out. As for the rest, I just waited, as I imagined everyone else just waited, for something to happen that would put an end to this bad dream.

April 1945: People in the Hotel

There came a turning point for me about a month later, on April 1, when I turned fourteen. The doorbell rang, and when I opened, there stood before me a Brown Shirt who handed me a sealed letter covered with postmarks. I opened it and read that further attendance at school for first-degree *Mischlinge* was forbidden upon attainment of the age of fourteen and that I was to seek out an apprenticeship for myself. Should I fail to find one by the end of that day, I was to report to one of the locations listed for special assignment. Should I fail to appear, I would be delivered there. It was all my mother could do to calm her anxiety, for we had heard a great deal about these "special assignments," which usually turned out to be one-way trips. She told me I had no time to lose. The first thing I did was to go to the employment agency to find out through testing what my special aptitudes were. I had to wait and got nervous, since time was pressing, but after a few hours of waiting I was admitted. A gentleman had my file on his desk and asked me what I intended to become in life. I responded "an architect," since architects, it seemed to me, would have the best employment opportunities in the wake of so much destruction. "My boy, you have to be realistic," he harrumphed, "for that you have to study, and there's still plenty of time for that." Then he looked at the file and said tersely, "Actually, in your case that's not even an issue. It says here you're a half-Jew. So there's no question of study." I replied that I wanted to take an aptitude test, but he said in his opinion that wasn't necessary since I had Jewish blood in my veins, and all Jews were only out for making money, as history had shown. Whereupon he wrote down for me on a piece of paper the address of a company that was looking for mercantile apprentices. He dismissed me with the disclosure that he was actually doing me a favor, since the company in question was located not far from our apartment, on Gerichtstraße. So I went smartly on my way, as it was already 1 p.m. and I only had a few hours before they would, as I was convinced, come and get me. The company was the great paint factory, Decken, on Müllerstraße, not far from Seestraße. I introduced myself and tried to make a good impression. In this I succeeded, besides which I had the advantage of having attended a *Gymnasium.* My knowledge of Latin also probably played a roll here, as the chief clerk asked me if I could give his son some private lessons in the subject. I promised him I would take his son under my wing, which gladdened his heart, convinced as he must have been that he had stumbled on a low-cost tutor. Then I went proudly home and told my mother everything. I had scarcely finished when the outer doorbell rang. I opened the door and standing there was a runner for the company with a letter for me. I opened it and read that the company was an Aryan business and that it could not hire anyone who was unable to produce Aryan identification. This took place on April 1, 1945, the last full month before the end of the war. Again I was back at square one.

It finally came down to a quick discussion with my mother, who thought I should apply for an apprenticeship in the hospitality trade, maybe as a cook, since I was always hungry. So I was on my way again. I looked in the telephone book, and right there in the first column was the Adlon Hotel. So I went over to Paris Square, checked out the hotel, which stood just east of the Brandenburg Gate, and headed for the personnel department. There I was told that all apprenticeship positions were already filled. Just at that moment, Frau Hedda Adlon happened to be passing by. She asked me what I wanted. I told her the truth, that I needed an apprenticeship if I was to avoid being "detained." She stepped into her office and phoned someone. Then she told me that a position as a chef's apprentice was available at the Hotel Continental, but I would have to apply in a hurry before it was filled. I rushed out of the magnificent Adlon hotel and over to the no less imposing Hotel Continental, which was located in the vicinity of the railroad station on Friedrichstraße, not at all far from the Adlon. Once there, I again went right to the personnel office, was asked what I wanted, and in a few minutes had the job. To make sure I wouldn't be picked up, I asked for permission to start immediately, and so I was sent forthwith to the main kitchen, located on the ground floor. I got in just under the wire, as the clock now showed almost 5 p.m.

My first workday or training day lasted a mere two hours. I was handed a white apron and introduced to the head chef, who in turn called his sous-chefs over and introduced me around. It was all very polite and according to Hoyle. Scarcely had the head chef gone off when one of the assistants, a Frenchman like most of the others, came by and gave me the name "Gérard." He hustled me over to the stove, which was very long and had over twenty hotplates on it. He shoved one of the copper pots aside, removed the burner rings, took my hand, which was already balled into a fist, and pressed it directly over the open hearth. The hand turned red and already had some blisters. The chef pressed it lower and lower, almost beyond my endurance. But I didn't cry. Then he took an entire handful of butter from a vat and smeared it over my damaged hand, after which he asked me if I liked to eat butter. When I nodded yes, he took a second handful and, while another chef held me from behind, opened my mouth and shoved the butter inside it. I had to swallow all of it. My initiation into the culinary fraternity thus concluded, I was permitted to take off my apron and go home. On leaving I was told to report for work next day early in the morning. I realized that it wasn't easy to become a chef. Later I considered that the whole business was unlikely to have been an anti-Semitic act, but rather just a hard, though pedagogically effective, means to familiarize me with my new occupation. As for butter, so abundant in the hotel kitchen yet accessible to the people only through food stamps, after this experience I didn't go near it for quite a while.

Next day I was back again. I was assigned to the seafood chef or *poissonier.* My first assignment was to clean a turbot, a kind of diamond-shaped flatfish. It was thoroughly frozen and huge; I was shown how to make an initial incision high up from head to gills, then the same on the bottom, though without separating the head entirely. Then you had to pull the head tightly and all the entrails would come out as it came off. Since the fish was frozen through and through, my hands got cold fast, but I didn't want to say anything, having had all the hand-warming I could stand the day before. Anyway, I quickly found my rhythm and went through about twenty fish on my first day. That may sound like a lot, but the hotel was filled to capacity and the dining room was always full to bursting. The reason for this was that the SS held their parties in the hotel and took their meals there as well. For the next few days I had to clean roach (*Plötzen*). I approached these fish with high expectations, since they were local and I knew the *Plötzensee* (Roach

Lake) from swimming in it. To be sure, I had never actually laid eyes on a roach before, much less cleaned one. They were quite unforgiving fish, as it turned out, covered all over as they were with scales, which you had to scrape off before you could steam them. Nor was I aware that these fish had belly scales. They were tough to spot, being white, just like the belly itself. And so it happened that the not quite scale-free roach were served, resulting not merely in complaints but almost in my death. One of the high brass came charging downstairs into our kitchen snorting fire and asked the head chef who was responsible for cleaning the fish. The chef pointed to me and the officer walked over to me drawing his pistol. He intended to shoot me, believing I'd wanted to choke him. Reflexively I raised my hand in a Hitler salute and apologized as best I could. He reconsidered his action, either because my salute confused him or because my apology softened his heart.

Another time a mishap occurred that was not my fault. One of the waiters came into the kitchen white as a sheet, carrying in his trembling hands a silver tray on which lay something covered over. He lifted the serviette and we saw a small rocket that had probably been shot out of a *Minenwerfer* (mine thrower) or a *Stalinorgel* (Stalin organ).[33] This projectile had apparently dropped through an open window into the dining hall, lodging itself in an empty easy chair, the single empty chair at an otherwise fully occupied table. The waiter told us that one of the officers had discreetly called him over and politely ordered him to remove the projectile with care. The waiter did exactly as he was told, with great caution and dexterity, intending then to exit the restaurant with the offending object. But the headwaiter held him back and asked him if he had completely forgotten his training as a waiter. He handed him a tray, covering the projectile as he did so with a clean linen serviette; only then was the waiter permitted to leave the dining room. After showing it to us, he deposited it on a heap of rubble not too close to the hotel. That was my first lesson in the dangers and risks attending the waiter's vocation, but, as it turned out later, not my last.

Around mid-April and despite the never-ending alarm, I was walking with my mother across Nettelbeck Square when an American fighter plane suddenly dove down and strafed the people on the street with the fire of the machine guns attached to its underwings. Everybody scattered, seeking protection against the walls of the houses, my mother included. I, of course, had slipped my hand out of hers and just stood there staring at the departing airplane, totally fascinated. It was a scene I had heretofore viewed only in the weekly newsreel. Now, all of a sudden, I was not only witness to such a scene, but also its focus of attack. At that point the plane made a turn and headed back in my direction. My mother screamed out to me as if possessed, "Son, come here! Get over here!", but, even though I wanted to obey my mother's command, I was unable to put one foot in front of the other; I was as if frozen stiff. The plane fired again, the salvos ricocheting off the pavement left and right in front of me; then it turned away and disappeared. And there I stood, somehow still in one piece. As I ran over to my mother across the square, she was livid that I hadn't listened to her and gave me a resounding slap, hard enough to cause one of the bystanders to remark, "Aw, leave da kid alone, willya, it coulda been woise. Jus' be glad ya still got yer sonny boy witcha. At's betta den if 'eda been laid out in da big box." Later it occurred to me that something or someone must've held me still and thereby saved me, because, if I had run away, one of the salvos would surely have hit me and I would certainly have wound up in "da big box."

The next day I was back in the hotel, after being told that we had no days off to look forward to for the foreseeable future. All at once we heard the howling of artillery fire through the open window of the sawtooth roof. Our head chef knew what to do. He assembled all his cooks and assistants and told them that the Russians were now intensifying their attack on the Reich's chancellery. It was now my job to listen for the whining of the rockets and to warn the others whenever the hits came too near. The kitchen offered no protection, since the diagonal roof that spanned it was made of glass, with only a few windows here and there for ventilation. A few days later, when the rocket fire intensified, I had to lather the tiles of the kitchen floor thick with butter, so that whenever I shouted "Take cover!", everybody would slide across the floor right into the protected corridor where they felt safe.

Looking back, I must admit that, at the time, I failed utterly to appreciate the absurdity of this situation. To me it wasn't absurd. Perhaps it was my drive for self-preservation that allowed me to perceive such moments as quite normal, because whenever I would try to process all this chaos mentally, I'd become confused. Then too, I was anything but a hero. I didn't cause any trouble; I was just a boy who wanted to belong and not be too conspicuous, who knew how to adjust smoothly to a new situation, and who simply wanted to survive. Now and then I would bitch and moan, but only to myself. My self-confidence was also at ground zero, having been told over and over again that I wasn't a true German, that I was merely tolerated by them, and that German was no more than a foreign language for the likes of me. And so I would flee again and again into the world of illusion and sometimes dream that I was Old Shatterhand or Kara Ben Nemsi: [34] both were heroes who stepped forward and took upon themselves the struggle against all evildoers and somehow always managed to win it, in spite of the hopeless situations in which they usually found themselves. One big difference between us was that I was not as religious as the two of them.

In the condition of alert, in which we virtually lived, things looked different, especially during this period in which the SS-officers held their bacchanals in the hotel's festival hall. The situation was lethal, since at any moment a rocket could hit our sawtooth-roof and put an end to our lives. But we didn't think about that; we just went on busily cooking in the midst of the shelling. We put on steel helmets and covered all pots and pans with lids. I was there to climb one step higher in my training and was entrusted with the honorable task of setting up a mushroom soup. First the mushrooms had to be washed and cut into thin slices. Then you had to melt butter in a big copper pot, after which you floured and steamed sliced onions together with the mushrooms. At that point the soup chef, or *Potagier*, took over the preparation, filling the whole concoction with broth and tasting the soup, which he thickened with salt, pepper, sour cream and various spices. What astonished me was the quantity. My mother made mushroom soup too, but she used no more than half a pound of mushrooms and a small onion; in this kitchen mushrooms were used by the kilo in a soup intended as the first course for some 120 persons.

My favorite job was assisting the cold-dish chef, the *Gardemanger*. His job was to prepare cold appetizers or hors d'oeuvres and set up cold plates for the buffet. I was permitted to help with the cheese platters, and I learned to arrange the different types of cheeses very artistically, also putting the finishing touches to everything with parsley and radishes. Since I did all this very well, I was then allowed to put together cheese platters for the chefs themselves for their meals. The chefs baked their own white bread, which they didn't slice up but simply broke off by the piece; to this they would add huge chunks of cheese they had cut up, washing everything down with red. Following that they would eat a kind of endive salad, which they dressed with nothing more than vinegar and olive oil, garlic and a bit of thyme. The salad was too bitter for my taste, but the chefs goaded me to eat the same food they did. So I slowly accustomed myself to it, and actually it doesn't taste bad when you add a few olives and some feta cheese to it, as I later learned.

The Last Days of the Third Reich

The rocket fire was especially bad on April 20, Hitler's birthday, nor did it let up in the days that followed. Now we were cowering more than ever on the kitchen floor, and preparing meals became even more difficult, since there was so much dust and we couldn't always cover the pots quickly enough. I was also concerned about how my parents were doing, so I told the head chef I had to go home. He eyed me briefly and we parted company, well aware there would be no returning to this place. On April 29 I grabbed my bike and pedaled in the direction of the Weidendamm bridge. Pedestrian traffic was tremendous, since so many people had formed what amounted to a tribal migration to the Gasag-bunker on Reinickendorferstraße, toting their possessions behind them on handcarts or flatbed handtrucks. The thick walls of the bunker offered a degree of protection from the heavy shelling, heavy because the street led directly to the Reich chancellery. On the middle of the bridge, we were attacked by a small Russian plane flying towards us very low to the ground. It flew just over our heads, ejecting as it did small bombs, which I assume were made of cement since they didn't explode. An elderly married couple walking in front of me were trying to reach safety, but it was too late. The man was hit and lay motionless. The old woman wept, and I told her she'd better hurry or she'd end up suffering the same fate.

When I got to the bunker facility on Reinickendorferstraße, I was pulled over by an officer and led to a group of young men. He gave us all an optimistic-sounding speech climaxing in the declaration that the future, not only of Berlin, but of all Germany rested on our shoulders. The army under the command of General Wenk was expected to arrive at any time; until then we must defend the city against the advancing Bolshevic hordes. He then gave each of us a *Panzerfaust* (literally "tank fist"), an anti-tank bazooka that rests atop the shoulder and fires rockets at armored vehicles and even larger tanks. He also gave everyone a pack of Juno cigarettes and a copy of the *Panzerbär* of 29 April 1945, the last newspaper in Berlin before the surrender. The headline read, "HEROIC STRUGGLE: NEW ATTACK FORCES AMASSED DAY AND NIGHT," and the article on the title page confirmed what we already knew: "Battle for heart of city rages." I laid my *Panzerfaust* under a clump of bushes, unarmed once again as I'd been before the bunker; unprepared to carry Germany's fate on my narrow shoulders, I pedaled home disburdened. When I showed up, my mother was happy to see me again, but her joy also had an ulterior motive.

We had nothing more to eat, and the other tenants in our building were in similar straits. Since all the young men were away in the military and even the older generations in the *Volkssturm* were supposed to be busy leading the homeland towards final victory, it fell to me with my fourteen years to help them. I hit the street and went straight over to a large grocery store right next to our building on Gerichtstraße. Its windows had been smashed and its wares plundered. I hesitated for a moment, afraid of getting shot, but then I made my way into the ransacked store. Everything was gone except for a sizable cardboard box full of ration cards sitting next to a large sack of salt. I took both with me and hurried back to the apartment with my booty. Earlier in our hallway, I had found a large suitcase full of banknotes next to the body of a soldier who'd been shot. He had probably stolen them from a bank safe. I pulled the body out into the street where it could easily be found, took the note-laden suitcase with me and thought myself quite rich. At home I checked out both suitcase and box with ration cards, and then got the idea to take the flatbed wagon of a neighbor and go shopping again, this time completely legally.

From my mother I knew of a store on Adolfstraße and knocked on its rear door, its front door being boarded up. A man opened and asked what I wanted. I answered that I'd been sent to buy groceries for my entire building and showed him the ration cards I'd already sorted out. He looked through them, took a large ledger book and carefully pasted them in. I then purchased at least twenty pounds of meat, six pounds of butter, a big cheese wheel and much else besides, paid for all of it with the money I'd found, loaded my treasure onto the flatbed, which scarcely accommodated the huge load, and headed home. There I distributed my most lawfully acquired goods among the tenants, and my mother roasted the meat on a small spirit stove, which she had also used in the garden, since we no longer had electricity. We ate, and immediately afterward had to head for the cellar, but at least we were full. When I later thought back on this experience, it occurred to me that the principle of order must indeed be deeply rooted in my fellow citizens, since I could scarcely think of another people that, in the face of such total annihilation and the complete collapse of all external orders, would take the time to paste ration cards neatly into a book and calculate monetary sums down to the penny. As for inner order, on the other hand, there were some who did manage to hang onto some sense of it a while longer. This pasting of stamps was, however, in vain, as the Russians were on the street the very next day, cleaning out the whole store, and quite without ration cards or cash, needless to say. Later I did come across the book with the pasted-in ration stamps again; it was lying in the gutter virtually reduced to mush by the rain. Thus does the grandeur of the world pass, or as I learned in my Latin class, "Sic transit gloria mundi." Nor was this an isolated case.

The next day I was back on the street scrounging up bread, now regarding myself — justifiably — as the provider for our domestic community. Just a few streets away stood the August Wittler bread factory, and this I took to be my opportunity. When I got there, hundreds of people were standing in front of the big building, all lined up in disciplined double columns, the discipline maintained, however, by several SS-soldiers manning a machine gun. The problem was that some agile Russian T-34 tanks were parked on the same street no more than thirty meters away directly in front of the breached road block and were shooting over them. Behind the barricade, made up of rubble, iron rods and sandbags, lay two young men, each equipped with a *Panzerfaust* and a *Panzerschreck* (tank rocket rifle), the latter, like the former, a rocket launcher just under two meters long . They were firing at the tanks, one of which had been hit and could only move its turret. It was merely a matter of time before the soviet tanks would overcome all street barriers. We just stood there stoically, waiting to enter the building, and when my turn came, we marched slowly one floor up to the ovens, turned in our food stamps, which were promptly pasted into a book, paid the requisite low price and went quickly home.

Later that day my mother and I went outside in front of the house and spoke with some youthful looking soldiers who had just dug a trench next door to us. My mother told the soldiers, all of whom looked wet behind the ears, that they should go home and that she could even give them some civilian clothes, since the war would soon be over. To this the youngest responded, "We can't do that. We've sworn Nibelung loyalty to the Führer. Do you know what Nibelung loyalty is?" My mother shook her head, while expressing the view that, all things considered, they'd be better off getting the hell out of there while they still had their heads and holing up somewhere in safety. Whereupon the young man pointed to the street light standing across the way on Gerichtstraße, from which hung the body of a young man of similar age, who had doubtless intended to desert. Affixed to his chest was a large cardboard sign which read: "I have betrayed the fatherland." Standing beside the suspended body was a woman, most likely the soldier's mother, who was pointing to an SS-patrol just then passing while wailing repeatedly, "*You're* the criminals. But God will punish you." Apparently the youthful soldier's Nibelung loyalty wasn't grounded in political conviction but in the terror of meeting a like fate.

Before going back upstairs, I ran around the corner to Lindowerstraße. There I saw a crowd of people standing in line in front of a big herring storeroom located in the basement of the building. The SS stood guard, now and then waving a few people inside while sternly warning them to take no more than a handful of tins of oiled sardines. These tins were stacked in hundreds of crates in the storeroom. The man standing in front of me saw fit to disregard the warning, grabbing an entire crate and running out of the place like mad. To no avail, as one of the soldiers raised his automatic pistol and shot him from behind, causing him to fall forward. As he stumbled, he took another bullet in the back of the head and a third in the back, the net result being a spattering of blood in all directions. The crate was flung forward from the impact, right in my direction, breaking open and scattering tins of sardines all over the street. Quickly I shoved about a dozen tins into a steel helmet I'd found. Then I went home where we feasted royally on Wittler bread and sardines in oil.

But alas, we had nothing to drink, as there was no more running water. I knew, of course, that not far away, on Reinickendorferstraße in front of the Mampe schnaps distribution center, there was a pump still in working order. The Russians had discovered the liquor center, packed with bottles of Mampe Half and Half, of which they'd already had more than their fill. The SS had taken up a position two streets over, on Nettelbeck Square; they too had filched several bottles from the center. The pump stood exactly between both locations. Screwing up my courage, I made my way into this no-man's-land, pumped up the water and let it run into the two buckets I'd brought with me. As I turned to go home, I saw the Russians take aim at the one bucket as a target and proceed to shoot right through it. Naturally, it wasn't long before the spectacle repeated itself from the other side, the SS shooting through the other bucket, so that now water was streaming out of several holes in both. I remained standing, pointing angrily at first at the one bucket, then turned around and pointed at the other. The shooting stopped, I went back to the pump and ran home as if possessed, not out of fear, but just to save as much water as I possibly could. Arriving home, I could see that everyone was anxiously waiting for me, and I divided the water up among the families. I thanked my destiny that neither the Russians nor the SS had managed to nail me, but my mother suggested the reason for my survival might well have had nothing to do with destiny, proceeding then to quote that delightful jingle:

Eyes a problem,
Go see Mampe,
Drink up till you're feeling crampy.
If you can see two of me,
Ruhnke, then, you needn't see.[35]

This "seeing two" in that situation probably also saved my life.

Later the same day I went back to Nettelbeck Square and witnessed the following scene: At the periphery of the square stood a group of trees bound together by rope. Three horses stood within the space thus formed, probably belonging to the cavalry, which had also been deployed in Berlin for its defense. A grenade was exploded in the midst of the horses as they stood together, and all three animals lay on the ground, stomachs torn open, from which they struggled to rip out their entrails with their hooves. A soldier walked up to them and gave each the mercy bullet. Hardly had this taken place when many nearby house doors opened up simultaneously, as if by magic, pouring out the inhabitants who forthwith fell upon the horse cadavers with knives and buckets. They carved large chunks out of the still steaming and twitching bodies, returning then to their homes, where they all no doubt prepared grand dinners. Just then I watched a straggler come by, an old crone, who limped cautiously over to the slaughtered cadavers and proceeded to cut off the tails with a large scissors. When I asked her what she intended to do with them, she merely smiled, saying, "Dat stuff's goin' inta my pillars, ya know, horsehair's terrific fa sleepin' on." When I saw her again later on and asked her if she was satisfied with her pillow, she answered, "Dat's a good ting I done. Ya know, a good conscience is a good pillar, as da sayin' goes. An' dose pooa animals was all gone awready anyways, an' it wudda been a shame ta bury dem tails wittem."

That happened on April 29, 1945. On April 30 we were occupied. My mother told me the Russians were already in the house next door. They had skipped our house, she reasoned, probably because our whole entryway had been secured against errant splinters with piled-up bricks, making our entrance door hard to spot from outside. I was skeptical of my mother's logic as we went into our upstairs kitchen together. As we leaned out the window, we saw Russian soldiers in the rear of the backyard next door; then all of a sudden a gunshot rang out, shattering our window frame, just inches above our heads. We needed no further proof to grasp the significance of our changed situation. What then took place, my mother related to me as follows:

I can still remember it all quite well, when the Russians came in. Earlier they were at the post office, where the Volkssturm was just having lunch, and they took everybody prisoner. Then they let everybody go again, since it was just a bunch of old men who could hardly walk anyway. And then they shot at us too, while we were standing at the window, and that bullet is still stuck in the window frame. When the Russians showed up in our cellar, you were the one who was supposed to be shot first. One of them aimed his automatic pistol at you and said "Hitler Youth." At that Frau Groggert jumped up hysterically and screamed, "Gerd, tell them no!" She actually saved your life by doing this. The first wave that came into the cellar was very nice, but the second wave, the reinforcements, they were bad. They caused so many women so much "suffering," as the rapes were then termed. Frau Rauhut, who owned the drugstore in our house, gave Gerd a silver chest containing her cutlery; a Russian came by and snatched it away from him. I just looked at Frau Rauhut and said, "Ah well, Frau Rauhut, after all, it's war." And everything was very loud. The Stalinorgel [rocket launcher truck] was set up in front of our cellar window and was firing at the Wedding railroad station where soldiers had dug in. The Russians didn't get any closer, as the railroad station was on the way to the Reich chancellery, which they wanted to protect at all costs.

The first group of Russians we encountered in our cellar was perhaps not what you would call friendly, but they weren't dangerous either. A somewhat older Russian took a shine to me, accompanying me into the neighboring cellar where he gave me vodka to drink straight from the bottle and a cigar. I had to light it but immediately began coughing violently, since I'd never smoked before. The Russian laughed and said in his broken German, "Hitler kaput. War over soon. Vodka good and cigar good." Then I had to fondle him all over his belly, which, judging by the expression on his face, pleased him enormously. Upon hearing some explosions outside, we climbed to the top of the cellar stairs where he placed himself in front of me to check out the situation. In that instant a small grenade exploded directly in front of us; it had been shot out of a mortar (*Minenwerfer*) in front of our house, sailed onto the roof and immediately fallen back down to the ground. The Russian standing in front of me was hit and fell back down the stairs where he lay motionless on the cellar floor. I bent over him and opened my suitcase, with its bandages and glucose pack, in order to administer first aid, but all help was too late.

It wasn't long before the so-called second wave came, as my mother put it, and this time we were not treated so congenially. They ransacked the cellar, took our watches from us, including the Junker watch given to me for confirmation, and herded the women and girls into the adjacent cellar from which I had just come and which had a bed. It availed the women nothing that they had dabbed their faces with soot and put on dumpy old clothes ahead of time to make themselves undesirable. The Russians saw them, bleated their "Dawai! Dawai!" and "Woman come!", and pulled the resistant females into the adjacent cellar. My mother was fortunate that she "didn't have to suffer all this," unlike most of the younger and even not so young women in the cellar. One might even describe her as unfazed in that she noticed the Russians were sparing women with small children and cleverly had me sit on the laps of different women. I shifted quickly from one lap to another, was cuddled by each "mother" and felt very important in my role. She surreptitiously briefed me as to whose lap I should sit on next. My mother based her decisions on the simple moral principle that good must be rewarded and evil punished. For instance, there was a choice between Frau Groggert, who had always been helpful to us, and the owner of the Brown Store, who for years had been insulting and accosting my mother and me. Without hesitation she decided in favor of Frau Groggert, who as a result had the good fortune to be spared by the Russians. When I asked my mother later on whether she was at peace with this decision, she merely said, "My boy, that one was easy enough. We're all human beings who have sinned, only some of us sin more than others, and these people must reap just what they've sown. That's in the bible."

Notwithstanding all the violence, only a single shot had ever been fired in our cellar; alas, it was at my bird Peter. My mother had taught him to greet all people in uniform with "Heil Hitler," out of self-protection and protection for me, it being her belief that this was the best way to demonstrate we were an Aryan household. Peter saw the Russians, in their uniforms, and belted out his Hitler greeting to the troops. One of the soldiers was dumbfounded; he opened the door to the cage, and Peter, as always, flew straight to me. Only this time he didn't quite make it, as the Russian took aim at him and, under a hail of bullets, my loyal bird exhaled the last breath of his tiny life. He hadn't learned to distinguish uniforms by their colors. This was one thing I'd never been able to teach him.

On May 1, my mother's birthday, we had to evacuate our building, a consequence of the stubborn defense of the Wedding railroad station. The SS had dug in hard at the station, the Russians had taken up a position just around the corner from our house, and the bullets were zinging back and forth. All of us, my aging father included, had to get out of the house, which was supposed to be blown up, and we literally crawled from the house to the nearest side street. To stand up would've been suicide. Moreover, my mother was very uneasy because she'd heard that the SS was supposed to have blown up the *Landwehrkanal*, releasing the waters of the Spree into the rapid transit (*S-Bahn*) and subway (*U-Bahn*) tunnels, putting them completely under water. But that was precisely where thousands had sought protection from the shooting, among them a close acquaintance of my mother. A school behind Seestraße took us in; we stayed there for four days. Since my mother wanted to know what had become of our house, I went back there on my own and saw to my delight that it was still standing, minus the top floor in which a grenade had gone off. The door to our apartment was ajar, and inside I saw three men rifling through the clothes closet. They were former concentration camp prisoners, probably looking for something to put on. The apartment looked ghastly. The Russians had sliced up all the clothes and suitcases with their bayonets, the bathroom was filthy, and the glass panes of our kitchen cupboards were shattered. The apartment looked like a pigsty, but the good thing was we still *had* an apartment, even if one full of shattered glass and broken belongings. Things could've been a lot worse.

My parents returned the next day, on May 5, I believe, and we cleaned up, which mainly amounted to throwing all the rubble and broken dishware out the window. For us the war was now over. We didn't need any official notice, for we could see on the street Russian tanks passing by, followed by Russian soldiers pulling their machine gun behind them on a small flatbed wagon. On our street corner lay some swastika flags and Nazi propaganda writings, left there no doubt by Nazi sympathizers who all of a sudden no longer wished to be identified with the ideology of the Third Reich. My father had little to say to all this. Like Master Anton in Hebbel's tragedy, *Mary Magdalene*, he no longer understood his world, which in his life's course had now lost its moorings three times: 1918, 1933 and now, 1945. Doubtless he also felt too old to build anything new. He could scarcely sleep at night, having entirely run out of pain medication for his kidney ailment. Often he would complain that he couldn't even take his own life, since there was no gas. My mother was more optimistic. She made the best of the situation, scraping together a bit of food and seeing in the general dissolution of things a sign of divine providence, for to her the end of the Nazis was also the end of constant worry over me.

5. The Period from 1945 to 1951

Every Beginning Is Hard — Only Never Give Up

On May 8 the war was declared officially over. Germany had surrendered unconditionally, and it occurred to me later that the word "unconditionally" carried with it the same momentous meaning as the word "total," as in "total war." Now people were asking themselves how it all could've happened. There seemed to be no satisfying answer. From many sides I heard that no one had been aware of the atrocities committed against those imprisoned in the concentration camps, since these camps were kept secret. This not-wanting-to-understand, this flight from responsibility, I could not comprehend. People were picked up on the basis of their race or their beliefs, and many had seen such things take place. Had people not listened to the Nazis' propaganda speeches, in which the intention to "extirpate" all Jews in Germany was proclaimed quite openly? Had they not seen how brutally I was mistreated, or the suffering to which my parents were subjected? When I asked our neighbor, an unwavering Nazi-enthusiast to the bitter end, about this, he merely opined: "Gerd, you were in the *Jungvolk* yourself and marched with them. Do *you* feel guilty?" I could only reply that these were two completely different issues, yet for the longest time I couldn't help but ponder them. Later I thought that my guilt perhaps consisted in wanting to be a part of it and, consequently, in not asking any questions.

The war had been a calamity for all of Europe. But the calamity in Berlin was one you could actually see, and what you could see with your own eyes couldn't be denied. Living quarters were bombed out, and people suffered hunger and cold. Families were torn apart, the whereabouts of parents, sisters, brothers or friends being in many cases unknown. There were no universal modes of communication, and you'd often see among the ruins of leveled houses notes with such messages as, "Otto, where are you? Your Inge," or even death notices like, "Gerda Schulze here i[n] t[he] rubble. I'm still alive. Gerd Schulze, Adolfstraße." Now and then the laconic barb: "A. i. A. [= *Alles im Arsch*, or 'It's all up your ass']. I'm at Franz's." Total war had led to total collapse. Only one thing remained important: survival at any price.

We were all hungry, so once again I went downstairs and directed my steps without thinking to the one place I'd already had good luck — to the herring depot on Lindowerstraße.

Berliners on the march

The Russians had now taken over the depot and some Germans were loading crates with tins of sardine and other fish onto trucks, while the Russians looked on. When the work was finished, they opened up the cellar storeroom and a total mob, including me, plunged into it.

The cellar had a concrete floor upon which stood barrels of salted herring and cottage cheese; the crates of sardines in oil we'd been hoping for were, of course, all removed. The cellar mob was hungry and impatient, and they were using an ax to break open the barrels. Just next to me stood a couple of former concentration camp prisoners who were plunging their arms into herring-filled brine, pulling out the fish and devouring them from head to tail. When they noticed me, they must've thought I was one of them, since I looked exactly like them with my black eyes, dark hair, long nose and narrow face. One of them slipped me a herring, which I ate up just the way they did; in spite of the salt it didn't taste bad, and I had the sense I was in a place where I didn't need to be afraid of again being branded a marginal figure. Then we took our buckets and filled them with the cottage cheese the Russians had spurned. The buckets were full to the brim, and I had trouble maneuvering them out of the cellar. To make matters worse, the floor had become very slick, with the cottage cheese oozing out of the broken barrels onto the concrete floor which provided no outlets for run-off. One woman, who was holding a small child by the hand, was also scooping cheese into her bucket and, becoming absorbed in the labor, let go of her little boy, who instantly disappeared. I listened to her calling out for him again and again, until finally I packed up my precious culinary cargo and went home, where we divided up the cheese among the tenants. Later the rumor circulated that the boy had slipped on the greasy floor, fallen down and smothered under a mass of cheese. That may well be true, but the mother assured us later that her son had died a natural death.

We let it go at that. On the second day of the peace, I was watching the Russians as they bivouacked with their horse-drawn wagons on the street corner in front of our house. One of them was strumming the balalaika, and all the soldiers were singing a most melancholy song that sounded wonderful, since the singers had very good voices. The whole scene struck me as a bizarre paradox: here I stood in front of our house, no more than half intact, the apartment block across the street completely razed, people moving quickly past with their little flatbed wagons on which they'd loaded their scant possessions, the whole scene lit up by the moon, and I was listening to this wonderful song, a song sung by the same soldiers who only yesterday had raped those women and wanted to shoot me. Now the Russians struck me as simply human; they sat around in a circle, in the middle of which they had placed a cauldron on the fire they'd built with wood salvaged from the houses they'd destroyed. Every now and then one of the soldiers would get up and stir the irresistibly aromatic contents with a big ladle. One soldier noticed me, waved me over, ladled out a kind of porridge and gave it to me in a cup missing its handle. It was rice with lamb. It could've been horsemeat as far as I was concerned; either way, it was a banquet for a hungry kid who hadn't had anything hot to eat for days.

It seemed to me later on that I was learning at that time how to compartmentalize things. Compartmentalization is a technique whereby one encapsulates certain impressions and experiences from others so that they never come in contact with one another.[36] Even in my dreams, more precisely nightmares, I saw myself divided up and put together again from different persons. For instance, I would see one "I" or self standing at the casket of another self, all teary-eyed and curious as I gazed down upon myself, while my dead self stared straight up. Then I would even accompany myself to my own grave, where I would speak winged words about myself, moving all who had gathered for my burial to tears, just like me. Or I would be running like a man possessed to escape the mob pursuing me, the murderous pack getting closer and closer, while I viewed all of it like a film, sitting in my garden spooning ice cream. I believe this defense-mechanism of mine functioned extraordinarily well, perhaps even serving to preserve my psychic integrity, as I struggled to move beyond this period of my life.

Some days later I learned that the Russians were looking for workers to help clear out the warehouses at the western port. I set off on my way, on foot, all train traffic having been shut down. Knowing that the western port was located on the rapid-transit line, I climbed the embankment at the Wedding station and ran in the direction of Pulitzstraße. To get to the port, you had to cross the Spree, no mean feat, as the SS had blown up the bridge. The Russians had cobbled together out of wood a narrow emergency bridge, which you could use to cross the river quite handily. One of the officers saw me and gave me permission to cross over. This I did, arriving soon after at the locked entrance gate of the port. Many men were gathered in front of it, waiting to be let in. I joined them and waited two days until I was finally called in with a few others. Never before had I seen the many silos, filled to the very top, then as they are today, with valuable foodstuffs. I and others were ordered to carry the sugar and flour sacks out of the warehouse and load the trucks parked outside with them. One man came over to me and asked if I was sympathetic to the Russians. I said no, since they had raped many women, shot my bird and stolen my watch. Whereupon he gave me a knife and indicated that I was to cut a slit in the sugar sacks at the bottom end, allowing the sugar to seep out slowly, thus sabotaging the Russian effort. I walked over to the huge mound of sugar sacks, which were stacked up in staggered or interlocking rows, and began pulling them out of the bottom rows and carrying them to the truck. It wasn't long before I had opened up a fair-sized cave. Then I pulled out my knife and began slitting the sacks from the ground up — not deeply, since I had to carry them outside, just deep enough to ensure that most of the contents would never arrive at their destination.

When I was just about finished cutting my way slowly up to the top of the stack, I heard voices. Keeping still, I listened to the dialog that took place between a Russian and a woman. The Russian was asking for sex, while the woman was demanding in exchange a can of pork in its own juice. I couldn't see either of them, but I recognized the woman by her voice. She lived only a short distance from us, with two small sons and a husband still in a prison camp. I also knew her to be very devout, and she had on several occasions chided my mother for not going to church, but only to the city mission. After a protracted negotiation, the two came to an agreement, and the act was carried out directly above me, that is to say, directly above the cave that had formed through my withdrawal of the sugar sacks from the bottom rows. I had just finished slitting the sacks over my head a moment before they arrived, and now with each thrust I had sugar sprinkling down on me. The Russian was no spring chicken, and the whole business seemed to take forever. I was at wits' end, aware that I'd never get out of there alive, should I be discovered. Soon I was up to my knees in sugar, and the sacks above me, full and rounded just a few minutes earlier, were getting flatter with each movement. To prevent the couple from plunging down into my cave, I reached up and supported the backside of the woman, who probably had no idea what was happening to her. That alleviated the worst danger, and the moment the transaction was completed, the woman hurried off with her loot, while I set about carrying out the sacks of sugar, now only half full. The upshot of the incident for me was that sex remained for a long time intimately bound up with sweetness, and every time I sugared a dish, I couldn't help but recall this experience. Later, encountering the same woman once again on the street with her now-liberated husband and her two sons, I felt as if she were looking at me knowingly and imploringly. Maybe Arthur Schnitzler was right when he said that women are closer than men to the abysmal bottom, better yet bottomlessness, of life, and can therefore experience much more intuitively than they.

Punishment followed hard on the heels of the incident. After finishing my work, I filled my rucksack with flour and, in addition, two sacks I'd brought along with sugar, now lying all over the floor. Staggering outside with my burden, I dropped the rucksack, which had become too heavy for me, unceremoniously onto the loading dock. Right next to it the Russians were sitting in a circle cooking rice with meat in a kettle. Just then a gust of wind came up, churning up a cloud of flour that blew straight into their faces. A few of them jumped up in fury, bellowed and took the rucksack from me. That was a shame, because it didn't belong to us, but to our neighbor who had made a point of telling me to make sure to bring this family heirloom back safe and sound. Left to me now were only the two sacks of sugar, each of which weighed about ten pounds. Coming again to the destroyed Spree bridge and intending to cross over on the make-shift, I was refused permission despite all my entreaties. I was told I'd have no trouble getting to the other side via the planks. Planks — I hadn't noticed any — but then I spotted them. The train tracks were still attached to the wooden planks and were suspended like a rope over the river. The gravel track bed was, of course, missing, and the vertical iron supports, completely detached, loomed up out of the water like little rocks, all pointy and dangerous. I placed one of the sugar sacks between my teeth, swung the other one onto my back, bent over and groped my way from plank to plank on all fours, all the time trying not to look down, as I'd had a fear of heights ever since my experiences in Altwerder. All of a sudden the plank-track tightrope began to sway, and I thought my last hour on this earth had arrived. I closed my eyes, losing the sugar sack from my teeth out of fear, the sack falling and impaling itself onto one of the protruding iron stanchions, the sugar in turn slowly trickling down into the Spree. At last safely reaching terra firma on the other side, I took the one sugar sack still remaining to me firmly in hand and made a beeline for home.

Once there, I fell to thinking things over and doing a sort of mental inventory. I'd come out of that situation intact, no one had picked me up for "special assignment," my parents were still alive, I had a home, I was healthy, and somehow we'd managed to avoid being run over or under ground. All in all, we were better off than many others, and I thought of myself as leading a "charmed life." Not all enjoyed the same charm. The S*A-Blockwart*, who like Inge had so often warned us of raids, was shot by the Russians in the hallway of his own house. A fellow tenant had gone to the Russians and denounced him. Many people in the neighborhood dropped by our apartment to assure my mother and me that they'd never meant any harm towards me and that they had nothing at all against Jews, indeed, that many of their friends were non-Aryan. My mother regarded all of these assurances with suspicion and merely responded that people were singing a different tune before the war ended. In any case, she'd had more than enough of these times. She concludes her interview with the words, "I wouldn't care to live through that whole business again. But it could've been worse."

The First Turning Point: Film, Theater and Starting School

Then something radically new happened. The first thing to rise up from the ruins was artistic life. First came the films. The first film I saw, in June 1945, was Russian, portraying the battle for Stalingrad. One scene in it made a deep impression on me: a young, mortally wounded Russian soldier held some torn telephone wires together in his mouth to enable communication between groups to take place. Later I found out that the Russian town major, Colonel General Bersarin, had already given permission for the movie houses and theaters to be reopened on April 28, 1945, even though fighting was still going on in Berlin at that time. Somewhat later came the films of DEFA (=Deutsche Film-AG, or German Film, LTD.), which were made in 1946 in the newly established state film studio of the GDR in Babelsberg. The first of these was Wolfgang Staudte's *The Murderers Are among Us* (1946), a film directed against the evasion and repression of the guilt question.[37] Also among the important films of this period was Gerhard Lamprecht's *Somewhere in Berlin* (1946), which, along with a homecoming drama, depicts the conditions of children who grow up amidst the ruins of Berlin, learn their way around the black market and play with the dud bombs lying everywhere. Another good one was Erich Engels's *The Blum Affair* (1947), a crime thriller with a social critique recalling the Dreyfus affair. It presents the fate of a Jewish factory owner who becomes a victim of racist justice. All these films were also discussed in our classes in school. There were, in addition, the French films with Gérard Philip, Yves Montand, Jean Louis Barrault, Danielle Darrieux, et al, which I saw with a classmate almost every week in the cinema on Stein Square. A new day had dawned, and the best thing about it for me was that there was nothing to be afraid of. I was a typical teenager, just like so many others.

Theatrical life too arose from the ashes. Right after the war, I saw, either in the German Theater or in a studio theater, a piece that made a strong impression on me. It was *The Adding Machine*, written by Elmer Rice. The central character of this piece that takes place in the 20's is a married bookkeeper by the name of Zero. Zero is aptly named, a man with two children who has done nothing more with his life than work/s. He defines obsequiousness and expects to be properly rewarded for his 25 years of service. Against his expectations, however, his boss breaks the news to him that he is to lose his job and be replaced by an adding machine, all part of a move to modernize the business. In the office he picks up a letter opener and stabs his boss. Condemned to death, he is taken to a laboratory where men in white lab coats are busily flitting about. One of them approaches him and holds up a test tube, in which a white flake can be seen dancing up and down, explaining that this flake will evolve into a human being, that he, Zero, is this human being, who in the fullness of time will be born again on the earth, have the same parents as before, marry the same wife as before, have the same children as before and do the same work as before. He will then have the experience of being replaced by a machine, whereupon he will stab his boss and again find himself in the laboratory after his condemnation. The man resists in desperation, to no avail; as the curtain falls, the audience hears the first cries of a new-born baby. The viewers sat transfixed in their seats, for here they were witnessing the eternal return of the same, allowing no way out of the present situation, out of the world of rubble that awaited them outside.

In the Fall of 1945 school started up again, as the Heinric-Schliemann-Scule. The problem now was how to get there, since the rapid-transit line to Schönhauser Ave. was shut down, and the were no street cars:

A burnt-out streetcar

I remounted the tires on my bike (I had removed them to prevent a theft by the Russians) and rode through the Humboldt grove to school. Along the way I came to the huge bunker that had been one of the four defense bunkers of Berlin. Even now, with its seven stories and its flak towers, it looked powerful and dangerous. Its interior was also elaborately appointed, as it was intended to serve not only defense purposes but also, and especially, women and children as an air-raid shelter. I was stopped at the bunker by the Russians, and my first thought was that they wanted my bike, but they weren't interested in my mode of transportation. They looked me over, one of the soldiers nodded, and I was led with some others to a few mounds of dirt where we had to dig up the remains of soldiers who had been hastily buried there. There were no tools for the labor; we had only our hands. As soon as I finished this most unpleasant job, I was allowed to continue on my way. Even then I thought cremation was a good deal more aesthetic than burial. Who knows if anyone would be around to dig me up?

Arriving at school, I headed straight for my classroom. On my way there, I passed by a room in which a dead horse was lying. I had no clue how the horse could've gotten up the two flights of stairs, concluding only that the school must've been a haven for animals as well as people. Our classroom was a disaster area, and we had to spend several hours cleaning it up. We heaved lots of rubble down to the street, since the room's windows were without glass panes, or had at most a few jagged edges jutting out from the frames. I cut my hand open on one of these; the wound quickly became infected, but when I got to the doctor, there were no medications. He pierced the large blister on my hand, the pus drained out, and the dead skin hung down, which he then neatly trimmed off with a scissors. The scar on my hand is a present-day reminder to me of this procedure. Looking back on it, I'm very glad I have such a sound immune system, which allowed me to recover quickly. I learned from this experience that you don't feel any pain when somebody cuts away your dead skin; the whole episode cured me of my fear of death, which I realized would do no more than turn my entire body into just such a feelingless piece of skin.

Yet another experience intrudes on my memory. My father's nephew was now running a hauling company with two damaged army trucks equipped with wood gas generators. In the Fall of 1946 we rode in one of them to the authorities, where my mother wanted to have me classified as an *OdF-Fall* (Victim of Fascism case). The gentleman responsible for such cases gave her to understand that I was in fact no such case. "Your son is not a full Jew, but only a half-Jew. You have a Jewish nose, however, o you could really be a full Jew. But you were lucky since you having been raised as such in an Aryan household," he pronounced. He then proceeded to explain that half-Jews, though their lives were anything but easy, nevertheless had never been in mortal danger, nor were they shipped to concentration camps, like so many others. "In view of this," he airily concluded, "your son does not fall into the category of 'the damaged,' and may therefore lay no claim to compensation." He went on to say that he personally knew many half-Jews who had actually fared quite well in the Third Reich; too bad I was not one of them. All our objections and entreaties fell on deaf ears, so we glumly headed for the exit. Later on I would amuse myself with this paradox, that I was regarded as a Jew up to 1945 but ceased to be one thereafter. The experience familiarized me with what is sometimes called "attitudinal change." But after all was said and done, survival was all that mattered.

Cold, Hunger, Rubble and Refugees

The best thing was that your sleep was no longer disturbed by air raids. Of course, there were other problems, such as the increasing cold, the scarcity of food, the cleaning-up of a sea of rubble and the accommodation of so many refugees from the East. The winter of 1946-47 was unusually cold. Apartments offered little protection, since they had no window panes, just cardboard coverings with a bit of glass in the middle to let in some light. The cardboard, of course, got all mushy when it snowed, letting the bitter cold in. In our apartment the kitchen now had an outer wall on one side, since the adjacent room had been destroyed by a bomb. By December this wall had become entirely covered on the inside by a thick sheet of ice. To make matters worse, we'd run out of materials to burn for heat. I ran over to the railroad freight depot a few times where dump trucks with coal would sometimes be parked.

I'd toss a few pieces into the street and collect them later when no one was looking. This was not without its dangers, since the freight cars were guarded by soldiers who would sometimes actually fire their weapons, though usually intending only warning shots. My father and I also went rummaging among the demolished houses, pulling old wood out of the rubble; later we deforested trees in different parks. Berlin was and is known as a city of parks, but at that time the parks were empty. Some people even began chopping up their furniture and feeding it to their ovens. Parts of our roof disappeared; for the most part, the tiles had already been blown away anyway by the air pressure of the bombs, and the exposed roof beams soon found their way into people's ovens. Sections of stairway banisters served as firewood, carefully sawed off during the night, not, of course, by my father or me. For a short time it would become warm in our room, or more precisely in our kitchen, it being smaller than the large Berlin living room with its high ceiling.

With the roof now almost completely stripped, we gained, above and beyond a supply of wood, the advantage of an increased procurement of foodstuffs. Berlin was now ruled by famine, and people were trying, by fits and starts, to supplement their daily rations, which for normal consumers[38] were limited by ration cards to 800 calories per person. Every square foot of ground was turned into a vegetable garden, and we were fortunate that several of our tenants could now cultivate a little plot on the roof. All we had to do was bring up soil and cut up a few potatoes, and nature did the rest. Every day I would go up to the roof garden to check out how quickly everything was growing and to make sure no one else was harvesting the crop. The following year, however, I laid out a little plantation with tobacco plants, since you could trade the dry tobacco leaves for potatoes on the black market:

Closer to the sun

Around this time I received my first care-package from Sweden. It contained, in addition to a ladies' fur jacket, a decorative bra. The reason was, as the sender wrote me, that in her country the name Gerd can also mean Gerda, leading her to believe that I was a budding young lady. I immediately made her aware of her mistake, and in the second package I found a set of tails, together with the requisite patent-leather shoes, a starched shirt and white gloves. The next time I went to the opera on Friedrichstraße, I donned all this finery and felt like a king. I was the only one at the opera so festively dressed, but that didn't really matter to me. The one discordant note in my appearance was my growling stomach.

I also had good fortune in my relationship with a woman by the name of J. W. Rose, an elderly American living in Anderson, Indiana. She had pulled my name out of a basket at her church and sent me, initially, a big package containing Corn Flakes, Rice Krispies and a bible. That didn't help much, as we had neither sugar nor milk, only milk powder, which couldn't be used for mixing. So I wrote her that I'd rather have cigarettes, which I could use to purchase groceries on the black market. And she sent me some, wrapping them up in a few dollar bills, which I exchanged for marks at a good rate. I have never met this woman, without whose help our lives would've been much harsher.

The paltry food rations were especially hard on growing children, and on hard-working women as well. Since most of the men had either fallen in the war or been incapacitated by it, not to mention the many who were still in prison camps, women between the ages of 16 and 65 were pressed into service to clear away rubble. They were classified as "assistant workers in the building trade," and, in addition to a small sum of money, were granted category II status in food rations, whereas women not so employed were listed in category V and had to make do with less. The work was very hard: first some garbage heaps were leveled, then tracks laid on which large dump trucks were placed. The women then set about chipping the mortar off the stones lying all around, then shoveling the stones into the trucks, bracing themselves against the trucks, shoving the trucks to an open area, tipping them over and stacking the stones up again, so that they could be reused in the reconstruction effort. My mother too pitched in, and sometimes I would help her pass on the mortar-free bricks in a relay line.

Another problem was the influx of Eastern refugees and displaced persons. Many of them came in 1946 from the East to Berlin, among them my half-Aunt Emma and her husband. The city could provide only limited help, having few means at its disposal to ease their burden. And so in August, 1946, it promulgated an "appeal for donations for Eastern refugees," which was posted everywhere on the advertising pillars still standing and whose opening paragraph read as follows: "Appeal to the population! The first transports containing Eastern refugees have arrived in our city. Once again the city administration confronts difficult tasks. A small part of the many thousands who were forced to leave home and hearth, scarcely equipped with even the bare essentials, are to be given a new home here among us, a decent residence, work and bread." I don't know how much was donated, but I doubt it was more than a pittance, since the people themselves had little to give. My relatives were now living with us, but only for a while, for both soon died of typhoid fever, as did many others.

This was also a time of suicide, with so many older people unable to adjust to the transition. It was suicide by the clock, since gas was available for only four hours a day, and the exact time at which the gas was turned on varied. An elderly woman next door, who had lost both her son and husband in the war and who was seriously ill, opened up the gas tap during the rationing period and was found dead in her kitchen the following day. My mother was angry and didn't go to the funeral, since in her mind such a way out of this valley of tears was a crime, entailing as it did a colossal waste of gas. Gas was a rationed precious commodity, one we all needed to stay alive. Many a night my mother would have to get up and cook, knowing that the gas would only be on for four hours.

Foraging Trips for Two

For the first three years after the war my attendance at school was extremely irregular. The reason for this was the foraging trips (*Hamsterfahrten*) necessitated by the scant allotment of food permitted by the ration cards, which got you out of bed in the morning hungry and put you back in bed at night in the same condition. Foraging at this time was not a matter of laying up food for later, for some approaching period of distress. The period of distress was now, and the foraged items were quickly consumed. Foraging meant hustling, and what you hustled wasn't luxury items but necessities of life like potatoes, bread, vegetables and sometimes butter, eggs and bacon. Since these foods were in minimal supply in Berlin, you had to head out into the surrounding rural areas in search of them, each time further away from home, since all too many hustlers were crisscrossing the local countryside with their backpacks on their backs, grazing for anything edible. In my own case there was no choice anyway, since my father was sick and needed nourishment and my mother was too afraid to ride in the over-filled trains. The upside of it was that I would at last be getting out of Berlin, for I was familiar with only a small section of the Baltic and the Warthe region.

Of course, getting out of town was no easy matter because the Russians used most of the engines for their own purposes. Just before the opening of school in the Fall of 1945, I went with my rucksack to the Stettin station, intending to take the train to Neuruppin, since someone had told me you could get potatoes there. The train, sitting there on its track, was so full it had passengers hanging out the windows; a lot of people must've heard about the cheap potatoes, I thought.

To get on this train, you had to climb onto either the running board or the roof, no mean feat for older people. Inside the train several people had locked themselves in the toilet and refused to come out, even if someone from a compartment had to use it. The most coveted place, of course, was the caboose, which was, so to speak, hooked onto the rear of some cars and had a door that was insulated against the wind. But any train has only a few cabooses, and sometimes people would come to blows trying to decide who got in. Only once was I myself lucky enough to enjoy such a secure ride. More typically, I would get a good spot on the roof, where you could even position yourself over the air shaft in the middle. And since it was still the Fall season with its pleasant temperatures, the cold wasn't much of a factor:

As long as it moves

The first time I went on a foraging trip, the locomotive was missing; the Russians had separated it and attached it to their own train. So we were stuck at the station for three days, and whenever nature called, you'd ask your neighbor to keep an eye on your spot on the roof, climb down and head for some nearby patch of devastation where you'd do your business, meanwhile keeping a sharp eye out for vagrant homosexuals who would exploit such opportunities to assault teenagers. But at last the train moved out, and when we arrived in Neuruppin a few hours later, I was lucky enough to hustle some fifty pounds of potatoes. It wasn't so much money that interested the farmers, the Reichsmark being almost worthless, but rather items of exchange, and the more expensive the item, the more you could get for it; sentimental attachments to objects were irrelevant. Farmers were particularly interested in such valuables as gold jewelry and precious stones, also porcelain and rugs. We had none of these things. But I'd heard that salt was also a scarce commodity in the countryside. Since I'd brought a whole sack of salt with me, which I'd "liberated" from the grocery store shortly before the war's end, you could say I'd now "struck gold" in the truest sense of the term. For half a pound of salt I got my potatoes, with which I immediately headed back. I can't count the number of times I had to schlepp that hundred-plus-pound sack on my shoulders more than a dozen kilometers all the way back to the railroad station, but the elation of returning home with food always spurred me on.

Back at home, my mother stretched the precious potatoes as far as she reasonably could. And like the alchemists of old, she conjured up edible gold from virtually nothing. She made a soup from raw, grated potatoes, which she threw into hot, salted water and quickly brought to a boil; then we'd eat the thickened soup as fast as we could to get the feeling of a full stomach. Sometimes my mother would squeeze the grated potato pulp to get the water out of it and form little balls that would wind up as floating additives in the succulent soup. She also knew how to make a lard spread from semolina, which she would season just so with thyme. It was outstanding on bread. And the pie she made from grated potatoes was first-class. It contained a minimum of calories but a maximum of taste and was made only on special occasions. For dessert we would occasionally have a kind of whipped cream, which at that time, of course, wasn't made up of milk or cream but of chemicals. And they didn't call it "whipped cream" (*Schlagsahne*) either but "whipped crème" (*Schlagkrem*). No doubt it was delivered straight from the city's chemical laboratories, a triumph of better eating through science; but at least it came in a variety of colors. The other women in the neighborhood were also culinary creative, and I later thought that people generally become inventive in times of necessity, as per the proverb, "Necessity is the mother of invention." To this I would add that profound necessity makes one extraordinarily inventive.

In 1945 Felicitas joined our class. (I'll have more to say about her later.) We became fast friends and wound up making foraging trips to the country together. Her father had not survived the war, so that she too had to provide for her family, i.e., her mother and two younger brothers. On our first foraging trip together, we grabbed a nice spot on the roof, one with a beautiful view, and rode to Sonnenwald, where a daughter of my father lived. From the train station, I had to hoof it almost ten kilometers into the village, but I was rewarded for my trouble with homemade sugar-beet syrup and three liters of milk. The trip home was anything but pleasant. Again we rode the roof, but this time it was very cold and we were hit by heavy rainstorms. We were sitting directly behind the locomotive, which was being fueled by coal dust, coal itself being so scarce. So the smokestack was belching out not only steam but also a ton of soot, which was turning the people riding the running boards into chimney sweeps. Just before reaching Berlin, my can with its three liters of milk tipped over on the roof, sending the milk spilling more or less equally over both sides and briefly bathing those standing on the sideboards below in white. But just briefly, as the continuous stream of soot stuck to the white liquid, soon making them look as if draped in mourning clothes, with the one difference that the grief of mourning was replaced by rage. They shook their fists up at us, promising to beat our asses black and blue the moment we climbed down, so that we wouldn't be able to sit for weeks. You could tell by their tone of voice that they meant it. But they looked so cool in their three-layered make-up of soot, milk and again soot that we could hardly hold in the laughter, which of course made them even more furious. After the train pulled in, we waited a whole hour until the very last passengers had drifted away before daring to get off. Alas, the milk was gone, but it could've been worse, since I was also carrying the two-liter can filled with home-made syrup, and who knows what would've happened, had I knocked *this* can over.

The syrup was the last sustenance my father took. He had lost a good deal of weight, since he was always giving me part of his share of the little food we had. It was his opinion that growing boys needed to eat hearty. Then he began having attacks of pain and had to go to the hospital. He wasn't there long, and I visited him on the day after his admission. Like many others he lay on a gurney in the ward corridor, since all beds were occupied. Later he was diagnosed with volvulus (intestinal obstruction), but there were no pain medications. The doctor came, and I watched him raise my father's shirt and pinch the folds of his stomach, which no longer smoothed out when he let them go. Responding to my questioning glance, he told me my father was dying and would not live to see another day. My father weighed very little when he died, desperately undernourished as he was. Not many people came to the burial. It was a "little corpse," as my mother was wont to call such funerals, at which only a few people showed up, in contrast to a "big corpse," which we would sometimes observe from our window and which usually led to traffic jams. On the day after the burial, I went foraging again.

Only once did my luck turn bad on a foraging trip. I knew a farmer who had a dim-witted daughter who liked to smoke. Since I had a pack of American cigarettes on me, all specked yellow with nicotine, the farmer behaved very amiably towards me and gave me a hundred-pound sack of potatoes for the pack. I carried the sack slung over my shoulders some six kilometers to the train station, but this time I ran into the VOPO (*Volkspolizei*, or People's Police), who were waiting for foragers at the station. Not only did they confiscate the potatoes, they also insisted on knowing where I'd gotten them. When I refused to give up the farmer's name, they locked me up in the fire-engine house, which besides a few bales of hay and a barred window had only a bare cement floor. I was given nothing to eat, neither the first nor the second day. Rather, two men came to see me, who demanded I reveal the farmer's name, but I refused to do so. I was terrified, not only of punishment, but also of the rats that were running all around me. The second night of my incarceration a hand reached in through the bars and gave me a bacon sandwich. This gift came from a farmer who probably took pity on me. Such gifts-through-the-bars became more frequent, and soon I had enough to eat. But I also had to make sure I wasted no time scarfing down the sandwiches, since I wasn't the only one who had taken up residence in the fire-engine house. At one point I saw Felicitas and her mother pass by outside and became painfully aware of my isolation. On the third day the VOPO came for me and took me to my farmer friend, whose identity was betrayed in the meantime by the initials on his potato sack. They confronted me with him, but before I could say anything, his dim-witted daughter walked over to me, gave me her hand and asked me if I had any more cigarettes for her. Now the cat was out of the bag, and I was allowed to go. Whatever became of the farmer, I don't know, and since I never had any further dealings with him, I never found out.

I had better luck on another trip, but it took a while. Once again I made my way through a series of villages starting from Meyenburg, which lay at the end of the Berlin-Neuruppin train route, but every farmer I asked for potatoes wanted to know if I had anything of greater exchange value than salt and salted herring. I did have some flint stones, which I had removed from a dud, and some saccharin in both tablet and powder form, but these things too were generally spurned. It began to look as if I might be returning home empty-handed. Finally, as I was passing by a large farmhouse, I noticed near the barn some large stacks of potatoes, and, next to these, a few iron poles lying around a forge. I took one of them, waited till about midnight and ran over to one of the stacks to break it up. This was anything but easy, as the stack was covered over with frozen earth, and underneath that was a layer of straw; but under the straw were these gorgeous potatoes. As a wedding celebration was going on in the farmhouse, I thought I'd be able to do my work undisturbed. But all of a sudden, the door opened and a young, slightly tipsy couple came out of the house. Of course, the young farmer had something special on his mind, something best carried out on the potato stack. Alas, he picked a spot on the pile directly opposite me. Since the stack was built like a pyramid, he couldn't see me, but I sure could hear him and his partner. The mutual giggling told me that the cold was having no effect on either of them. I remained as quiet as a church mouse, well aware that, if he spotted me, I'd be driven to flight with my own crowbar, if indeed it didn't lead to worse. The bizarre similarity of my present situation with the seeping sugar in the silo came to mind, with the obvious difference that it had been a lot warmer there. As the couple went back into the house, I breathed a sigh of relief, filled my sack with potatoes, laid the straw and earth back over the restacked potatoes and took off for the station, where I had to wait till dawn for the train. By 8 a.m. I was back in school, struggling in Latin class with the bridge-building episode in Caesar's *De bello Gallico*, a passage that required looking up every word to get a clear sense of the text. Thank God I had a trot, a German translation of fairly literal precision, which allowed me to do at least a modicum of preparation before class. Naturally I doubted the utility of agonizing over Latin texts, there being so many other things that were so much more important, and I soon came to the cynical conclusion that the saying, "Not for school, but for life do we learn," could be read in either direction.

The Black Market

Without the black market it would've been impossible for me to do any foraging, since I had to peddle some of the potatoes on the market to get the money it cost to make trips to the countryside. The minute I was back home with my wares, I headed out to the market, which was always bustling only two streets away, stretching from Adolfstraße up to Schulzendorferstraße. The ritual unfolded as follows: if you had something to offer, you'd walk along the street slowly, murmuring "cigarettes, cigarettes" or "potatoes, potatoes." Someone else might be intoning "bread, bread"; only rarely would you hear someone offering, or trying to buy, eggs or butter. It wasn't money that determined the value of the wares, but other wares, although cigarettes came close to being a kind of standard currency, especially American brands like Camels, Philip Morris, Lucky Strike and Chesterfield. So, for example, you'd exchange a hundred pounds of potatoes for four loaves of bread, or you'd get a loaf of bread for a sack of beets. The entire transaction took place relatively quickly, with supply and demand holding sway and trade agreements come by easily. The one thing you had to watch out for was the raids regularly carried out by the French M.P.'s, since the black market was, of course, illegal. Yet without it many would've starved, and many of the military on patrol showed their humanity by looking away from the transactions taking place right under their noses.

Only once did it happen that someone came close to being killed on the black market, and I was right there, though only as a bystander. In the Fall, many would come from the rural Eastern region to peddle vegetables, of which we in the West had very few. One day, after popping the E-string on my violin, I went over to the market to pick up a new one. Across the street from me, I saw an older man carrying two cabbages in a pouch, which he was offering to another man. Just then, two French M.P.'s came by, looking like Laurel and Hardy in uniform, the one rotund, the other a stick. There was, however, nothing funny about them. They asked the man with the cabbages for his ID papers, which the latter either didn't have on him or didn't want to show. First they took away his cabbages, then his pouch. When the man asked them at least to give back the pouch, the fat one punched him in the face, and as the man lay on the ground, the fat MP slammed his foot squarely onto the man's chest. The man on the ground cried out in pain, but the MP did not remove his foot. Then something quite extraordinary took place: the crowd on the street fell silent, such that you could've heard a leaf flutter to the ground. Then a circle slowly formed and began to contract around the two M.P.'s. All of this happened without a sound. The stillness was lethal, and even the man on the ground stopped whimpering. The two M.P.'s looked around and could only see a mob slowly encircling them. One of them drew his revolver from its holster and shot into the air, causing the people standing closest to him to draw back a bit. I was standing on the other side of the street on top of a small mound of gravel, able to watch the whole affair. I drilled my eyes straight into the face of the fat one, so consumed with hatred that I felt I could've killed him with them. The Frenchman noticed me, bulled his way through the crowd, came up to me and arrested me. That dissolved the tension a little, and the crowd found further release through blustering and cursing. The Frenchman then turned me over to some German police just then passing by, and they took me to the precinct station where I was kept for two days. The police lavished every comfort on me, feeding me well and playing skat with me for hours at a time. My mother was quickly informed of my arrest; she showed up at the station all upset, but couldn't do anything. As I was being released, I was told that I needed to be careful with my eyes, because they tended to draw the looks and attention of others to themselves. And this did indeed prove to be the case on many future occasions, long after I had put my black market activities behind me.

Nowadays, when I think back on this episode with the Frenchmen on the black market, I try to understand their behavior. There's no doubt these two soldiers acted wrongly, since the man with the cabbages was merely offering them for sale or trade, and represented no danger to the general public. On the other hand, I could also see it from the French point of view, since it was not only under Hitler that they had suffered terribly, rather Hitler was the culmination of three German attacks on France within a seventy-year period, each attack a successful invasion and occupation. No wonder the French had by now become mistrustful of the Germans, just as the Germans, after Versailles, bore no great love for the French. It would take time for the mutual strain of relations to abate; and it would take the currency reform, or rather reforms, to sound the death knell of the black market. The reforms also contributed significantly to a thaw in relations between Germans and French in our particular area.

The Blockade, Currency Reform and Traveling in a Divided Germany

The currency reform(s) brought an end to the black market. The military governments of the Allied Powers announced the reforms on June 19, 1948, and put them through in the Western zones on Sunday, June 20, 1948.[39] A few days later, the new *Westmark* made its debut in the Western sectors of Berlin, and, along with everybody else, I too received my allotment at the exchange counter. Next day all the store display windows in the Western zones were full of wares, albeit with hefty price increases. It was obvious that the merchants had been holding back their inventory until just the right moment — which was now. Two days later, on June 24, the soviet military administration followed suit, enacting its own currency reform in the Soviet Occupation Zone of Germany (*Sowjetische Besatzungszone*, or SBZ) and in the Soviet sector of Berlin.[40] The net result was that we now had not only two Germany's, but two currencies as well.

Everything in Berlin was now more expensive. Wares there were aplenty, but we couldn't buy them. We heard reports from various people that the same products were a good deal cheaper in the Western zones than in ours. It might pay, then, to go to West Germany to shop and then hold on to some purchases back here, while selling others, in order to cover travel expenses at least partially. The problem was getting into the Western zone, since the Russians had, as of June 24, 1948, imposed the blockade on West Berlin in order to prevent the formation of a West German state. All connections to West Berlin were interrupted, bus and train connections ended in Magdeburg, and all border crossings were stopped. So I quickly made up my mind to try to get into the Western zone, hoping to come back to Berlin laden with groceries. I told Felicitas of my plan, to which her immediate reaction was, "I'm in." The other tenants also gave me money, asking me to bring them back something — anything. And so we bought tickets to Magdeburg, the end of the line at that time. We got off and seemed to be having luck, since there were all these trucks parked in front of the train station, whose drivers were offering, for a small fee, to take us right up to the border. We were ecstatic, but our joy was short-lived. After a short ride, the trucks pulled up to a VOPO barracks. The offer, it seems, had been a ruse; we had fallen, better yet driven, right into the hands of the police. I was interrogated by a VOPO and a Russian who happened to be present. They asked me why I wanted to go to the West. Here I sensed a chance to appeal to the humanity of the two soldiers, and told them all about my Jewish father who had succumbed in a concentration camp. I told them how I just had to get there in order to find out exactly what had really happened to him. The Russian was convinced by my story and let me go, naturally with the proviso that I not show my face around there again.

Meanwhile it had grown dark, and since Felicitas was waiting right outside, we took off immediately. Recent events had naturally made me mistrustful, so I took my shoe off and stuck my money, all 250 DM of it, under my sock. After putting my shoe back on, I undid my wristwatch and hid it at the bottom of my rucksack. We headed toward the next city, which was Helmstedt, located in the Eastern part of Lower Saxony. Helmstedt was a major border crossing between the Federal Republic of Germany and the German Democratic Republic, and it lay en route to Hannover, the city Felicitas and I were trying to reach. The route was simple, once we decided simply to use the train tracks as our guide. Along the way, we met a group also heading for Hannover. These people had been assembled and were being guided by a hustler, who came over to us and suggested we join his group, for a fee, of course. We turned him down flat. Since we already had the tracks as a guide, what did we need *him* for; besides, how could we be sure he wasn't just another con-artist in the employ of the Russians? But we did stick close behind the group anyway, and it wasn't long before the very thing we were afraid of happened. A group of three armed Russians came up to us and ordered us to show our ID's. One of them took mine, glanced at it briefly, without actually reading it, and let it fall into the grass. Then he demanded our money, and it became obvious the three of them were out and about committing larceny. Most of the people in the Hannover-bound group were afraid and gave the Russians everything they demanded, but I had nothing in my pocket to turn over. My money was under my sole. The Russian was clever, though, and stuck his finger down into my shoe behind my Achilles heel, intending to feel my sole; however, I spread my foot out as best I could, and that, combined with the thickness of the Russian's finger, made it impossible for him to get down under there. Then the Russians told us to hand over our watches, and even Felicitas, who'd already lost her money, was now separated from her watch as well. But suddenly she begged them to give it back, protesting that it was an heirloom from her deceased father. The Russian holding it was inclined to yield to her request — on the condition, of course, that the two of them have a quick romp in the bushes. But there was no romp, quick or otherwise, and we were finally able to resume our trek to the West, to Hannover via Helmstedt, the walk now a bit lighter for the many who'd been relieved of the excess weight of their money and watches.

Finally arriving at the border railroad station, we bought two tickets and waited for the train. All of a sudden, we heard a woman cry out that her handbag had been stolen. Before you could blink, we were surrounded by police, the difference now being that it was the Western police. They took us with them on guard duty and confiscated our ID's. Everybody had one, of course, except me. Mine was lying on the ground somewhere in no-man's-land, wherever the Russian soldier had dropped it. I suggested I be allowed to go back there and look for it. My suggestion was accepted, but only on condition (always a condition!) that Felicitas remain there to guarantee my return. While I was gone, they used her to sweep out and clean up the rooms in the station house. I headed right out in search of the spot, as far as I could tell, where the Russian had dropped my ID. But everything looked different now. Dawn was breaking, the whole area looked by day as if I'd never been there before, and besides, both the Russians and the Americans began shooting at me, fair game since I was in no-man's-land. I assumed they were just firing warning shots but dropped to the ground anyway and crawled to safety. When I made my way back to the station empty-handed, the officials merely nodded ironically; it was obvious to me they believed I had made up the whole story. They took me, together with the other detainees, and marched us to the bridge that was the local connecting link between East and West.

As we stood midway on the bridge, they turned us over to the VOPO, who proceeded to return the men among us to the same barracks in which I had been a "guest" just recently. Only this time my visit was neither so pleasant nor so brief. The windows were all nailed shut, sealing off all daylight, probably to discourage escape attempts. There were about thirty of us packed into a small room, most having already done their shopping in the West and now toting their supplies homeward in cloth bags and rucksacks. One man had candles, which he lit, while everybody else unpacked his edibles, each one a delicacy for me in the truest sense of the term. But I was not invited to take part in this feast, neither on this day nor on the following three during which we were cut off from the outside world. The *Volkspolizisten* knew about the provisions the detainees had on them and, consequently, gave us nothing to eat, which, of course, was to my dire disadvantage, as I now had no access to food at all. Next day a few of the men, including me, were fetched from the room and put to work drilling the shaft for a well. This project proceeded as follows: we paced slowly in circles, like oxen, tethered behind a heavy horizontal pole, in the precise middle of which a perpendicular drill stood, such that through our circular movement the drill penetrated deeper and deeper into the earth. It was a long time before we struck any water; it must've been between eight and ten hours. Without a break and without food. As soon as the work was done, it was back into that snake pit of a room.

I'd befriended my neighbor, who was eighteen, and asked him what we had to look forward to here, as I wasn't relishing the prospect of spending the rest of my life running around in circles behind a pole. And besides, I was without my partner, since only the men had been locked up, while the women were let loose on their own somewhere outside. The young man answered that we would soon be interrogated and that those without ID's would probably be returned to Aue,[41] from which some had escaped, himself included. He'd thrown away his papers so that he couldn't be identified. When I asked him why in the world he had worked in such a hellhole, he told me he'd actually volunteered, but that after a few months he'd started having breathing problems and that the doctor diagnosed *Steinlunge* (lit.: "stone lung," i.e., pumiceous lung), the consequence of inhaling too much dust. He was told in no uncertain terms to either quit or get his affairs in order.

The next day an officer came to collect our ID's. Having lost mine somewhere in no-man's-land, I could only turn over my monthly pass for the city transit, on which I had registered my name. When my name was called out, I literally stumbled into the interrogation room, having eaten nothing for days. Sitting before me were two of the very men I thought I had successfully conned earlier, the VOPO policeman and a Russian officer. The VOPO seemed happy to see me again, and I was totally convinced my next stop would be Aue. At that point, a profound exhaustion came over me, causing me to wobble on my chair, then to hit the floor in a dead faint. The hunger and dehydration were too much for the organism, added to which was my terror over the prospect of being sent to the uranium mines. The Russian discontinued the trial, came over to me and gripped me by the shoulders. Then he said I was free to go. But I couldn't quite trust this acquittal and pointed to the VOPO, lamenting as I did that he (the VOPO) would surely arrest me again as soon as I set foot outside the room. Whereupon the Russian took me by the arm and led me out of the room. Felicitas was sitting right outside the door. She'd spent the entire time there and had eaten as little as I. I was sure she would wait for me, since she had informed me she would. To this day I haven't been able to figure out how that came about. Later she told me she'd written a brief note to that effect, giving it to the Russian guarding the door with instructions to see that it reach the hands of a young man with black hair. Overcoming an initial reluctance, the Russian took the note, and the next day I discovered it in my pocket, where he had presumably stuck it while I slept. Since there were a good many young men with black hair in the snake pit, I have no idea to this day how he was able to single me out.

So then Felicitas and I stumbled along together into the next village to beg for food among the farmers. One farmer was generous, observing from our condition that we hadn't eaten for quite a while; he permitted us to share the slop in the pig trough with our porcine hosts. Potatoes have never tasted so sublime as in that moment. We trekked on to Magdeburg, where we had to wait in the station lobby for our connection. A man was selling country bread there, and I bought a six-pound loaf, for which I paid over a hundred marks. I had no intention of going back to Berlin empty-handed.

The blockade ended in May of 1949, but prior to that something happened that gives a vivid impression of the general mood among West Berliners at that time. It was on my birthday, April 1. It seems the Berlin newspaper, *Der Telegraf*, decided to play an April fool's joke on its readership in that day's issue, announcing that the blockade was over, as an enormously long tunnel had just completed construction, extending from the West and running underneath GDR soil to Berlin. Indeed, supplies were already on their way to Berlin through the tunnel, due to arrive at the radio tower at any time. As you might expect, we were all ecstatic, and many of us, including yours truly, hurried over to the radio tower, only to learn that someone in the employ of the publishing house had permitted himself a very bad joke. The people's rage over this sadistic attempt at humor was tremendous; some even went to the publishing house and stoned it. In times of great necessity, even normally intelligent people can become gullible, and that was certainly the case here.

Felicitas, Homer, Karl May and the Era of Mass Demonstrations

All this happened while I was going to school, which I did only sporadically during the early post-war years. Our class had only seven students, some having transferred; we became known as "The Banner of the Upright Seven," after the novella by Gottfried Keller. Crassus was the one I admired above all; he was prodigiously well read and outstanding in both contemporary history and German. His actual name was Dietmar, but the students called him Crassus, after Marcus Licinius Crassus, a Roman general and politician who became fabulously wealthy through land speculation and later formed, together with Pompey and Julius Caesar, the First Triumvirate. To be sure, my classmate was not fabulously rich, but he did always have money on him, which he enjoyed lending to us. Eventually he was accepted as the third member in our own little triumvirate, made up of him, Felicitas and me.

Felicitas was the only girl in our class. She was different from the other girls who were now integrated into our original group of seven. She had a short hair style, large expressive eyes and a somewhat slow, deliberate way of speaking; she mulled over each word before uttering it. It wasn't long before the other boys in the class began regarding her with desire, and whenever she would spend an inordinate amount of time in conversation with one of them, that would generally be regarded as a coup. That she sought my company totally baffled me, as I was not her intellectual equal by any measure. In any case, we formed a friendship, a bond that we wanted to seal through the brotherhood of blood, just as Karl May had described it in his novel, *Winnetou*. That meant we had to draw blood from a finger with a sharp knife and press it onto the other's finger so as to mingle the two. But when I set the knife tip to my finger, I found myself unable to penetrate the skin; on the contrary, I felt on the verge of fainting. Somehow our friendship found a way to endure, even without the charm of this ritual.

Felicitas also invited me to accompany her to her semiweekly piano lessons given by a Frau Böhme in Weissensee. Her piano teacher had spent the years of the First World War in Edmonton, Canada, and had also given concerts and recitals in that country. Later she returned to Germany, married and earned a living through piano instruction. The apartment house in Weissensee belonged to her but had been expropriated by the GDR. On occasion, we would ask her to play, and it was thus that I was introduced to the world of classical music: to the etudes of Chopin, Beethoven's piano sonatas, piano transcriptions of Sibelius' tone poems, and much else. These evenings left their mark: to this day I'll rarely miss an opportunity to attend a concert featuring any of these beloved works. As I listen, my mind will drift back irresistibly to those days when I first heard those wondrous tones — in counterpoint, as often as not, to the basso profundo of my growling stomach.

Frau Böhme was a widow; her husband was buried in the cemetery in Weissensee, not far from Rölkestraße. One day in conversation, when I happened to mention to her the value of heavy metal, for which scrap dealers were paying a lot of money, she told us to go and take the big copper angel that was adorning her husband's gravesite. She just gave it to us. Of course, moving it off its pedestal was no mean feat. Felicitas and I borrowed a large two-wheeled handcart from Frau Groggert and headed out with it to the cemetery. We'd contacted a construction company ahead of time, which was already at the gravesite with a winch by the time we got there. The job went very quickly: the angel was taken down from its base and laid in the cart. We immediately took off in the direction of the Western sector. The trip was complicated by the fact that the angel had these long outstretched arms that stuck out from underneath the cover spread over it, leading passers-by to assume we were transporting a cadaver. (You could tell they were thinking this by the way they gawked at us.) It was a long stretch from Weissensee to Gleimstraße, where the Gleim tunnel formed the boundary between the Eastern and French sectors of the city. Another problem was that the Eastern side was being guarded by Russian soldiers and the Western side by French. Felicitas, who was fluent in Russian, lured the soldiers into a conversation not far from the tunnel; they, of course, fell right into our plan of distraction by feminine wiles. The way was clear and I took off like a shot toward the Gleim tunnel. I was a little more than halfway when all of a sudden I heard the *Stoy* (Halt!) so familiar to me since 1945. But I did not halt — I kept running. Then suddenly a shot rang out, splitting the wheel hub, and the wagon listed to one side as the angel slid slowly down. Immediately I heard a second shot from the

French side, this one no doubt in warning. I couldn't help but think of the situation in 1945 when I was caught in no-man's-land between the Russians and the SS, only this time one of the uniforms had a different color. Not knowing what to do, I just sat down on the angel.

All of this played itself out in the French sector. A small squad of French soldiers pulled up, looked the situation over and commandeered a truck from the next rubbernecking scrap dealer to drive by. He loaded the angel onto his truck, along with the handcart, and we drove off to his property. After so much effort and frustration, I was expecting a nice piece of change, but I was sorely mistaken. The scrap dealer handed me a sledge hammer with which I proceeded to strip the angel of its copper raiment, more precisely its copper-tin raiment, as the angel's innards were made up of plaster of Paris. My mother offered the following commentary: "Young man, let that be a lesson to you. First of all, not everything that gleams is gold, or even copper, for that matter. Second, never forget there are a lot of people running around who feel they just have to make other people so white that they look like angels. That's all so superficial, because on the inside those people are hollow or filled with plaster." In my life I've made the acquaintance of many such "plaster people." Later on, in my study of the Viennese *Fin de Siècle*, in which the *Schein* and *Sein*, or appearance and reality, problematic assumes great prominence, I often felt reminded of this experience and of my mother's classification. And the money I got for the angel fell far short of what I wound up paying for repairs to the handcart.

It was truly an adventure to go on foraging trips with Felicitas. Once we had to wait several hours for the train home. We were just lolling in a haystack, and I decided I wanted to show her I was a man. As I made a move to embrace her, she just looked at me with her big, round eyes and asked me if I was normal. That, of course, is exactly what I was trying to prove to her, but the tone of voice in which she put the question told me I'd definitely have problems putting my plan into action. I felt mortified and wanted to end my life. I knew there was a lake nearby, so I ran straight for it, found it and meant to plunge right in. But it was night, and on my way there I had tripped several times, or at least often enough to suffer a slackening of my death wish. Also, close up the lake looked a lot smaller and shallower; I guess it wasn't really a lake at all, but more in the nature of a pond. Nevertheless, I wasn't about to let myself be dissuaded by these sobering facts and stepped into the water, gingerly placing one foot in front of the other. A few feet out, while trying to get my bearings, I slipped down off a flat stone on which a frog was sitting that I accidently stepped on. I fell lengthwise into the water, and since even here the pond didn't seem to be getting any deeper, making it less than an ideal body of water for drowning, I dragged my sorry ass back to the haystack, where Felicitas was sleeping peacefully. This made me even more furious: while I was making this absurd attempt to punish her with my heroic death, she was sleeping the sleep of the just. She graciously let me rest by her side, and after a short nap the train pulled in, with which we took our leave from this — for me at least — unhappy place. We got into Berlin in early morning and just barely managed to get to class on time, albeit unprepared.

The faculty in our school was outstanding, and the school's academic standards were extremely high. One reason for this was the fact that we were a humanistic *Gymnasium*, of which there were precious few in the Eastern sector of Berlin; another was the recent addition to our class of one Georg Ebert, whom we called "Osch." He was the son of Friedrich Ebert, Jr., who became mayor of Berlin in 1948, which means he was also the grandson of the first *Reichspräsident* of the Weimar Republic, whom I'd heard about from my father's stories. Since our class was so small, they merged it with another one, so that we now totaled about 25 students. The new students were several years more advanced in English than we were, making it hard on us beginners, as our reading list began with the sophisticated tales of Oscar Wilde and rose only a year later to the elite level of Shakespeare's *King Lear*. It was only for instruction in classical languages that the original seven and the new students split up, which allowed us originals to continue our more advanced study of Latin and Greek. All in all, the integration of the two groups worked out very well, both academically and socially. Previously, we'd had only one girl among us, Felicitas, and now in one stroke fully half the class was female. Friendships formed quickly, not a few escalating into love affairs, which in turn led to marriages. The political discussions we had were especially stimulating, not only because of Osch, but also because some students were quite expert in the history of the workers' movement.

Our Greek teacher was Herr Sierke. Rumor had it that he had taught at the prestigious state school, Schulpforta, whose illustrious graduates included F.F.G. Klopstock, J.G. Fichte, A.F. Möbius, L. von Ranke and K. Lamprecht. It was also gossiped that he'd been transferred to our school because of his membership in the party. He could translate fluently from Greek into Latin and vice versa, and we were introduced by him to all things Greek, not just the language, mind you, but the culture and mind-set of the ancients. We became, in a word, Graecophiles. Herr Sierke stimulated in us a hunger for extra reading, reading beyond the syllabus, which we typically did in the afternoons in our study groups. He passed on to us a foundation that was to shape our entire future development. We had but few books then, and for that reason I had to learn many passages by heart, passages that remain with me to this day. We discussed Plato's *Apologia* and the myth of the cave, and had great fun reading Homer. Homer in particular fascinated us, especially *The Iliad*, since we already knew of war from our own experience. As we recited the tripping hexameters day by day, we found ourselves standing with the Greeks before Troy, suffering with Priam and Hecuba and holding up Helen as the standard by which to judge feminine beauty.

Sometimes, in the shivering midst of an ice-cold winter, we would stand on the street corners and bellow out to the passersby in ancient Greek all our hope, as symbolized by a passage from Homer which, in the English translation of the Voß translation, reads as follows: "Soon the day will arrive, on which the hallow'ed Troy falls asunder, and Priam as well, and the men of the expert lance-wielding monarch." This "Soon the day will arrive" helped us through this time, a time in which we would do our homework in the bar across the street from school, with a plate of no more than two herrings in front of us, to be divided equally among "the Seven." Now and then I would smile as I recalled the parable of the loaves and fishes, which, in the Bible, sufficed to feed thousands, but, alas, the religion of miracles was of no help to us then and there. We went into that bar hungry and came out later just as hungry. What kept us going was our idealism and our fierce hope in that day to come on which all would be different. We believed in that day with all the unflappable hope of youth.

To be sure, our day of salvation was anything but soon in coming. As the weeks and months in class stretched on, so did our gnawing hunger, and we took up smoking to get our minds off it. We began with Machorka, a Russian tobacco made from the cut-up stalks of the tobacco plant. Cigarettes were rolled with blotting paper that would always catch on fire when you inhaled, forcing those around you to frantically blow it out. Our classroom was so blue with smoke that, half the time, you couldn't see your own hand before your face. Thank God the glass panes were blown out; the windows were, at best, hastily rigged with cardboard, allowing the smoke to drift out at the sides. Later on we advanced to Stella cigarettes, which I would usually bargain for on the black market and sell there as well. They were of Bulgarian origin, did *not* catch fire when inhaled and tasted a lot better than Machorka, though not nearly as good as the Russian *papyrossi*. Only occasionally could we afford Abdullah cigarettes, which were oval-shaped, came in a gold-bordered box under fine silver paper and gave off a bluish smoke that aroused fantasies of the wonders of the Orient, of the sort depicted, say, by Karl May in his novel, *Through the Desert*.

Nor was Karl May left on the shelf, even in this period of higher education. Our geography teacher, a Dr. Klenner, who was very friendly with us, used Karl May for instructional purposes when we discussed the geography of North America. He read passages to us from *Winnetou* and *Old Surehand*, passages containing the most plastic and vivid descriptions of the continental landscape, and it was not only I, but so many of my classmates as well, who dreamt of one day backpacking across the North American prairie, protecting a squaw from wild animals, and smoking a peace pipe with the Iroquois. One morning, when I was surreptitiously reading May under my desktop during Latin class with Fritz Plagemann, he snatched the book away from me and scolded me, saying life was too short and one should not waste it perusing such tripe. He said there were so many other books from which to learn so many valuable things. He was right, of course (all due respect to May), and so began for me a new reading phase, together with Felicitas, who, biologically speaking, was my age, but who was by far my better half in terms of maturity. We began by reading Stefan Zweig, then Arnold Zweig, followed by Hermann Hesse and Thomas Mann. A whole new world opened up before me, and I read my way into it. I even became politically active, but that was more a result of external pressure than a free commitment. It came about more or less as follows.

Our school was in the Russian sector, but border traffic to the West, especially to the adjacent French sector, where I lived, was lively. So I wasn't exactly surprised when Osch came to me one day and asked me to go out into the street with him. We went down together, and the minute I hit the street, somebody stuck a red flag in my hand, and I became part of a demonstration against the capitalistic West. The march went down the street, heading for nearby Nettelbeck Square, and I was at its head, carrying my red flag before me. In this moment I had the rare experience of feeling important, for it had not been so long ago that I was at the head of another crowd, that one in hot pursuit, just salivating to beat me to a pulp, whereas now they were following me as their leader. I waved my flag back and forth, but not for long. The West Berlin police were already in place, waiting for the demonstrators, and they proceeded to disperse the crowd with a water cannon. I was stubborn and kept going. When I finally turned around, everybody had scattered. After two days' detention at the police station, in which I remembered having been held once before, I was released to go home. During this stay, however, there had been no friendly invitation to play a fast game of skat.

When I gave my mother a blow-by-blow about the incident and told her how good it felt to head up the parade with flag in hand, especially since the flag had this beautiful pink area in the middle to offset the surrounding blood red, she merely snorted, "My boy, the flag was an old swastika flag. What with raw materials being so scarce, they cut out the cross in the middle and replaced it with some red bed sheet. Before, all the people ran around behind the swastika flag, now it's the red flag—you know, I think people always have to have some flag or other to follow, otherwise they're not happy." These words never failed to come back to me later on, as a gentle irony, whenever I would take part in a demonstration march.

And marching was one thing we had to do in school, especially on holidays. The first of May, 1949, was just such a day, and participation was obligatory. Our class assembled at the Bornholm bridge with thousands of deputies of the Free German Youth (*Freien Deutschen Jugend* or FDJ), and marched toward the *Lustgarten* (Pleasure Garden).[42] For me the name *Lustgarten* signified much more than just a place for mass rallies; it also meant burgeoning sexual desire, given new and copious nourishment on this day, as would become evident in the course of the march. The demonstration moved in closed formation behind the red flag, which in this instance displayed no pink area in its middle. We'd been underway for about an hour when it suddenly began to rain heavily. It came down in sheets, soaking us right through to the bone. We refused to be put off, but just kept marching and singing. Some of the songs were familiar to me from having sung them in the *Jungvolk*. I was marching alongside a beautiful girl from Saxony, whose blue blouse was a little too small for her. All at once my gaze was transfixed by the miracle of that blouse as it slowly shrank in the rain and turned from blue to a pale transparency. Actually, I was well acquainted with this process: the same thing had happened to my confirmation suit, and it made no difference whether it'd been put together from the *People's Observer* (*Völkischer Beobachter*) or the *New Germany* (*Neues Deutschland*). And as the blue color continued to fade, and the blouse became ever smaller and filmier, you could see more and more clearly just what the blouse was meant to conceal. I stared in fascination at the demiglobes of my marching partner, wishing the rain would never end. After the rally, my little pioneer asked me if I had a pullover at home, since there was no way she could go home looking like that. When my mother saw her, she said sharply, "Girl, you can't run around like that. You can see everything." She gave her a few things to wear and made us a *Muckefuckkaffee* (ersatz coffee),[43] which we also called *Blümchenkaffee* (lit.: little flower coffee),[44] after which the girl went home. Glumly I thought it was a shame we had to part, as such an opportunity to educate my eye was not likely to present itself again anytime soon.

The Abitur, Analytical Geometry, Thermodynamics and the Ladle

The year before the *Abitur* exam, I made an effort to fill in some gaps in my knowledge of mathematics and the natural sciences, and I must say I succeeded to a fair extent. I especially liked geography, taught by Dr. Hugo Rosendorf, as I'd always been fascinated by the idea of travel to foreign countries. Once I had to present an oral report on lagoons, and I told the class that a lagoon was a flat body of water sealed off from the sea and that there were both fresh-water and salt-water lagoons. Then I went to the blackboard and drew an island with a pond. Since the island looked empty, I filled it in with a few palm trees here and there. Still, I had the feeling something was missing, so I went on to draw a beach chair, on which you could barely make out the curvy outlines of a woman. Then I added a house with garage in the background, and with this finishing touch my lagoon dream-island was complete. Now I was "cooking with gas," which was just when I was told to take my seat. But the drawing remained on the blackboard for the entire period, and we all starred mesmerized at this dream-island, particularly at the beauty reclining on the beach chair, who seemed to be waiting longingly for each of us.

My Achilles heel was mathematics, but that was less my fault than our teacher's, who couldn't abide me; it probably had even more to do with the math classes I had to cut on account of the foraging trips. My relationship with my math teacher was like that between the positive and negative poles of a high-voltage electrical circuit. When the time came for promotion from the 11th to the 12th grade, I had problems, since I'd received a "5" in math and was told my good grades in Greek and Latin would not be enough to compensate for it. With the help of some tutoring from Felicitas, I raised the grade to a "3." This got me admitted to the senior or *Abitur* class, to the obvious consternation of my math teacher. He'd give me harder problems to solve than he gave to his pet students, and when I couldn't solve them, he'd just lament, tongue in cheek, of course, that I'd never get it, that my prospects were hopeless. This led me to reflect on just how much times had changed, for, during the Nazi period, I would always have to hear how smart Jews were in calculation, but now, all of a sudden, it seemed we weren't so good after all. But maybe it had to do with the fact that I was only a half-Jew, and so they could pigeonhole me this way or that according to their needs or convictions. My mother was in despair. Her whole life she had worked to provide her son with better schooling and a better life than she'd been able to have.

Just before the *Abitur* exam, she got the idea to put me in touch with a neighbor of ours, a former math teacher at a *Gymnasium*, who, owing to his former party affiliation, was now allowed to teach — paradoxically — only religion. This man gave me private lessons, and almost immediately I was able to understand so much more than before. Then he gave me a practice test. It contained two problems, both of which I found very difficult, since they presupposed an understanding of differential and integral calculus, as well as a solid basis in analytical geometry. I managed only partial solutions to the problems, but my tutor had the patience to walk me step by step through the complex calculation process.

On the day of the written math exam, our teacher walked into class, gave out the bluebooks and opened the envelope containing the problems. Earlier he had turned in a list of several possible problems to the school administration, which then selected the ones to be solved on the exam. When I received the sheet with the problems, I saw there were three altogether, of which I was to work out two. I couldn't believe my eyes when I saw on the sheet the very same two problems I had carefully worked through with my tutor only the week before. I had a very good memory and no trouble recalling the precise route to their solutions. When I turned in my bluebook (the first to do so), my teacher eyed me with profound suspicion, as he was convinced these problems were beyond my powers. A week later he called me into his office and had my bluebook on the desk in front of him. He stared at me for a while and said, "I can't imagine how you pulled it off, but your exam is a perfect "1." I know there's something shady going on here. Don't think for a moment that this will be your final grade. You could, of course, push for a "2," but if you do, I'll rough you up so badly on the upcoming oral exam that you'll drop back down to your "5," which is the grade you deserve anyway." I accepted the "3" offered me and left, confident I'd escaped the nightmare of an oral exam in this subject. Of course, the man couldn't dismiss me without casually mentioning that I wasn't any great shakes in physics either, and that one might just find it worthwhile to poke and probe me in this area as well, which, he had no doubt, would lead to the exposure of numerous "dead spots." Later, when I asked my tutor how it was that I was given the same problems on the exam that I had worked out with him, he just laughed. He opened his filing cabinet and pulled out a notebook, decorated with a swastika and containing test problems that he had used as a math teacher in the Third Reich. He was fairly sure my teacher had the same notebook and had taken the problems from it. Fair enough, I thought, but still, there were close to a hundred problems laid out in the notebook, so it was still something of a miracle that precisely these two were selected — not only by both teachers but by the state school board as well.

Then came the day of the oral exam, which in the year 1950 was to have a somewhat different format than usual. What was different was that the entire 11th grade was allowed to be present, in order to see for themselves what would be expected of them when their turn came. As for myself, I knew not only that I would be tested in physics, but tested so as to bring out my weaknesses rather than my strengths. I also knew that only one other candidate was to be tested in this subject. Since the exam was scheduled for 9 a.m., I made sure I was there in front of the doors of the exam auditorium by eight. Nervous as I was, I opened my textbook for a little last-minute cramming. Around half past eight the beadle showed up, and I watched him as he carried two covered pieces of equipment into the examining room. Just by their shape, I could tell they were a galvanometer and an X-ray tube. So I could be fairly sure that I would be getting questions on one or the other. Now I had a more specific use for my physics book: I found a peaceful corner and reviewed everything I knew about these two devices.

When my name was called, I entered the examining room. Seated in the front were the examining committee and the representative of the Soviet municipal commander's office, and in the auditorium orchestra some fifty pre-*Abiturienten*, for whom the whole business was probably a pleasant dog-and-pony show. Someone stuck the X-ray tube into my hand and told me I had fifteen minutes at a side table to prepare myself for questioning. They would test Crassus in mathematics ahead of me. Unfortunately, math was not his forte. Since I'd already prepared for my own exam, I spent my fifteen minutes observing closely how Crassus maneuvered his way through the questions. And it was here that I learned something important: a bit of flimflam I would spin out in my own future exams, just as my own students, whom I was to test in years to come, would do. One might say this trick or technique is a defense mechanism with archetypal roots. It's one you use to show you're not an idiot, even if you don't exactly know the answer to the question being put to you.

Crassus was asked to illustrate a parabola on the blackboard and then describe it. The first part was simple, with Crassus drawing a quite beautiful geometric figure. But he couldn't explain it any further than that, despite the hints offered, such as directrix and focus. The correct answer was, as I well knew, that a parabola has only a single focus and that all points on the parabola are equidistant from this focus, as well as from the directrix. Crassus mulled it over, but no illumination came from above. Finally, he fell back on this old trick, which consisted in simply shifting the question to an area in which he was much more at home. To stall for time, he asked them please to repeat the question, and was promptly told to describe a parabola. With these few seconds to think, however, he managed to spin out his flimflam, "The concept of the parabola has a long history. It is not only a geometric figure, but has played, as 'parable,' just as important a role in *belles lettres*. In literature it is an allegorical narrative and is employed especially in works of a didactic nature. Events are reported, the significance of which the reader can discern only through analogical reference. A classic example is the parable of the ring in Lessing's drama, *Nathan the Wise*, in which an appeal is made for tolerance in the sense promoted by the Enlightenment," gravely intoning the word "tolerance" as he gazed at the committee long and imposingly, "the Enlightenment being, of course, the era referenced by Kant in his essay, 'What is Enlightenment?'" And so it went on for a while, Crassus deftly spinning out ideas by association. The committee, of course, was not especially impressed by this demonstration of the candidate's humanistic knowledge, least of all our math teacher. But the latter, desiring to bring the whole business to a positive conclusion, simply asked what field parabolic calculation belonged to, having, of course, analytic geometry in mind. Yet when this question was put to Crassus, he hesitated. The teacher tried to help: "What we're testing here is geometry, right? And when we analyze geometry, what is *that* field called?" Crassus remained mute. Teacher: "Look, if you regard one of these two words as an adjective and the other as a substantive, what is the resulting combination?" At once Crassus's face lit up as he said, "That would be a geometric analysis." Instantly correcting himself, he finally blurted out "analytic geometry." All present breathed a sigh of relief, and the candidate was dismissed, promptly beating a hasty retreat to the door.

I was next. X-ray tube in hand, I came over to the table, where I was asked to take a seat. In doing so, I happened to place the tube on the table less than gently. My teacher flared up, "Be careful with that apparatus! Don't break it, as you already have done several times in the past! It's very expensive, and this is the only one we have." Then came the first question, which, of course, required me to identify and describe the object at issue. At once, my thespian proclivities kicked in: miming the ignoramus, I faltered just a bit with my answer. That had its intended effect, as I could easily see from my math teacher's expression. I continued to (pretend to) hem and haw, but then it all burst forth from me like a tidal wave: I described the Röntgen rays or X-rays, the construction of an X-ray tube, the difference between cathodes and anodes, the poles at which the oxidizing processes run down and those for the reducing processes, the discovery of rays, and the applications of Röntgen rays to medicine. All of this information came straight from a few pages in my textbook, but the way I brought it all out made it sound completely original. This was my greatest hour, and I shone. Not expecting anything like this, my examiner tried to interrupt me, but once cranked up, I was not to be stopped. When I finally finished, at first there was only silence. Then my examiner said, "Yes, yes, fine, you do know a thing or two about the Röntgen tube, but now tell us something about the three fundamental laws of thermodynamics." I was prepared for this, or so I thought, and I recited the first law, that energy always remains constant and can never be lost. The second law, I continued, adds the idea of entropy, since not all heat is preserved in a closed system, as heat can pass through a cold body, but not vice versa. The third law caught me cold; for the life of me, I couldn't remember that the equation, $T=0=273.15C$, is designated as an absolute zero point, which, of course, according to the third law of thermodynamics, can never be reached. A lethal hush fell over the room, and I found myself hoping for a miracle, that maybe, say, a gigantic hole would open up before me. I would fall into it, only to reappear on the other side of the earth on a South See island, by the side of a lagoon dotted with palm trees. A beautiful native girl reclining in a beach chair would be waiting there for me, smiling as I approached her.

No hole opened up before me, but a miracle did occur nonetheless. The Russian sitting in on the proceedings took matters in hand, perhaps sensing something of the tension in the relationship between teacher and candidate or because he felt pity for me, or both. He asked me, in a German of native fluency, why, in the essay describing ourselves and our desired careers we'd all had to turn in, I'd said I wanted to become a chef. I answered him truthfully, that a career in the hospitality industry interested me and that cooking was not only essential to people's well-being but could also be very creative when you invented new dishes. This answer seemed to please him, and he then asked me the following question: "Let's assume you're the head chef in a kitchen and you want to test the soup. How do you go about it?" I replied that I'd take a ladle, fill it with soup and sip some from it. To which he replied, "But the soup is much too hot, and you would burn your mouth. So what would you do then?" My answer was that I would blow on the soup until it cooled off. With his next question the Russian made a seamless segue to the field of physics, as he set me the task of explaining this process in physical terms. Now I was on my own turf, since I'd already put up soup once or twice in the Hotel Continental. I explained to him that I would blow away the steam forming in the ladle just above the soup, in order to take some of the heat out of it, which would help to establish a temperature enabling me to test the soup without burning my mouth. I laced my explanation with a few mathematical formulas, from which we proceeded to the field of thermodynamics; and in this general context, the correct answer concerning the third law of thermodynamics came to me without effort, which I just happened to "throw in" at the end of my remarks. Pedagogically speaking, the Russian examiner was light years ahead of our math teacher; and later in my own career, when I tested candidates, I would often think of this man, who blended practical knowledge, pedagogical ability and empathy so well.

After the oral exam, we were expected to march proudly into "real life," as the public myth so grandly envisions it. But just before this march there remained the graduation celebration. We were invited by the Eberts to hold our party at their home. And so off we went that evening in our relatively decent clothes. The house was in Pankow, in the government district, where most government officials resided. It all began very politely and cordially. We were served potato salad and wieners, as was customary on these occasions, and were permitted to drink beer. The beer tasted fine, and, since there was so much of it available, we did not stint. Meanwhile people were stepping outside to cool off. I decided to join them, accompanied by my beautiful tablemate, who at this point was more than happy to fling herself into the arms of "real life." After two bottles of beer, she discovered this life in yours truly, and as we strolled around the block, she took possession of more and more of my arm, until it began to feel more like dragging than walking. But before I had the opportunity to "devote" myself to her, I heard the clumping of boots on the pavement behind me. I turned around to see, to my astonishment, two armed VOPO's running towards us, one of them with a submachine gun perched on his shoulder. When I asked why all the fuss, since we hadn't done anything, or at least not yet, they told me that this was a government district and that they would screen any unknown person just as warily. This was enough to cool my ardor, and I just asked them for a light for my cigarette, which they readily gave me. Grinding out the cigarette, I went back to the party with my tablemate, who by now was suspecting that "real life" was not quite so glorious as she'd imagined it to be. The party was now in full force. Bigger and better bottles of beer, so it seemed, were brought in, and the mood brightened with the popping of each bottle cap. Then somehow a chair collapsed, the noise rousing the master of the house, who came into the room livid, in his pajamas, and, without further ado, kicked us all out. Escorted by the VOPO, we turned our backs on this government utopia and headed happily for home. All in all, it was a terrific celebration.

Alas, it was not long before the seriousness of life beckoned to me. I wanted to study architecture, which was logical in view of the ravaged city we had to face every day. When I went to the Free University, I was told that, for the first two years, I would have to pay for everything myself, since there was no money available for scholarships. This I couldn't do. On the other hand, I didn't want to study at the Humboldt University, even though I had an offer, since I lived in the Western sector and no longer wanted to commute back and forth between the sectors. But I was not to remain unemployed for long. In the Fall I received a letter inquiring whether I would be interested in becoming a relief worker. With the coffers at home as bare as they could be, I accepted the offer, and therewith commenced yet another new phase in my life.

An Intermezzo: Relief Work 1950-51

I was assigned to a work group charged with building a little connecting street in the Reinickendorf district. The construction job was undertaken by the firm Lehr for the municipal building department, and the pay was the same for everybody: just over one DM per hour. The financing came from various U.S. funds, so we were told, and the purpose of the whole program was not so much to build anything new or important as to get as many unemployed men off the street as possible. Young men above all, who, unable to find apprenticeships, were just hanging idly around. The street we were to build first had to be cleared of rubble, and for that job we had a machine that didn't always work. So we often had to do manual labor. Since I was already experienced in clearing rubble, the work was familiar to me: we laid tracks for the truck cars and filled them up, first with debris and later with sand for the new street. The work wasn't hard, and we didn't exactly kill ourselves either. The pay was a pittance, especially if you smoked, a habit I had unfortunately picked up through my black market activity.

Since I was the only one there with an *Abitur*, I moved up quickly and was appointed secretary in only my second week. My job was to go around and note down the number of filled trucks, for which the building contractor was paid from the fund. It wasn't until later that I learned that the engineer in charge of the project always raised my numbers by a few trucks before turning in the paperwork, which of course was signed by me. Eventually, with the exposure of the swindle, he was prosecuted and the firm went belly-up.

It didn't take long to recognize that class differences dominated the atmosphere on the construction site. Almost all workers lived north of the city. Most of them either came from the working class or had previously worked in an office. *Abiturienten* (*Gymnasium* graduates) were few and far between and were mostly regarded with mistrust. This I was to learn quickly. Some made obnoxious comments to me, and one day, while we were eating our lunch in the contractor's shed, it happened that somebody surreptitiously removed the *Wurst* from my sandwich and slipped a dead rat (one of the many on the site) into it. I was challenged to eat my sandwich, and when I refused, the whole gang guffawed. Among other things, the prank was probably a reaction to the "egghead intellectual" who had so quickly been elevated to the exalted position of a secretary and, as such, no longer need get dirt under his fingernails. It was at this point that Franz came to my aid. He lived on Köslinerstraße, together with an alcoholic mother and four siblings, all in one room. He was someone you didn't want to rub the wrong way. He took me under his wing, maybe because he felt we were both outsiders. When he took a seat next to me, all the teasing stopped and I had no further problems.

Franz accepted me fully, no strings attached. He was what you'd call a crook, and he would occasionally bring some of his stolen booty to work to show us. Once I was given an especially beautiful little radio set that he'd filched from some store on one of his nocturnal capers. My pleasure was short-lived, however, as my mother sent the tainted goods right back to him. His friend, Wolfgang, who lived in the same house as he, was his opposite number: soft, delicate and an "egghead," who already had a number of semesters at the Humboldt University under his belt. Wolfgang wanted to become an ophthalmologist. It was his dream to emigrate to the States and make a life for himself there. But the dream had to stay on hold for the time being, as he had no money for the passage; he also had a wife and two children. Later I would see Wolfgang with his wife and children in New York, where he'd established himself as an optometrist and drove a luxury car. But that all took place several years later, with the relief work well behind us.

Much water was to run under the bridge, before Wolfgang would realize his dream. Relief work gave us an opportunity to earn a little extra money. This involved salvaging the felled streetlights from the rubbish, sawing them up and then selling the pieces as cast iron. Essential as they were to reconstruction, metals brought good money, and raw materials were very scarce at that time. Only one time, late one night when my two friends wanted to saw down some still-intact streetlights, did I bow out. I never did find out whether they went ahead with the project without me:

My buddies and I (center)

We stayed at this construction site for about a year, even though the street we built was very short. The reason for the extended period was that the site first had to be cleared; then it had to be excavated, which could only be done by hand. The trucks were then piled high with sand and, as I observed, moved back and forth, since in one place the foundation for the new street would be too low, while in another too high. No doubt the (ir)responsible engineer, to up profits, cooked the books in calculating the amount of labor required to move the trucks back and forth. Then the earth was flattened out with a steamroller and the flat foundation covered with bricks, which were tightly packed. The bricks were in turn covered with sand, which was again steamrolled flat. After that, still more bricks and more sand. Gaps were filled in with crushed stone, until the street was smooth and dense and so firm that you felt it would last for centuries. Next came the tar wagon, and so many buckets of tar were poured out onto the street and smoothed with trowels. When the street was almost finished, they tore one side of it right up again, since they'd forgotten to lay the electric and telephone cables. All this happened while the workers, leaning on their shovels, looked on in fascination to see the results of all their effort, of which they were very proud, destroyed. Then the whole dug-up area was filled in again, the steamroller did its job, buckets of tar were poured out and the tar once again evenly spread. The street was finally finished, but, alas, not for long, as now the other side was torn up so the sewer pipes could be replaced. My two friends and I didn't mind any of this at all, since we continued to be paid and could spend the extra hours rummaging through some nearby ruins for leveled streetlights, which we'd then, as usual, saw up and carry off to the dealer. But eventually the street actually *was* finished. All pipes were laid, the street surface looked fine and we were told to pick up our last pay envelope.

This I did, and found myself back on the street, which didn't look anywhere near as beautiful as the one I'd just helped to build. My mother's advice, to pay another visit to the employment office, seemed sound. So I headed over there. When I arrived, they told me the first thing I needed to do was take an aptitude test that would pinpoint my strengths and, doubtless, also my weaknesses. So I sat down for the test, filled in lots of little boxes with x's, did a few exercises and wrote a short essay describing my previous experiences. The test was evaluated immediately and my name called out. The man assigned to me began the interview with the remark that my test showed unequivocally my strong aptitude for math, but just as well an inclination to creativity. When you considered these two traits in connection with my previous experience in construction, it was clear, he opined, that I had an aptitude for architecture. So, back to architecture! When I told him that this field required a long period of study for which I didn't have the money, he shrugged his shoulders. Before leaving, I asked him if there were any openings in the hotel business, since I also had experience as a cook. He checked his book and said he thought the Hotel am Zoo might be looking for an apprentice waiter. I could apply there, he said, although I was probably too old and overqualified for such a position.

Next day I went to the Hotel am Zoo. It was located at Kurfürstendamm 25, right next to the Filmbühne Wien. I climbed the hotel steps and entered the study of the owner, a Dr. Joseph Köhler. He interviewed me, along with a Herr Klingemann, whom I took to be an investor who was routinely consulted in hiring decisions. The conversation went well; I was able to show off my best side, deftly dropping casual allusions to my extensive knowledge of Greek and Latin. This, they told me, was of little use in the hotel business, as I could expect to meet very few guests who spoke ancient Greek or Latin. Thereupon I demonstrated to them my fluency in English, which made a better impression. The only serious downside they could see in me was my age, I being already 19 years old, which is really already too old for an apprentice waiter. Of course, there was also the fact that I had the *Abitur*, and, truth to tell, *Gymnasium* graduates tended to be too independent-minded, preferring to follow their own ideas to carrying out the directives of the headwaiter. What finally settled the issue was my previous hotel experience and the written recommendation I was able to present for the month I spent working in the Hotel Continental's kitchen. And so I was given the three-year apprenticeship as a waiter, therewith beginning a new and interesting chapter in my life. I went to the employment office with my mother, and there they gave me the necessary papers, which I immediately filled out and turned in.

6. Life in the Hotel am Zoo 1951-1954

My Training as Ganymede [45]

In April, 1951, I began my training at the Hotel am Zoo. I had to bring my own apron and jacket, which my mother had quickly stitched together for me, as there was no money to buy anything new. First, ten other apprentices and I assembled in a room equipped with a large refrigerator for the wine bottles and a sink for the wine glasses. The headwaiter, Gronwald, who for decades had been maitre d' of the five-star hotel restaurant, as well as of the Konditorei Kranzler Unter den Linden, a pastry shop on the corner of

Friedrichstraße, introduced us, and immediately thereafter began giving instruction. The first thing we were told was that, for the time being, we'd be staying right where we were, in the wine kitchen, and wouldn't be allowed to assist in serving until later. So we got to know the different types of wine glasses, those for red and white wines, for *Sekt* (champagne) and liqueurs. Then we were shown how to wash, dry and inspect them, to check for water stains that might dim the luster of the polished glass. Once, in my first month, I remember washing and polishing some 250 glasses in a single stint. Soon enough the headwaiter came by and inspected them. Catching a tiny water spot on one, he grabbed a bottle of ketchup and emptied it over all the glasses. Then he told me to clean them all again, a job lasting over three hours. Something similar had happened to me in the Hotel Continental in 1945, the difference being that in this instance I wasn't forced to hold my hands over a hot stove. Maybe this sort of thing is part of an initiation ritual for trainees in the restaurant business.

That Fall, the classroom part of our vocational training began. Every Monday we sat in class from 8 a.m. until well into the afternoon. The subjects were all job-related, and we learned such things as how to shop differently in different seasons, how to calculate profit, what legal rights one has in case a guest either can't or won't pay the bill, and how to set up an annual budget. Our instruction in food that Fall was oenology. First, we took up the history of wine, from the time of the Romans to the modern era. Then we were introduced to the various wine-growing areas. We learned that you can tell just from the color of the bottle whether a wine comes from the Rhineland or from the Mosel, Rhine wines being bottled in brown bottles and Mosel in green. We were taught to discriminate between table wines and wines of quality, and the terms of designation that were tossed around were all new to me: *Kabinett, Spätlese, Auslese, Beerenauslese, Eiswein*, and the highest, most expensive level of quality: *Trockenbeerenauslese*. Then we learned how to test a wine for such qualities as harmony, elegance and maturity, and to assess the influence of the aging process on the aroma of a wine. For instance, you should drink a *Kabinettwein* within two or three years, whereas you can wait up to ten with *Spät*- and *Auslesen*, giving the wine more time to mature.

All this expertise was presupposed in the selection of a wine for a given meal. Between a wine and its meal there prevails a delicate relationship, as not all wines are suitable for every meal. A wine can enhance the aroma of a dish or do the opposite. We learned that one serves dry wines with light dishes, as, for example, a *Königinpastete* or *vol-au-vent*, and strong, even heavy wines with chateaubriand in Roquefort sauce or a sirloin steak. At one point we were assigned the task of recommending a wine for any dish listed among the specialties of the hotel restaurant. That was no problem for me, since our head chef had enriched our international menu by one delicious dish: veal steak Singapore. You brown a veal steak lightly in the pan and serve it on a bed of rice. It's topped off with a sliced half-banana and half a slice of pineapple, both browned in the pan. Everything is then draped in a mild curry sauce. This dish is best accompanied by a *Traminer* or *Gewürztraminer,* whose golden-yellow hue picks up on the yellow of the curry sauce and, in general, accents the color palette of the dish. But the olfactory also comes into play here, as the commingled fragrances of roses, honey, violets and acacia blossoms native to this wine enhance the tastes and textures of the meal profoundly. While our teachers articulated all of this in theory, there were also plenty of banquets at which wines were served, wines we could sample, since we were at this time one of the foremost hotels on the square.

Wine-tasting was not an exercise in mere swallowing; rather, you had to be able to describe the taste and aroma with precision. This entailed mastering the proper vocabulary. Thus a wine can taste flowery, or: full, elegant, racy, tender, balanced, insipid, insouciant, fiery or even bitter. The vocabulary was sensual and often led the imagination along seductive bypaths; in the description of a wine, you'd find yourself indulging fantasies of things other than the wine itself. Our headwaiter was an expert, and to this day I am grateful to him for introducing me to the field of oenology, until then completely unknown to me. One time we took the liberty of playing a practical joke on him that involved putting his expertise to the test. We gave him a glass of wine that we had secretly adulterated with a touch of vinegar and asked him to identify both winery and vintage. Never will I forget the glower that shot out of his eyes at us. Our "reward" for this little bit of devilment was two weeks of doing nothing but washing and polishing glasses. After graduation he gave us each a taste of a *Trockenbeerenauslese*, and when we asked him how he would judge the wine, he said, "It tastes just as if an angel were peeing over your tongue. But that's not a professional appraisal, and it's not something you'd ever say to a guest. But I'm telling you, it's right on!"

Near the end of our second year of training, we had our own little wine-tasting session, which, as you might expect, degenerated into something approaching a debauch. We had to fill the wine cellar with correctly placed bottles that had just been delivered, a difficult job, as the truck carrying the wine had been in a collision, leaving most bottles cracked or broken. An insurance official was on the scene as we opened up the crates containing the broken bottles; after a while, he wrote off the whole inventory. We took the broken bottles, filtered the wine still in them through a fine sieve and proceeded to feast on the noblest varieties of the grape, wines that are normally prohibitively expensive. There were so many of them. When we were finished, I went upstairs to the restaurant, where I was to wait on the owner, Dr. Köhler. He recognized my condition immediately and had me walk along the seam in the blue rug that covered the entire floor of the restaurant. I couldn't do it and just reeled from one end to the other. He sent me home to sleep it off. The following week he issued an intermediate evaluation of me that I had to present to the school. I was worried that my Dionysian condition might be mentioned, but, to my astonishment and shame, read the following: "Herr Schneider is honest, very diligent and reliable; we are extraordinarily satisfied with his accomplishments. On the basis of his modest and friendly self-presentation, Herr Schneider has succeeded in winning our respect and that of our guests." Signed May 14, 1953. In the wake of the previous day's "wine tasting," I found the description, "friendly self-presentation," to be more than generous; a more objective characterization would've been "self-humiliation" or "self-abasement." Still, after that fiasco, I always strove to become worthy of the accolades I didn't deserve at the time, to keep the gratuitous laurel wreath from withering, so to speak.

At home life was different, and it was often hard for me to bridge my life in the west with my life in the north, or life on the Ku-Damm with life in Wedding. At home there was no wine and no beef stroganoff, just a simple goulash with potatoes and red cabbage. We couldn't afford wine, and my mother thought I should drink *Gänsewein* (Adam's wine or water) anyway, since it was healthier. The contrasts between the hotel and home were jarring, but I did attempt on occasion to try out my new knowledge at home. On my mother's birthday, I prepared a dish that was new to her. Her only condition was that it had to be simple. We only had a small gas stove, and expenses had to be kept to a minimum, since my salary as an apprentice was itself minimal: in my first year as an apprentice I earned only 35 DM per week, in my second 45, and in my third and last year 55. That wasn't much at all, when you consider that a pack of Juno cigarettes cost two marks and that I was a heavy smoker. So you had to apply your creativity to the financial realities.

And so I made a simple and — for my mother at least — novel meal. For an appetizer I served beef tartar, something I'd had to put together many times in the restaurant. My mother had made this for us on occasion, but only in the "good bourgeois" style, which meant spicing up the meat with an egg, onion, salt and pepper. I refined this recipe by taking some finely ground tenderloin, along with an egg yolk, salt, pepper, garlic, paprika, a spritz of Worcestershire sauce, a chopped anchovy and a touch of English mustard, mixing it all together and shaping it into a ball which I garnished on the plate with a sprig of parsley. The dish was accompanied by a slice of toast cut up in quarters. The main course was a fine Viennese-style chicken fricassee in a wreath of rice. For this I took a chicken, removed the innards and cooked it with parsley, finely chopped celery, half an onion and carrots. In a small frying pan I sautéed sliced mushrooms, after which I fried the chicken liver. In another pot I steamed a few stalks of asparagus and florets of cauliflower. Then, taking some butter, flour, and the chicken broth, I made a *sauce blanche* or white sauce. I had to boil it very slowly so as to avoid clumping. Then I de-boned and chopped up the cooked chicken, cut the liver finely and put the whole concoction, now in bite-sized pieces, into the sauce, to which I'd already added a dash of lemon juice. Since I still had a little leftover tartar meat, I mixed it with breadcrumbs and put these little meatballs in the sauce as well. This last ingredient was not Viennese style in the strict sense, so I expanded the name of the dish with the phrase, "à la maison" — "in the style of the house," *our* house. I let the whole thing cook another ten minutes, tasted it one last time, mixed a scrambled egg yolk into the sauce (another "à la maison" gambit) and served it with the rice. For dessert I served *Pêche à la Melba*, or peach Melba. That was fairly simple, since all you need for it is vanilla ice cream, a few halved, ripened peaches and raspberry sauce, which latter is easily made with raspberries, water and sugar. The sauce is boiled quickly while stirring, put through a sieve, tasted, reduced and finally poured over the halved peaches lying on their beds of vanilla ice cream.

The festiveness of this birthday dinner was further enhanced by the pecuniary wallpaper in our living room. Since our apartment had not fared well in the war and the wallpaper had even come loose from the plaster and was hanging down from the upper walls, my mother saved up and had the room re-papered. First the paperhanger pulled down the old crimson wallpaper, which had always had bubbling in certain spots anyway, and as he proceeded, we discovered that, for all these years, we'd been living in a room worthy of Croesus. Since most original bare walls were very rough, people strategically added newspaper to them, so that the final wallpaper would show no unevenness. In our case, however, even the newspapered wall was still so rough that some earlier paperhanger had been forced to cover it up with a second layer of paper to get a reasonably smooth surface. Since the room had last been papered in the 20's, a decade during which the value of money decreased almost daily, the paperhanger, doubtless out of depression or cynicism over his disappearing bank balance, had used some of those huge, virtually worthless bank notes for one wall, pasting them onto the concave spots in a row from top to bottom. Only then was the actual wallpaper pasted on. My mother and I sat at the table and gazed at the columns of bank notes, all impressively lined with zeros, and she remarked with a satisfied expression, "Now, not only are we enjoying an expensive dinner, but we're also millionaires." I corrected her, pointing to the zeros that in fact made us billionaires. When I asked her how she liked the meal, she merely replied, "Better than the poor man's porridge we've had to make do with, much better. Let's hope we never have to go through that again."

Human — All Too Human

Not only was the hotel a new world for me in a culinary sense, it also offered a panorama of human behavior. It wasn't until our second year that we were permitted, under the watchful eyes of our *chefs de range*, to serve guests. The first guest to order a bottle of wine from me was Sir Carol Reed, the director whose film, *The Third Man*, had made him a household name. He had selected an expensive wine, a '36 Erdener Treppchen *Spätlese*. Carrying the bottle to the table with the utmost caution, I immediately made my first mistake: I opened it without first showing it to the customer. The cork came out easily, and the fragrance released from the wine was almost intoxicating. I sampled it, most uncritically I must admit, since I was so nervous I couldn't tell what mattered and what didn't. Only then did I show the bottle to the guest, who merely glanced at it and sent it back. The reason was that it bore an SS-symbol on its label, indicating that the winery had been expropriated by the SS. I was instantly gripped by panic, as the bottle was extremely expensive and, open as it now was, not one I could bring back. At that point a gentleman, sitting with his escort at a nearby table, took pity on me and took the bottle off my hands. I later learned that he was the head of Olympia Film AG, which infused the situation with irony, since Olympia had financed films made by Leni Riefenstahl during the Third Reich. Among them the 1936 production, *Olympische Spiele* (Olympic Games), released two years later. That film's intent had been to show the world the openness and tolerance of the Nazi regime. Of course, these were qualities profoundly doubted not only by Carol Reed, in whose mind this vintage was likely linked with his dining neighbor, the games and the cynical propagandizing, but also, in due course, by me as well. But I will never forget the bouquet and the taste of this wine, for here the vatic utterance of my headwaiter was fully validated: "The wine tastes just as if an angel were peeing over your tongue."

Hitting the floors, so to speak, to take room-service orders or wait on guests, came relatively late in our apprenticeship. There were exceptions, of course, especially when the hotel was filled to the last room. And so it happened one day that a floor light went on in our common room, and since all the waiters were already occupied, it fell to me to go to the source of the light signal. I knocked and entered. Two gentlemen were in the room, one pacing back and forth trying to memorize a roll, the other relaxing, apparently somewhat bored. The latter said, "Waiter, we're very hungry. What can you recommend?" Having only recently gone over the chateaubriand with our headwaiter, particularly the style and manner in which this double filet is served, I answered with expert conviction, "If you're really hungry, you ought to order the chateaubriand." As I spoke the words, I let the aristocratic name glide over my tongue with sensuous delight, as if it were something rare and precious. And it certainly was that, qualitatively one of the best cuts of beef, taken right from the tenderloin, but, as I didn't know then, also quantitatively, since it was a double-sized fillet intended for two persons. This explains, if not excuses, my emphatic "No!" in answer to the gentleman's question whether the dish would suffice for two famished diners. "Why don't you order two, just to be sure it's enough?", I suggested to him, and he took my advice.

When I informed the headwaiter of the order, he asked me the room number. I told him, and he became apoplectic with rage. "Don't you know the gentleman staying in that room," he asked me. I did not, I said, and had this critical lacuna in my knowledge instantly filled in — it was Gustaf Gründgens, the famous actor and director, and his friend. I almost fell over — Gustaf Gründgens, who had made the trip from Düsseldorf to Berlin to attend the film festival. I handed the headwaiter the order, at which he could only mutter dejectedly that two chateaubriands were more than enough for four persons, especially considering the huge vegetable platter that went with it.

Now, it was an unwritten law among us that the waiter who responded to a room-service call must stay with that call to the end. In the hopes of averting a catastrophe, the headwaiter briefly reviewed with me, yet again, the procedure for cutting a chateaubriand, emphasizing to me over and over to cut against the grain and not to press the fork too heavily against the meat, lest the blood run out. I became nervous, since now I was really being challenged to show what I could — or couldn't — do. The dinner tray needed to be arranged most artfully, as there had to be room on it for two large silver platters, one containing the meat, the other the vegetables. Moreover, Gründgens's friend had ordered two large glasses of orange juice and two portions of toast, the latter sitting, wrapped in a white napkin, in a silver wire basket also placed on the tray. There were, in addition, three large pre-heated plates, one for cutting the meat and two for serving the meal. Then too, salt and pepper and two wine glasses. The whole tray weighed upwards of seventy pounds, as the big silver platters also had heavy covers on them to keep everything warm.

A *commis* accompanied me to the door, carrying the wine cooler with the bottle in it and a silver *rechaud* to keep the food warm. He knocked and we went in. The room was littered with manuscript pages, so I set the heavy tray down on the bed covers, placing it precisely in the middle. That was a big mistake, as the puffy bedcovers collapsed under the weight of the tray, causing the two glasses of orange juice to tip over and empty their contents onto the platter with the chateaubriands, thus partially washing the Bearnaise sauce from the meat. Oh yes, the toast also slid off the tray. The assistant vanished instantly, (I hoped) to get fresh juice and toast. Gründgens was too absorbed in his role to pay any attention to my little comedy of errors, and his friend was too flabbergasted to say anything. Making a snap decision, I picked up the two chateaubriands, ran into the bathroom and washed the orange juice off them in the sink. Then I took them back to the warming plate, laid them out and carved them. At first I searched desperately for the grain or the fibers, but in my dither I couldn't find anything. So I cut the meat just as my mother would: first vertically from top to bottom, then a few times across to form smallish pieces. But even this was hard to do, as I'd also neglected to remove the warming plate from its position atop the other two plates, so that the pressure of carving caused it to slip traction back and forth. When I'd finally arranged all the small pieces on the serving platter as best I could, I saw to my horror how much juice and blood had been squeezed out of these sorry steaks. Then I took salt, pepper, a shot of Worcestershire sauce and a pinch of garlic, stirred it all up expertly and drizzled it over the chateaubriands. I served the pieces with the vegetables and the juice and toast, the latter two brought in fresh in the meantime by the *commis*. When we left, he could only gape at me and say, "Had Gründgens noticed you, he'd have given you a roll in his play." Later, I came back to clean up and retrieve the tray and actually received a tip of five marks.

Gründgens wasn't the only luminary to grace the Berlin film festivals; there were many other celebrities of the international film world. A particularly exciting moment for me came when I had to serve Gina Lollobrigida breakfast in her room. She had a single room, as her husband, a Dr. Milko Scofic from Jugoslavia, had taken a room on another floor. She was in bed reading a letter as I walked in, but she then got up to show herself at the window to the journalists outside, all of them exuberantly calling for her. As she stood there looking out, the incoming light framed her beautiful figure beneath her gossamer silk wrap, and the breakfast tray I was carrying began to tremble. The beautiful film actress turned to me, smiled and said, "Bring the tray over here, and come back in a half hour and clean up." Which is exactly what I did, and I was the happiest waiter in Berlin! Later that evening, I saw her arm in arm with Sophia Loren, who seemed very tall next to Gina, and my eyes just wandered from one beauty to the other.

Another actress to whom I felt an attraction was Maria Schell. She came to Berlin in the spring of 1954 to attend the world premiere of her film, *The Last Bridge*, directed by Helmut Käuthner. I saw her for the first time on an afternoon in the little dining room, which was separated from the large room by a set of double doors. She was sitting at the last table, studying a role. At first I just watched her from a distance, not wanting to disturb her. Finally she looked up and waved me over. For a brief moment her beauty took away my composure. She noticed my embarrassment, smiled and asked, "Waiter, can you recommend something good and fast? I'm not really hungry, but I would like something." At that time, calve's brains were my favorite dish, since we never had anything like it at home. I gave her the choice between baked calve's brains with tartar sauce or fried with scrambled eggs. "How would *you* prefer it?", she asked. Being familiar with the baked dish, I suggested the egg style. She ordered it with a cup of tea. As I was about to serve her the meal, she said apologetically, "Waiter, now I seem to have lost my appetite entirely. Please take the meal back. Naturally I'll pay for it." As I looked at her, it was instantly clear to me that she knew perfectly well that this meal would never see the kitchen again. I went to the common room and ate the delicious mixture of brains and eggs on a piece of toast. That evening, just before the film was to begin in the Filmbühne Wien, I saw her standing in front off the causeway that connected the hotel to the cinema, in tears with anxious anticipation. I went up to her and gave her a clean napkin with which she dabbed at her tears and then smiled again. Since then I've seen many of Maria Schell's films, and when, in 2005, I read reports of her illness and poverty and subsequent death, I felt a profound sorrow.

Life in the hotel didn't merely train me, it educated me. Normally I worked until ten in the evening, and since nothing much would usually be going on at that late hour, I was often the only one in the common room. One evening the room-service light came on, and I hurried up to the room in question. A gentleman in middle age, sitting at a table, asked me if it was too late to order something hot. I told him yes it was, the hot kitchen was closed at that hour, but the cold kitchen was still open. The guest ordered a cheese sandwich and a bottle of beer. When I returned with his order, I was shocked to see that he had used the intervening moments to strip, so as to present himself to me buck-naked. Naïve though I was, I knew what was up here, that this man was out for a good time, and not with a girl either, but with a man, and that man was yours truly, since there was no one else available. I put the sandwich and beer on the table and made as if to leave. "Oh, please stay a few minutes," he said, "please, won't you sit down?" I did so, perhaps out of curiosity to know how the whole thing would develop. He apologized cordially for shocking me that way, but he was just so fascinated by my eyes that he couldn't take his mind off them. Perhaps, he said, he could show me just how fascinating I was if I would undress too. I wasn't having any of that, but neither did I want to snub him, since he was after all a guest, and "the guest is always right." I replied that I had a girl friend, whom I loved very much, and that I had vowed to be faithful to her forever, a vow I took very seriously. The man sensed it wasn't going to be easy to get what he was after, and proceeded to "interview" me: what school had I attended, what did I like to do, and such. I answered him truthfully, that I had been at a humanistic school and that literature fascinated me. "No doubt you've read the Greek classical writers," he speculated, to which I nodded yes. "Then, of course, you would know that the Greeks preferred pederasty, the love of boys, to heterosexual love. And do you know why they did?" I said no, though expecting his response with intense interest, since he was, as had by now become plain, highly educated. He then held forth, explaining that Greek men preferred homosexuality because, unlike women, men had no hidden agenda.

At bottom, he said, women want to get married and exploit their beauty in an egoistic way primarily to snare men. With increasing age, however, the woman's beauty fades, yet the woman remains. Schopenhauer saw this clearly, he continued, highly recommending to me the philosopher's essay, "On Women." The erotic connection between men was something altogether different, he offered, it was a love that, while validating and incorporating the physical, nevertheless existed primarily on a spiritual plane. That was why most of the ancient Greek literary and intellectual immortals had relationships with boys. He suggested I read Thomas Mann's *Death in Venice*, as this was a writer who understood deeply how to give sensuous expression to the feelings he had just endeavored to describe. I won't deny I found this man's disquisition on the essence of beauty and homosexual love interesting, and I promised him I would read Mann's novella. But later, I insisted, as I was much too tired at the moment and just wanted to go home. He let me go, but not without first asking if I would be on duty the following evening. I said no, but immediately added that another apprentice would be at his beck and call. As I later found out, he had more success with that fellow, and the German and Greek poets and thinkers didn't even enter into it.

My life in the hotel also brought me in contact with high-level politicians, sometimes in a way that did not exactly do me proud. My training included taking part in the *Kaffee-Jour* rotation, which meant having to get up around 4 a.m. and take the *S-Bahn* via Westkreuz to the *Zoo* station. There I would begin my shift at 5 a.m. First, I had to carry the silverware, cups and saucers upstairs to the restaurant from the wash-up kitchen on the ground floor. Now and then I would find the rear door of the restaurant locked, which meant I'd have to enter through the front, frowned on by my superiors though this was. The main marble stairway of the hotel, numbering about twenty steps, led straight to the connecting passage to the restaurant and the rooms on the second floor. Since the trek from the wash-up kitchen to the restaurant was rather long, we would normally take some sixty saucers up at a time, covering them with a table napkin and balancing the wobbly tower as we went. One time, when I was almost all the way up the stairway, I stumbled, and the tower of plates fell over, right onto the top step. All the saucers cascaded down the stairs one after another, spinning their way down on their own axes. It was a tremendous clatter, a true cacophony. Soon enough, a door opened and a gentleman in pajamas came running over to me, livid with rage: "There's no getting a night's sleep in this place! Do you have any idea who I am?" I had no idea, but he wasted no time giving me one, informing me, "I'm Kurt Schuhmacher, and I know Herr Dr. Köhler very well, I can tell you that. And you can bet your last mark I'll be telling him he should toss you the hell out of here." I had just begun the second year of training and was aware that I was by then under the protection of the *Lehrlingsausbildungsschutzgesetz* (law protecting apprenticeship trainees). When I told him that, he stormed back into his room, slamming the door behind him. The fact is, I felt sorry for him, because I knew how important sleep must be for someone holding so important a position in the SPD (Social Democratic Party), and I was terribly upset when I learned of his death not long after this incident.[46] For quite some time I was bothered in conscience that I might've played some part in his demise.

Soon after that I was permitted to serve at table for the first time. They had me set the table used by the Rotary Club, a regular patron, for its luncheon, which usually featured a guest speaker. On this occasion the speaker was Ernst Reuter, incumbent mayor of Berlin, a man popular and beloved among its citizens. The menu was simple, consisting of eggs sunny-side up, fried potatoes and spinach, a dish well known to me from the Thousand Year Reich. Before serving, I figured it might be a good idea to practice using the server's silverware a bit. This was not simple. You had to place both a spoon and a fork in your right hand and then use these to pick up the food items you wanted to lay on the diner's plate. The problem with fried eggs was that you had to proceed with extreme caution: too much pressure between fork and spoon and the yolk would break, too little and you'd drop the egg, as they were fried in lard and were very slippery. To prevent the latter faux pas, you had to move the heavy silver platter, which contained around ten servings, two eggs per serving, in close to the diner's plate, thus facilitating the transfer of eggs. Of course, all this was explained to me after the fact, when it was too late. Beginning with the guest of honor, Ernst Reuter, I lifted his eggs with my implements, but in doing so held the platter much too high. The eggs fell from between spoon and fork, landing splat on Reuter's shoe. Without missing a beat, I carried on, serving him another portion, then continued serving around the table until the platter was bare. Then I went back to Reuter, apologized, and asked him whether he'd mind if I cleaned up the mess. He just nodded, yet he seemed curious to find out how this was going to play out. I knelt down in front of him and saw that the broken egg yolk had seeped through his shoelaces onto his sock. I pulled off his shoe, then the sock, and left the room to wash everything out thoroughly. Then I laid the sock over the heating unit. In doing so, I noticed that, not only did the sock have a big hole in the sole, but the sole of the shoe had one as well. I thought he must've been doing an awful lot of walking. At that point, he launched into his speech about the construction, expansion and the advantages of the various Berlin transportation services, in which he also held a high office but for which he seemed to have little personal use. He delivered the speech wearing only one shoe, the other still too wet, the sock no less. By the time he finished, the sock was dry. I put it on his foot, followed it up with the decrepit shoe and stuck the two-mark piece he tipped me in my pocket.

Certainly there's much about those days I've forgotten, whether intentionally or not, but one episode in particular sticks in my memory. One evening a party of ten or so came in from the theater or the opera. Pilsner beer was ordered all around, which I was to fetch and serve on a beer tray. Now, a beer tray is a very smooth and shiny thing, and one must take care not to lose one's balance with it. As I began to serve, I noticed that the first lady I was to place a glass in front of was wearing something with an exceptionally low-cut neckline, one that accentuated her beautiful semi-global forms, especially when viewed from the waiter's perspective, i.e., from above and behind. Which, of course, is exactly what I was doing. As I set the beer down in front of her with my right hand and peered down into her cleavage, my left or "tray" hand rose way too high and all the beer in the remaining glasses cascaded down like a mini-waterfall right into that cleavage. Dumbfounded, I put down my tray, pulled out my napkin and made as if to dry off the young and beautiful woman. Her escort, however, was disinclined to allow that, telling me in no uncertain terms he'd rather do it himself. I explained to him I'd been bedazzled by the lady's beauty and apologized. Everybody laughed and they all ordered another round, even paying for the one they didn't get. Of course, I made sure to put the tray with the next order down at the table's edge and pass out all the glasses from there.

I now had half my apprenticeship behind me, and it was time to transfer from the French restaurant to the floor below, to the *Kurfürstenkeller*, which also belonged to the Hotel Zoo. The rationale was that apprenticeship training called for experience in all forms and branches of service. Naturally I enjoyed just as rich and varied encounters with the "human-all too human" down there as I had upstairs in the posh restaurant. There too I learned that all the "official" people, the public *personae*, who came in masked real people, individuals who could on occasion permit themselves to show genuine feeling or, even more important, humor.

Homo sum; humani nil a me alienum esse puto.[47]
What Qualities Must a Good Waiter Have?

Shortly thereafter I began my training in the *Kurfürstenkeller*, a restaurant served by the same kitchen as our restaurant on the second floor. It was cozier here in this good middle-class establishment than upstairs, and the guests lingered over their meals longer. Unfortunately, the work was also much more difficult, since the *Kurfürstenkeller* opened onto the terrace, which, during the summer at least, was completely occupied. Being at this point in my last year of training, I was permitted to fill in for waiters on vacation, which meant that, every two weeks, I had to work together with a different *chef de range*. Between us, we had four tables on the terrace, but these four tables kept us, in the most literal sense, constantly on the run. Then too, it would sometimes happen that two or more separate parties would be sitting at the same table (something not at all customary in the USA), all ordering something different and maybe even showing up at different times. We ran around the whole day trying to keep the guests satisfied and scarcely had time to eat anything ourselves. Later, when I read Goethe's poem, "Ganymede," I came across some verses that poignantly captured my plight at that time: "I'm coming! I'm coming!/ Where to? Oh, where to?"

I learned a great deal, since all the waiters were very well trained, multilingual, and were experts who could answer any culinary question. I served Jan Kiepura and Martha Eggers, Hans Rühmann, Jürgen Fehling, Hildegard Knef, Wolf Albach-Retty, Paul Hörbiger and Paula Wessely; I guided James Mason into the Eastern sector of the city; and I celebrated my birthday with Theo Lingen, a famous German actor:

1953: Serving film star Theo Lingen and his family

The only celebrity I didn't particularly get along with was Hans Moser. He usually sat at the bar drinking Pilsner. Each beer made his mumbling a tad less comprehensible, until at some point I couldn't get a word. Many a night I swore I'd never go to Austria, convinced the German spoken by the Austrians was so in name only.

It was in the *Kurfürstenkeller* that I learned how to treat guests in such a way that, not only were they satisfied with the service, but also extremely grateful for it. A good waiter must not only know the dishes and their traditional accompaniments, but must also be able to prepare certain ones right there at the table; he must develop a reliable memory for the biographies of the guests so that they feel at home; he must be a good judge of character and a diplomat, as much is entrusted to him "under the table," so to speak; and he must be multiculturally informed so that he can introduce foreign tourists to German culture, though it be only the culture of food. Most of the waiters also spoke fluent English and French, some even Italian.

The following vignette will show what I mean. One evening an American female graduate student came into the *Keller* toting her briefcase and ordered artichokes as her main dish. I don't know why she settled on just this dish, which is usually a side order, but I suspect that price had something to do with it. When I served her the two artichokes, she just looked at them nonplussed. It was obvious she had no idea what she'd ordered, and now she hadn't a clue how to go about eating it. Still, as an American she was pragmatic, nor was she inclined to make a public display of her ignorance. So, taking up knife and fork, she cut off a leaf, cut the leaf in pieces, put it in her mouth, chewed it thoroughly and bravely swallowed it down. The waiter I was teamed up with saw all this, called me over and asked me what I would do in this situation. I told him I leaned towards a laissez faire attitude, as I found it unpleasant to intrude on the private sphere of a guest. Thereupon he went over to the young woman and said, "May I demonstrate to you, not only how one eats an artichoke, but also how one can truly enjoy it in all its succulent nuances?" She was obviously delighted to have someone come to her aid who knew what he was talking about; moreover, she was genuinely curious to know how best to eat the thing, and she nodded. So he took a leaf, sprinkled it with hollandaise sauce, put it in his mouth, sucked it flat and placed what was left of it neatly onto a napkin next to the plate. Then he pointed out to her how pleasantly meaty the outer leaves at the base were and told her that the receptacle was the best part of all. It was important for me to note that he didn't do any of this *ex cathedra*, as it were, rather he looked her straight in the face at every step to make sure he wasn't going too far. As he left, he folded the napkin together and took it with him. The woman smiled, thanked him and gave him a tip, which, to be sure, was quite modest, yet more than appropriate for her modest financial situation as a student. She learned how best to eat an artichoke, but I learned something as well: how to help someone using diplomacy and psychological finesse, and without in the least being importunate.

The necessity for a waiter to be able to think and act quickly, not to mention be physically, if not indeed athletically, fit, may be illustrated through the following anecdote. Once, when I was working with a waiter from northern Italy who was very tall, the following sequence of events took place. A table of four diners had ordered a goose, and since I was busy, the *chef de range* brought it out from the kitchen himself. The goose was relatively large and rested on a large, uncovered silver platter, which also contained five plates, along with side dishes of red cabbage and parsley potatoes. For optimal balance, the *chef* carried the whole load on the fingertips of his left hand. He held it high above his head and seemed not to notice that the chandelier, hanging from an already low ceiling, came, with its pointy hook-like features, perilously close to the goose, whose open rear end pointed forward. And, as if on cue, the inevitable happened: a chandelier hook bored straight into the rear end of the goose, taking it from the platter as the waiter passed swiftly by. Instantly the waiter dropped to his knees, at the same time cradling the tray that threatened to tip over at its rear, the end holding the plates and side dishes. Not a plate was broken, not a side dish touched the floor. Only the goose was left hanging all by itself from the chandelier, swaying ever so gently to and fro due to the jets of air constantly shooting from the swinging kitchen doors. The diners were astonished at the waiter's lightning-quick reaction and applauded loud and long. Then out came the manager with a small stepladder, lifted the goose a tad, pulled it from the hook, put it back on the platter and carried it back to the kitchen himself. After a while, the goose made a second appearance (I'm assuming it was the same one that was carried out). Finally, I was allowed to carve this noble fowl that had, as it were, taken flight one last time, never mind its roasted state.

It is above all the barkeeper who must be able to get along with the guests, since, under the alcoholic influence, they confide in him far more than they ever would sober. I had the great good fortune of having Herr Kadach for my trainer. He was extremely well read and very well versed in politics, not least due to the many politicians with whom he carried on extensive discussions at the bar during breaks in the Four-Power-Conference,[48] with our hotel as the center for journalists and the media. He also knew his way around the fashion world, as the fashion house Horn would occasionally stage shows in our hotel; and this is not to mention his extensive knowledge of the theater and cinema scenes, which stood him in good stead with the endless parade of actors and actresses stopping over at the hotel. He taught me how to size up a guest the instant she or he came in the door, and in most cases I found him to be right. Once he filled me in on the sad fate of a customer who would come into the bar every evening and drink his double Hennesey through a straw. Naturally I found that strange, until my boss informed me that this man, who was a Jew, had been so badly treated in the concentration camp that his nerves were now totally shot, something easily observable from his trembling hands. And so every evening, a large glass of cognac would sit on the bar in front of his stool with a straw in it, making it easier for him to drink. Paradoxically, instead of helping him to forget, the cognac seemed to stir up the painful memories. Mesmerized, I'd listen to him tell his grim tales of appalling mistreatment in the camp. And as I listened, I would ask myself if I would've come to know similar horrors myself, had the war, thank God, not ended in 1945.

I learned so much from my bar boss, especially in the area of human relations, and the high grades I later earned in my psychology courses at the university are to a large part the fruit of his mentoring. At the outset of these remarks, I said that we all have much for which to thank others, since "what one is one owes to others." Among these others for me are my trainers in the hotel.

Finishing Touches

In the latter half of my third year of training, I was transferred back to the restaurant upstairs. This was the culminating period of finishing touches, in which I learned how to prepare specialties such as crêpe suzettes and crêpes georgettes at the table, not to mention cherries jubilee, with which one must take care that the kirschwasser is sufficiently warmed up before pouring it over the cherries and flambéing them. And in flambéing itself, you also had to be very careful not to let the kirsch bottle get too close to the sterno flame, or the latter could easily shoot into the bottle neck and cause an explosion. I carved fillets of sole, saddles of venison, poulards (spayed hens), ducks and geese, even a pheasant. The pheasant didn't turn out so well: the breastbone of this bird tapers sharply in front. You really have to study a pheasant's anatomy closely before taking a carving knife to it.

The highpoint of my training came when, together with the headwaiter, I prepared a feast at the table for a number of Siemens directors. The meal lasted from 5 p.m. till midnight and had many courses to it. First, cold hors d'oeuvres were served, followed by turtle soup, the cups having previously been warmed with sherry. Next came the warm appetizers, then a salad, fillet of sole in Chablis with half-moon croutons and tournedos Rossini for the dark meat course. After the saddle of venison, cheese and fruit were set out, these followed by the final course, which was a specialty of our pastry chef: an ice-cream bomb Rothschild was served. It rested on a cubed block of ice hollowed out from the bottom up, in which glowed a small light bulb wrapped in pretty pink paper. All courses were accompanied, of course, by the appropriate wines, each one expertly characterized for the diners by the headwaiter, course by course. Some dishes came from the kitchen already prepared, it's true, but in each case the finishing touch was, so to speak, "performed" for the guests before their very eyes. All in all, a spectacular experience, one I have no trouble retrieving from the memory bank.

Although I'd been in training for only two-and-a-half years, I was told that my accomplishments warranted an early graduation. Since apprentices were examined twice a year, I took the exam with the earlier testing group. The exam for graduation had two parts: theory and practice. I was examined in the vocational school in the three theoretical areas of general competence, business math and business administration. I'd prepared myself well, especially for the trick question that, according to legend, had once been asked: "You're serving a bridal couple. The husband is significantly older than his young bride. What sequence of courses do you arrange for the wedding night?" I thought suggesting celery and oysters would definitely be a bad idea — you had, in any case, to come up with something in season. But they didn't ask me this question after all. My forte was business math, as I had an excellent memory and had learned very early on all the shortcuts to a quick and reliable result.

The practical part was given in the Schöneberg city hall. I had to set a table for ten persons, folding all napkins artfully, arranging the floral decoration in good taste and placing the wine glasses as prescribed. Then I had to serve the different courses. For the fish course, the apprentice chefs, who were sweating through their own exam in the kitchen, had prepared a sole à la meunière. I picked up the platter in the kitchen and brought the dish to the table, all set to fillet it. Now, there are two different ways to do this: you can either make a deep cut with a spoon from head to tail and then lift the fillet from the bones with the spoon, a process that must be repeated three times; or you can repeat step one above, but then, taking a fork, detach the ventral fins, press the fork through the backbone to the other side and pull off both fillets on that side of the fish. Then one had do the same with the other side. I preferred the latter method, as it prevents the fish from cooling off, since both fillets lie on top of each other. In any case, as I was attempting to detach the fillets via method #2, I realized that the apprentice chef had allowed the fish to fry in the pan for too long: the meat was dry and slightly blackened. Without hesitation I sent the whole platter right back to the kitchen, served the salad course and then the newly prepared platter of fish. I could see that this made a powerful impression on my examiners and may have contributed to my getting straight "1's" (A's) in all my courses, including a "very good" on the skills part of the exam. Even on the certificate issued by the training company, I scored straight "1's" in the subject areas of management, industriousness, punctuality, orderliness and accomplishments, with the additional comment, "exemplary". Dr. Köhler wrote in his reference letter: "Herr Gerd Schneider, born on April 1, 1931, residing in Berlin-N 65, at Gerichtstraße 54/55, is known to me as a man of unblemished character. He was in my employ for nearly three years and he has distinguished himself during this time, getting along well with our guests. He is goal-oriented and firmly committed to furthering his education. He has passed his final apprenticeship examination with distinction. Berlin, June 15, 1954."

Dear Homeland, Adieu!

And so my training came to an end. I received a few book prizes and was offered an opening at the professional hospitality school in Weinheim, which I turned down. I stayed on at the hotel for a few months, working as a *commis de range*, but then decided the time had come to leave Berlin. Since I wanted to broaden and deepen my education in the hospitality industry, my first priority was to go to a country where I could become fluent in French and English. That was Canada. Then too there were pressing personal issues. My girlfriend at the time was Lore, of whom I was very fond and who was always there for me when I needed her. I'd gotten to know her from baby-sitting her six-month-old daughter; I minded the daughter while her mother worked as a secretary. We went swimming together in Müggel Lake, went to Potsdam to visit Sans Souci palace, made music together (she adeptly accompanied my violin on the piano), went to the theater and the opera. When I would show up at her place after midnight following my shift in the hotel, she'd usually have something warm for me to eat, and her tin was always brim-full of delicious cookies. My mother was pleased with our relationship too, as she and Lore got along very well together.

But then Felicitas was also still in the picture, my old classmate, to whom I felt a spiritual affinity and with whom I had explored and come to love the worlds of literature and music. Without her my life would surely have unfolded in a totally different way. The truth is, I wanted to marry both of them, but since that wasn't an option, I decided the next-best thing would be to leave in the hope of reaching clarity in self-imposed exile. So I went to the Canadian, American and Australian embassies and filled out an emigration application at each. The Canadian embassy was the first to approve my application, and, shortly after that, the association of Lutheran churches came through with an advance to pay for passage on the Arosa Kulm's next voyage to Canada.

Just before I sailed, Felicitas came to visit. She'd fled the Eastern sector and was now being housed in a reception camp in the southern part of the city. Being penniless, she was forced to walk for hours to get here in time to say good-bye. It was nearly two in the morning when the doorbell finally rang. My mother opened and saw her in. When she saw us both together again, her eyes filled with tears; still, practical woman that she was, she quickly asked Felicitas if she had enough money for the return trip. Felicitas shook her head no, she didn't have a dime. My mother took off like a shot, running from apartment to apartment in her nightgown, asking the neighbors to come to our place on the double. And they all came, most of them half asleep and/or grumpy, but also curious to find out what was up. After hastily counting some thirty neighbors present, my mother began: "I've asked you all to come because there's someone here in need of your help. Felicitas here is a refugee from the East, and, believe me, she's a lot worse off than any of us. She has no money at all for transportation back to the camp or even to pick up a few basic necessities. I know we're all having a rotten time of it these days, but for some of us even 'rotten' is looking pretty good. And I know that many of us go to church to pray. But right here and now, God is giving us an opportunity to show our faith; here we can prove that prayers are more than just words." Then she picked up an old hat, dropped a bill into it and passed it around. The hat collected a tidy sum, just how much I no longer remember, but it was impressive. And I felt very proud of my mother. When, many years later, I read in Lessing, "The letter is not faith," I had to think of her.

When it came time to say good-bye to my mother, she said to me: "Gerd, since you're always hungry, you'd best marry a farmer's daughter over there, but make sure it's somebody who's a good cook — you know love travels on its stomach. And make sure she can speak good German too; I'm too old to learn English and I'd like to have a decent conversation with my own daughter-in-law. And if you have a son, I've no doubt he'll have hair down to his shoulders at birth, and dark eyes just like you. And make sure you give him a name I can pronounce and one the people over there are okay with too—I don't want the kids laughing at him the way they did at you. And then you can bring me over so I can have a good look at him. And never forget you're a special one, and some day you'll surely succeed in becoming a millionaire." I promised her I would always do my level best, and every good wish she sent me on my way with, I'm thankful to say, has come true. I kissed her and promised I'd come back soon, with or without attachment. Then off I went to the train station, suitcase in hand, which was very light, containing only two pairs of black pants and a few books, and wallet in pocket, holding no more than twenty dollars.

The trip to Bremen went via Dreilinden, Marienborn and Helmstedt, the usual route in 1954. I traveled with Fred, another erstwhile apprentice waiter from the Hotel Zoo who also wanted to try his luck in Canada. For three days we stayed in a camp with the other travelers and then took the bus to Bremerhaven. As I got in line with the other émigrés to board ship, a long-legged young fellow riding an old bicycle pulled up to the pier. He stopped by me and asked, "Is this the ship to Canada?" I nodded yes, and, after parking his bike at the anchor lock on the wharf, he joined us in line. When I asked him if he intended to leave the bike there, he answered in a serious tone, "Of course! I'm headed for Canada. By the time I get back, I'll be able to afford a car." We all nodded in eager agreement and went aboard the émigré ship that was to take us to the New World. We took one last look back and saw the bike standing all by itself on the pier. I'm sure many of us were thinking in that moment that we too would soon be returning and that a car would be waiting for us on the pier. But I'm guessing my particular fantasy trumped all, as my virtual car came with a chauffeur, or better yet, a gorgeous chauffeurette, whose face, to be sure, I couldn't quite make out. The ship set sail, as the little band on the pier played "Muss I denn…" and "Lieb Heimatland ade…."

I took one final photo of the Old World with my Agfa box camera, sitting down on the tarpaulin covering one of the lifeboats to get a good angle. As I went to get up, I couldn't. I was being firmly held back, as if a hand were keeping me rooted to the spot, as if some cosmic message were telling me not to leave this, my native land. Then it dawned on me what the problem was: the tarpaulin had recently been tarred, and I was sitting right in the middle of an area that had been softened and partially liquefied by the warm sun, but was now quickly re-solidifying with the falling temperature. To get down off it, I had to take my pants off and wound up standing there in my underwear. I went straight to my assigned quarters and put on the other pair — my last. Back up on deck, I cut the stuck pair loose with a scissors. They now had a hole in the seat rendering them useless. I felt a pang of gratitude for my mother for making sure I had two pair of pants with me. Somehow she knew that, for her son in the New World, one pair would just not do.

Part II

My Life in the New World

1. My Experiences in Canada: 1954 - 1962

Crossing and Arrival in the New World

The Arosa Kulm, as the ship was named, was old and setting out on one of its last voyages. Built in 1919, she went through a series of owners and ended up sailing between Bremerhaven and Montreal from 1952 to 1958; she was scrapped in 1959. The ship's main function was to transport German émigrés. All told, we were about nine hundred passengers, but not all of us were émigrés. Some fifty were vacationers, returning home on the cheap; the rest of us, on the other hand, were engaged in the emotional business of leaving home. Among the vacationers were a few of the female persuasion who drew most of the male attention. One of these no longer quite so youthful females had her eye on me, but I stayed true to my women. The voyage passed in relative calm. Only a few times, notably at the end of long evenings at the bar, when passions would heat up, were there fights or stabbings, but apart from these, all was well. The relative uneventfulness of the voyage probably also had to do with the fact that accommodations for the passengers were strictly divided. Those returning home had their quarters on the upper levels, while the much larger group of émigrés was assigned to the lower. I shared my sleeping quarters with about thirty other men, all of us bedding down in a common room next to the engine room. Not only was it loud where we were but also hot, since we had no portholes, situated as we were beneath the waterline with almost no ventilation. Two days out, I was asked to give instruction in English. My own English was bad, and heavily accented to boot, but the others spoke none at all, and among the blind, as they say, the one-eyed man is king. I had no end of difficulty with the American 'r,' which I could only pronounce gutturally, as a uvular trill. It wasn't until much later that I became able to produce this sound reasonably well, but in the early days, even after I'd been in Canada a fairly long period, whenever I'd order orange juice, the waitress would always ask me to repeat the order. Finally, frustration led me to change my order to Coke, a word I *could* pronounce, however much I hated this drink for breakfast. Anyway, on the ship I taught my faulty r-sound to the others, which instantly gave away their Germanic origins to the New Worlders.

Another problem was that I was full of misinformation. Before I began my journey, I'd taken a newspaper course in American English, a course published in the Berlin newspaper, *Der Telegraf.* The author made much of the fact that, in Canada and America, a form of English was spoken that differed in many important respects from British English. So, for example, to the question, "How are you?", one should respond, "Thank you. I am full of beans. I hope you are too." My knowledge-thirsty class drank down this "idiomatic expression" like cold beer on a hot day, and I can only hope it served them better than it did me: it was months before someone took enough pity on me to inform me that this expression can also convey the meaning, "to be a windbag," a meaning that, in this context, has nothing whatever to do with the German expression, "to *have* a windbag" (literally *Windbeutel*, metaphorically "cream puff").

Since we were all driven by the same hope, to find some way to "make it" in the new world and to amass wealth, an esprit de corps quickly formed among us. I was already sort of partners with Fred, the other apprentice waiter from the Hotel am Zoo, and the third member of our little band was Bruno, the fellow who'd left his bike on the pier. Since the trip was long and tedious, we killed time by playing chess. Bruno was slow, but he always won. After a while, he asked us if we'd mind if he played blindfolded. We said it was fine with us. He wrapped a blindfold around his head, and it was our job to let him know whenever his opponent made a move and what the move was, and then he'd plot his counter. After a few moves, he'd predict the number of further moves he needed and the square on which he would soon be calling checkmate. And so it would happen. Then Bruno progressed to playing several opponents blind at the same time, and he won every time. And he wasn't the least bit nervous, unlike Dr. B. in Stefan Zweig's "Chess Novella; quite the contrary, he made a sovereign impression on everyone. Later during the trip, he told us he had originally begun law studies in Germany, but after a falling-out with his family, had broken them off and was now bent on trying his luck in the New World. I lost sight of him but found out later that, after an entry-level job as a roofer in Vancouver, British Columbia, he established his own roofing firm, subsequently resuming his studies and eventually becoming a well-known attorney. But at the moment all that lay in the distant future. For now, we played chess, drank far too many bottles of brandy (cheap duty-free goods on the ship), and, during a storm that laid everybody else low with seasickness, the three of us, Fred, Bruno and I, stood on the ship's bow as it rose and sank, drank our bottles dry, flung them into the sea, then went up to the steering house, embraced the captain, kissed him and promised to invite him to a sumptuous feast as soon as we had our first thousand dollars in our pocket. Bruno, who had also written a poem to the captain, recited it to him and then kissed him, which moved us all deeply. After eleven days at sea, we finally arrived in Quebec.

After disembarking it was time to go our separate ways. Bruno took the train to Vancouver, while we were headed for Toronto. Since our train didn't depart till later that evening, we sought out a dance club. Spotting a young lady sitting alone at a table, I went over to her and asked her in my best French, "Voules-vous danser avec moi?" Not even casting me so much as a glance, she merely dragged on her cigarette and blew smoke in my face. I no longer had to struggle with my lame French, as I knew only too well what that meant. Turning then to the young woman at the next table, I put the same question to her. Since she didn't have a cigarette, she gave me no answer at all. I didn't have the heart to ask the question a third time. Doing an about-face, I made a hasty exit. It looked as if it wasn't going to be easy to assert myself in this country.

Waiter in the New World

We arrived in Toronto on August 13, 1954. As we stood there in front of Union Station, Fred and I gazed in awe at the imposing Royal York Hotel. Right next to it stood another tall building, and next to that a skyscraper. No one had come to greet us, as we had fervently hoped. All of a sudden I was feeling so small, and a spike of anxiety shot up my spine. How can a man assert himself in this country, I asked myself. Everything's so different, so alien, not to mention so much bigger. As this moment of panic subsided, I decided the first item on the agenda was to get myself a haircut, as the long crossing had allowed my hair to grow quite long. But where? I strolled away from the railroad station, after asking Fred to keep an eye on my suitcase, the only piece of luggage I had with me. Walking along the main street, it didn't take long to spot a storefront with a rotating red-and-white-striped pole. I stepped inside and got my first haircut, which turned out to be quite expensive. Obviously they could see the greenhorn coming from a mile away and fleeced more than my hair. Walking back to the station, I found Fred in conversation with a man who was looking for waiters for a club. The man examined our papers, passports and letters of recommendation and asked us to go with him. There we were, gainfully employed in the very first hour! Joy — at least for a few days.

The man who hired us was named Gossé, and he was the manager of this private club. He drove us in a very flashy car out to our new place of employment: the Toronto Hunt Club, 1355 Kingston Road. It was a country club with a golf course located in Scarborough, a suburb of Toronto, easily accessible by streetcar. It had opened way back in 1895 and stood right on Lake Ontario. As I got to know the place, I thought surely it must be a lot older than that, since most of the members behaved as if they themselves, or at least their forbears, had come over on the Mayflower. They didn't even deign to speak with the waiters, all Germans and Austrians, instead writing their orders down on a piece of paper that they would press into our hands. Sometimes we had a problem decoding these texts, since almost all the diners were old and wrote with palsied hands. It helped somewhat that the menu selections were rather narrow, consisting mainly of lamb chops, chicken, beef and an assortment of fish. Once a week there was a dinner dance, to which the young folk were invited. I had the distinct impression that the privileged youth of Scarborough would rather be doing anything else than sitting around with the old fogies.

Mr. Gossé drove us pretty hard. Mornings we cleaned the large dining hall, after which we served lunch; we then had off from two to five, finally reporting for the long dinner shift. When we spoke to Mr. Gossé, we'd usually drop the accented "é" from his name, which annoyed the hell out of him, since *Gosse* in German means something close to "gutter." However, we never did this when speaking with his wife, an extraordinarily pretty woman whom we all ogled lustfully, especially since, excepting the head waitress, she was the only female on staff. Occasionally she would help us with patient explanation when we'd struggle to understand the local ways and customs. One thing new to me was that you always had to put out cold sauces with just about anything you served; even for the salads there were these "dressings" that I found strange. For dessert we'd go around with this huge cheese platter on which sat large hunks of different cheeses, from which diners would cut themselves a piece or two. Some diners needed help with this task, as their shaky hands made any sharp knife a liability.

One cheese in particular almost caused my downfall. This was the Oka cheese, named after a small village in Quebec Province. It's semi-soft and has a fruity and nutty taste to it, but also exudes a strong odor not unlike a German Tilset. This cheese was declared strictly off limits to us, and the manager watched us like a hawk to make sure we didn't get near it. Now, the meals we were fed in the club weren't bad, mind you, but they weren't anything special either, so that we believed we had the moral high ground here. My roommate John and I worked together. He positioned himself directly in front of me, and since he was a large man, I was barely noticeable behind him. I then proceeded to cut several generous slices of the aromatic cheese, wrapped them in a napkin and stuck the napkin in my pants pocket. The whole caper had to be executed with speed and precision, and I must say we pulled it off brilliantly, without anyone suspecting a thing. I resumed my serving duties, smiling at the guests, but, oddly, they would only scrunch up their noses whenever I'd stand close by. Since the club rules prohibited their speaking with the service personnel, at first nothing happened. But of course a few days later I was summoned to the office of the senior manager, a Mr. Mason, who told me amiably that I needed to pay more attention to my personal hygiene, as some guests had complained to him that they could occasionally detect a most objectionable odor coming from me. I promised him I would shower every day; I also took the precaution of wrapping the offending cheese slices in *two* napkins.

Mondays we had off. We often went to the movies, which was very cheap and sometimes showed three feature films. We saw such films as *Betrayed, The Living Desert, Carnival Story, Ben and Me, Man with a Million, Blowing Wild, The Glen Miller Story, Young at Heart, Vera Cruz* and so many others, all of which I noted down in my diary. My first local excursion was to Niagara Falls, which made a great impression on me. We viewed the falls from the Canadian side and were told we just had to see them from the American side as well. But how to get to the American side? There was a border bridge linking the USA and Canada, and the four of us decided to cross it, maybe not so much to view the falls from over there as to be able to say we had set foot in America. At about the middle of the bridge we were stopped and asked to show our papers. With my dark hair I could pass for the stereotypical Frenchman, and we'd decided beforehand that, should circumstances call for it, I should do my best impression of one, since no native Canadian Frenchman was required to have papers. So I told the border official, in a lightly tinged French accent, that I was showing my friends the sights and would be bringing them back across to Canada that same day. The official looked me in the eye and asked me something in fluent French, which went way over my head. Back we went, and it would be years before I touched American soil.

Located on the shores of Lake Ontario as we were, we could also go swimming, which we did whenever possible. In the night of October 14-15, 1954, there was a hurricane. With its towering waves, it wrought massive damage, destroying some bridges in Toronto, leaving many casualties in its wake and ripping houses from their foundations. So naturally we decided to go swimming. We walked down to Lake Ontario, which to me looked more like an ocean, but, because of the storm, we had trouble climbing over the little knoll that abutted the beach. So we just dropped to the ground and let ourselves roll down into the water. Then we had a similar problem coming out, as the direction of the wind had shifted. It seems some lake or city employee had spotted us and reported us to the RCMP,[49] who pulled us out of the water and wrote us up for a citation, since it was a misdemeanor, not to mention lunacy, to swim in the lake during a hurricane. But it was all very exciting, and I felt just like one of Karl May's seasoned adventurers. I also learned that hurricanes had names; this particular storm in 1954, for instance, bore the pretty name, "Hazel." Later on, on being introduced to a woman of this name at a party, I looked at her in astonishment. I told her all about the storm, upon which she laughed and replied, pointing to herself, that "this Hazel isn't nearly so dangerous." I didn't stay at the party long enough to find out.

It was far less dangerous to go downtown. Toronto had much to offer. In November there was the Eaton's Santa Claus parade, the largest in North America at that time, with several thousand marchers.[50] Of course, I had seen parades numbering in the thousands before, but this one was by far the merriest, with its variety of inflated animals, all held down by their leashes and all looking so gay (in the old sense). On Young Street, one of the city's main drags, I met Duke Ellington in a place called the Town Tavern. I invited him to join me in a cocktail (a Manhattan) and told him all about the Bathtub, the famous jazz cellar in Berlin. Another evening, we brainstormed the idea of going downtown just as we were. No sooner thought than done. I had on only my pj's, others the same or in only a nightshirt, and thus attired, we went down to the Royal Alexandra where Tommy and Jimmy Dorsey were headlining. I wound up dancing with the vocalist, first on the table, then on the dance floor, and felt supremely happy to have such a beautiful songstress in my arms.

Still, I had no desire to kindle any further relationships with women. Felicitas and Lore each wrote me at least one letter a week, which I always answered promptly. I had an intense longing to see them again, but, as before, that longing was bifurcated. On only one occasion did I come close to violating my promise to remain faithful. One evening I went to the German Club with my friends. I had two glasses of beer, which made me slightly tipsy, since I don't tolerate beer very well. I asked a young lady named June to dance, whom I later described in my diary in the following words: "Going on 25, petite, athletic, very nice, very near-sighted, wears glasses, good in typing and shorthand, from Bishop Auckland in England, currently working in a household in Eglington, and just as lonely as I am." We went dancing a few times; then she told me I should take a room on Jarvis St. where we could be together. I paid three dollars for the room, and we went upstairs. We were in bed when suddenly we heard somebody enter a toilet right next door. It wasn't long before a powerful stench wafted over to us. Looking over toward the separating wall, we noticed that it didn't quite reach up to the ceiling and that the toilet was right behind it. She wanted minimum light in the room. Since there was no more than a single light bulb hanging down unshielded from the middle of the ceiling on a wire, I took my glove and put it over the bulb. Moments later we were accosted by another odor, this time of a burning quality, given off by my glove as the heat from the bulb began to break it down into its material components. At this point it was getting pretty near impossible, as Tieck so aptly puts it in his comedy, *Puss in Boots*, "to get into a decent illusion." We got dressed and left the place, heaping profanity on it.

A week later, we met again and laughed our heads off over our ill-starred liaison. June had a good sense of humor, a quality that attracted me to her. Later, after returning to England and satisfying her service commitment to the Royal Air Force, she wrote me asking if I'd like to come to London. She had inherited a grocery store considered fairly large by London standards and wanted to run it with me as her life partner. She also revealed in her letter that she was very attracted to me and that we could, if I was interested, more than make up for what fate had denied us that night in Toronto. But, as enticing as June's offer was, I had a very different vision of my future, however unfocussed that vision might be, so I wrote her back that I thought she was a terrific girl but that, all in all, it would be best if we didn't see each other again. Who knows what might've become of me if I had decided differently then. I might be hanging around the grocery today, cleaning and stocking produce.

The pay for my job at the club was a pittance; basically, we worked for minimum wage. My gross wages came to only 80 dollars a month, plus food and lodging. The dream car I had fantasized about on leaving Bremerhafen drifted further into the mists of memory. Then I was asked if I'd like to earn a little extra cash working as a night watchman. I'd heard that the previous watchman had been murdered and that the club was looking for a replacement. The pay was three dollars a night. I said yes, at the same time vowing to myself I would not put my life on the line, at least not for three bucks. The job involved checking out various strategic locations on the property, each location having a clock attached to a chain from which a key hung. I was supposed to insert the key into the lock-clock I'd brought with me and turn it. This proved that you were taking the job seriously. What I did was, I removed all the keys from their chains and went into the lounge with the TV, locking the door. I laid the keys on the table and simply stuck them into my watch and turned them, one by one, at hourly intervals. In the early morning I reattached all keys to their proper chains. Then my conscience began to bother me and I made two or three quick runs through all the dark rooms I hadn't bothered to check during the night. Having encountered no threatening presence, I made my prescribed rounds from then on by the hour without cheating. And in between, I would while away the time writing letters to my mother, Lore and Felicitas:

Lore

140

Felicitas

With the meager salary I was earning, not only did I have to support my mother (to the tune of twenty dollars per month), I also had to save some of it, since the church league that had advanced me the money for the trip over was starting to grumble. In February, 1955, six months after my arrival in Canada, I received the following notice from the Canadian Lutheran World Relief Fund: "Have you forgotten? Not long ago you petitioned us for aid and we granted your request. We no longer expect you to honor your promise . . . but do believe that this reminder will suffice to move you to remit a payment, to be followed by further such remittances." Then in conclusion with glaring red letters, making the warning impossible to overlook: "Please begin your repayment immediately, before we are forced to start charging interest!" The cost of my passage came to $185.85, a formidable sum considering my salary at the club. On the heels of this notice from the church, I received a letter from my mother telling me that the Lutheran church league had written to her, informing her that I had failed to fulfill my financial obligation and that it now fell to her to pay off my debt. So my mother had begun paying back five dollars per month, from the barebones public relief check she received and the twenty dollars I was sending her.

That could not go on. Saving more money from my salary was out of the question; the only prospect of earning more and getting ahead was some other kind of work. I'd heard that the Ford Motor Company was hiring, so I went there and took a test. In my interview with the personnel manager afterward, I was told they couldn't hire me. I was too intelligent for assembly line work, would be bored to death and quit in no time. In Toronto it was hard to find work, since so many émigrés settled there, causing the number of those looking for work to far exceed the number of available jobs. Then I got an idea. A relative of mine had emigrated to Canada shortly after World War I, settling in Edmonton, the capital of Alberta province. She'd once informed me in a letter that there were a lot of mines there that paid workers good money. I told John, whose father had been a party sympathizer in the Third Reich and whom I'd befriended, of my intention to head out there, and he said he'd like to come along. It remained only to give notice to the club manager. I went to him well in advance, as he'd always treated me very fairly, and informed him of my intention. I asked him for a reference, which he willingly provided. Part of it read: "Mr. G. Schneider has done his work in a thoroughly satisfactory manner and has been at all times a good worker and quite reliable. He leaves of his own accord with the intention of improving himself." These words were virtually an English translation of the boilerplate Dr. Koehler had used on my departure from the Hotel am Zoo.

The occasion for leaving the club came sooner than expected; it also unfolded quite differently than I would've imagined. The reason for this was a very old lady who held a highly revered position in the club, possibly because she was one of its founding members. One evening after dinner, when I was her waiter, I was serving her the mince pie[51] she had ordered in her written note. When I set the plate with the pie down in front of her, she touched the plate with her gloved hand, gestured to me and wrote on some notepaper, "I ordered hot mince pie. This pie is cold." So I took it back to the kitchen, stuck it in the oven for a few minutes and brought it back. She sampled it, and then, breaking the hallowed law of non-oral communication, said to me, "Waiter, you apparently do not understand English, and you definitely are unable to read it. The school system in Germany must be very bad, if you are any indication. I ordered hot mince pie. I will give you one more chance. If you serve me cold pie again, I will have you fired, because I know the manager very well." This made me livid, as it was obvious not only that her sense of touch at that hoary old age was dulled, but that there was no way she could tell through that glove whether a plate was hot or cold. Again I took back the plate with the pie, this time leaving both in the oven for quite some time, and served the dish again, now with two napkins wrapped around my hand. I set the plate down so as to leave its rim extending out over the edge of the table. Then I left the dining room, took off my apron and told the headwaiter I was quitting. Just then we heard the old lady scream, no doubt as she went to nudge the plate away from the edge. My friend John followed me, I phoned

June to say goodbye, and then John and I trekked over to the railroad station with our suitcases to catch the train to Edmonton, where we fully intended to amass our fortunes in no time. After all, we'd heard so often that, in this city, the streets were littered with dollar bills — all you had to do was bend down and pick'em up.

Go North, Young Man, Go North!

The trip took longer than expected. I had no clue as to the size of this country, which includes six time zones. We rode thousands of miles for days, across three zones, before arriving in Edmonton. It was the end of March, in Toronto almost the beginning of spring, but here still ice-cold winter. The temperature was forty degrees below zero, and at this point on the thermometer you don't have to convert from Fahrenheit to centigrade, since they're identical. The worst of it was that there was no wind, so that you couldn't accurately sense how cold it was. It wasn't long before somebody stopped me on the street and told me I'd best step into a coffee shop and warm up, otherwise my ears, already quite white, would fall off. This I did, and the first thing I purchased was a fur hat with flaps I could pull down over my ears.

The next problem we faced was money — we didn't have any. So the next day I went right over to the employment office and inquired about a job in the mines, aware that there were openings. The man behind the desk asked me if I had any experience as a mineworker. I said I did, and he asked to see my hands. He said in his opinion my skin was too soft and that I'd no doubt lied about having worked in the mines. He wasn't buying my explanation for the tender skin, to the effect that miners in Germany always wear gloves. What made the situation even more dire was that we weren't getting any unemployment insurance, since we had left our previous employment voluntarily. The positive closing comment in the reference I'd received from the club in Toronto had suddenly turned into a liability: "He leaves of his own accord with the intention of improving himself." John and I had already just about used up our meager savings; we'd arrived with only about forty dollars each. We'd taken a room in a house belonging to a Dutch family that had suffered enormously during the Nazi occupation. That fact may well go a long way in explaining their attitude towards us, which was no less icy than our room. In any case, it was getting along towards May, and the ice on the Saskatchewan River was beginning to break up with a thunderous din.

During this rough patch, I got to know an insurance agent who was known to find jobs for those willing to buy a policy from him. John and I did just this, all the more readily since the first premium wasn't due until after we received our first paycheck. The jobs that this Mr. Simmons of the Metropolitan Life Insurance Company found for us sounded fantastic. The hotel in Drayton Valley needed two managers for two day shifts; the managers were to see that everything ran smoothly. I had no clear sense of what "ran smoothly" entailed and no idea at all where Drayton Valley was. But I was soon to know both only too well. The place was about an hour's bus ride from Edmonton and, at the time, consisted of no more than a hotel, which housed the post office, some houses and a sea of drilling rigs, since oil had been struck in Drayton Valley. Finding a room wasn't easy, but John and I finally lucked out, taking a small basement flat for a high rent. It had only one bed, so we had to get used to sleeping together.

The next morning, I headed out for work — or at least intended to. The streets were full of mud so high, it poured right into the tops of my boots. I pressed on, but suddenly one boot got stuck deep and I never saw it again. So I had to keep going with only the other boot and went into the hotel that way. I introduced myself to the waitresses, who all eyed me mistrustfully. Then commenced the inevitable ritual of finding out who was really going to be the boss there. No more than five minutes could've passed before a waitress came up to me and told me I had to make a milkshake. I dismissed this, since, in the first place, I'd never in my life attempted such a thing, but also because I needed to prove that I was the boss and that making milkshakes was not among my responsibilities. The waitress scurried over to a man who was just beginning to dig into a massive steak, steak being one of the very few items on the menu. This dude was a behemoth; he looked as if his job in the oil fields might've been to pound the drill into the oil-rich sandy soil with blows of his fist. He grabbed me by the shoulders, lifted me straight up and said threateningly that the waitress was his girlfriend and that I'd best not get on her bad side. Since the customer, apparently discouraged by the long wait, had taken off without his milkshake, a period of relative tranquility ensued. But how brief this was, as I next watched another waitress shove the money a diner had just paid her into her pocket, instead of into the cash register. I went over to her and opened the register, gesturing to her that that was where the money belonged. After a brief verbal exchange, I noticed another behemoth heading my way, looking even more imposing than the first. Quickly deciding it was not in my best interest to wait around for him, I did an about-face and ran, still in my one boot, as fast as I could right the hell out of that den of thieves. Next day John and I were back in Edmonton. When I met up with John again at a hotel in Vancouver in the summer of 2005 and we waxed nostalgic over this fiasco, he smiled and said, "Gerd, those were our Wild West days — just without the six-shooters."

Legal and Illegal, Moral and Immoral in Edmonton, Alberta

A few days later, I saw an ad in the newspaper placed by a supper-club restaurant that was looking for a waiter, so I spent my last change to make the phone call. We arranged a time and met in a coffee shop. I showed my future boss my papers and he hired me. The next day, he picked me up, since his supper-club restaurant — Chick's Bar-B-Q--was located just outside the city limits. The location was important, since the laws outside the city limits were different from those within. During this period, Edmonton was very conservative. The pubs were divided into two sections, one for couples, i.e., men and their female escorts, and one for men only. Single women were extremely rare in this northern city; if you got to know a woman, typically it wasn't long before you'd be leading her to the altar. But a dance club outside the city limits was more liberal. Not that they served alcohol there; what they did instead was to serve so-called "set-ups," consisting of ginger ale and ice which the guests would then mix with whiskey from the bottle they'd brought in with them. There was a little dance floor, where, during the week, guests could dance to music from a jukebox, while on Saturday nights we'd have a live band.

But the best thing was the food. The owner, Al Hober, was a perfectionist and a smart businessman who operated on the principle that you should only have a few signature dishes on the menu, which, however, can be freely combined. So he would offer "Southern Fried Chicken," which you could have with another dish, say, spaghetti with meat sauce, or jumbo battered shrimp, cooked in the deep-fryer, which you could order with fries or spaghetti. Of course, the stars of the menu were the steaks, which came from grain-fed Alberta beef. All dishes were of the highest quality, which explains why the club, usually opening around 5 p.m., was almost always full. The tips were excellent: in two days I earned more than in an entire month in Toronto, which enabled me to pay off the loan for my passage quickly and also send more money to my mother. Tips were especially generous whenever there was a raid. Drinking in public establishments was only permitted under certain conditions, which in any case did not pertain to our club, since we didn't have a liquor license. So at least once a month we could expect the RCMP to come riding in on their noble steeds, which they would hitch to a tree trunk outside, and storm the joint from both front and rear entrances. We always expected them, since the boss would always be forewarned of their arrival. He'd give us a signal and the first thing we'd do would be to hide the bottles of those guests who gave particularly generous tips in a hutch in the kitchen. Then we'd warn all the other guests, who would immediately begin dancing to the strains of the jukebox or the band and totally ignore the frustrated exhortations of the police to return to their tables. After an hour or so the police would leave, the bottles would be retrieved, and the good times would roll again. It was a scene reminiscent of some of the finest black-and-white Western movies I'd seen since coming to North America. And you didn't even need to buy a ticket.

Working conditions were new for me, since I was only used to working with Germans and Austrians, my job in Toronto being no exception to this. Here it was a lot different. Sue, the other waiter, was a Canadian (male) of Japanese descent; the cook was Chinese; the cleaning ladies came from Poland; the cloakroom attendant was from Montreal; and my boss and his parents, whom I called "Mom" and "Pop," were of Ukrainian descent. They all spoke English, yet maintained strong connections to their countries of origin. They frequented their respective national clubs, listened to music of their homelands, read imported newspapers and magazines and enjoyed their native cuisines. Contact with so many different cultures led to a lively cultural exchange, not only at work but after it as well, whenever we'd go to Frankie's, a good Chinese restaurant. Frankie, himself a Chinese, knew us and made sure we were always served wonderful dishes, over which each of us would tell the others something about his country of origin. And the meal would go on and on, owing not only to the pleasant conversation but also the chopsticks we had to eat with. I wasn't used to them, and the first time I left the restaurant as hungry as when I came in. Sue showed me the best technique for using them, and the next day I practiced at home and quickly acquired, shall we say, a "near-native fluency" with chopsticks.

Sue was polite but very reserved. We divided the restaurant up into halves, he covering the one and I the other. Only once did he criticize me, when he said the Germans were cannibals who enjoyed eating raw meat. I answered this with the charge that the Japanese ate raw fish, which I found repulsive. Whereupon he proposed a deal: he would eat some raw meat, if I agreed to try raw fish. So I prepared a serving of beef tartar for him, following all the rules of the culinary art, while he filleted a whitefish and served it to me with soy sauce. It was surprisingly good, and with each bite I found my prejudice melting away. I gather my tartar produced a similar response in Sue, since I was to make him my recipe many times over the months to come. After this his behavior towards me also changed; he told me about his parents, who started out as fishermen in Vancouver, but then, in 1942, after the Japanese attack on Pearl Harbor on December 7, 1941, were evacuated inland and subjected to forced labor on a sugar-beet plantation in southern Alberta for next to nothing. Now they were living in Lethbridge, a town in southern Alberta. Sue also told me only partial reparation at best had been made to his parents for their property in Vancouver, a state of affairs that filled both of us with indignation. This intimate conversation broke the ice, and we got along much better after it.

Finally I was making some money, but of course I wanted more. So, as if on cue, an opportunity opened up for me to moonlight as a waiter at the MacDonald Hotel.[52] I worked the midday shift there, from 11 a.m. to 3 p.m. Then my boss would pick me up, and I'd work at the supper club till 5 p.m. as a janitor or cleaning man. After that I'd start my regular evening shift, which went till midnight, or 1 a.m. on weekends. On winter Sundays, our day off, my boss and I would drive either to Jaspers or to Banff in the Rockies to ski. Skiing wasn't totally new to me, as I'd flirted with it in the KLV camp in Altwerder, but here it was something entirely different. The mountain was so high, and the downhill stretch so long, that you couldn't even see the ski lodge down below. Still, after a few pathetic attempts, I managed it all right, and was proud of learning something new besides.

Only once did I have to miss a week of work, and that came about as follows. One Saturday I got a blister on my foot, which grew larger by the hour. Finally I took a needle, and, heating it over the flame of a cigarette lighter that was covered with soot, perforated the blister. Needless to say, this didn't help; the foot swelled up and I took my shoe off to continue serving, as the restaurant was very crowded. Not until the last guest was out the door did I let my boss drive me to the hospital.[53] The diagnosis was blood poisoning. I was given a shot and put in a ward with about thirty beds. I was told to apply a hot compress to the foot every few hours, followed by a cold compress, until the swelling went down. Walking was strictly prohibited. But of course I had the strongest urge to run to the toilet, since I'd had no chance for a bathroom break at the club. The instant the nurse left the ward, I made a beeline for the toilet, situated right next to my bed. Just then the nurse came back into the ward and, quasi Amazon that she was, literally lifted me back into my bed and threatened to tie me to it, if I tried that again. She said there was a pan for such purposes, which one could place underneath the relevant anatomy. I was having none of that. I threatened to go on a hunger strike, if they didn't give me permission to go to the toilet. Her reply was a magnificently indifferent "so what," so I acted out my threat, not taking a bite of food for three days. Then my stomach began to swell up, and the nurse started slipping me laxative tablets without my knowledge. They worked.

Wouldn't you know, it was right on Sunday afternoon, during visiting hours for all patients. It seemed there were at least three visitors per patient that day. There were also plenty of children playing, shrieking and running around the ward. I signaled the nurse that I had to go, and she set up a folding screen around my bed. At which point I carried out a massive evacuation. Up till then, I had no idea just how much of the stuff you can carry around with you, but boy did I have an inkling now. Besides, it gave off an awful stink. When I'd finally finished and rang for the nurse, she never showed up; it seems she'd left, and her replacement hadn't checked in yet. And so I sat there on my throne, unable to "abdicate" and forced to listen to the various and sundry comments of the visitors, none of which sounded friendly. One man insisted the doctor be informed, since it was clear the person behind the screen had passed on; you could smell it even a few miles upwind. Then a mother told her child to take a discreet peek. The child took a peek all right, but it was anything but discreet. He pulled the whole screen away, exposing me to the glares of all. Just then, thank God, a nurse walked in and helped me down from the bedpan, announcing as she did that visiting hours were over. Since most of the visitors had already left, driven out by the stink, those who'd hung in there were more than happy to obey her prompting. In a final effort to grasp the moment, the child asked his mother, "Mom, is that poor man dead now." She replied, "Not yet. But it won't be long."

I spent a whole week in the hospital, and, far from being bored, I learned and experienced much. The bed opposite me was occupied by a man with a rash. He had been instructed to powder the affected area on the hour, then wait an hour and apply a salve to it, then wash the area an hour after that and sprinkle powder again, and so on. The man developed this system of applying salve on even hours and powder on odd. Whenever anybody wanted to know whether it was one-thirty or two-thirty, all they had to do was glance at his bed and read the time. Then there was an old man who seemed to be at death's door. He'd been put in a bed with side-bars as a precaution to keep him from falling out. Every evening like clockwork, the nurses would give him a needle in the rear end, which the poor wraith didn't care for at all. One evening he'd managed to undo the lock for the bed-bars, and just as the nurses approached with his nightly needle, he let the bars drop with a crash, leaped out of bed, ripped the syringe from the nurse's hand and chased her wildly down the ward, waving the needle like a wrested banner. The nurse screamed, the man laughed the laughter of the mad, and all the rest of us from our beds egged the two of them on to run faster, faster! It was wonderful theater, on which, alas, the curtain came down all too soon. An orderly came in, subdued the old man, who continued to complain that they wouldn't let him die in peace, and put him back in bed. The man giggled himself into a peaceful sleep, from which he was never to awaken. Someone observed, "That's the way to go, man. That geezer had a ball before kicking the bucket. I should be so lucky."

Once in a while, I'd get a visitor. John came and told me he had a new job; my boss dropped by too, but all he did was hound me with questions about how soon I'd be coming back to work. One time a young Eskimo woman stopped by my bed. I'd seen her a number of times before, whenever she'd come to visit her old father who lay in a bed in the next ward over. To get to him, she had to pass by outside my door. She set herself comfortably on the edge of my bed and told me that I always looked so sad and wondered whether I didn't have a wife to take care of me. I was in no mood to play the proud, tight-lipped patient; besides which, I didn't want her to leave, so I answered that I was an "outcast" who meant nothing to the others. She just smiled at this and asked if I would like to hear a legend of her people. I was curious and said happily, "Yes, please tell me." And she proceeded to tell me the Innuit legend of the blind youth and the loon: [54]

A long, long time ago there lived a clan not far from the sea, which was covered by ice for most of the year. The men would often put to sea in the summertime to procure meat for the whole year, harpooning whales and other creatures, which they pursued with their small boats. All--but one. This one was still a child, but his youth wasn't the reason they didn't take him along, rather it was his handicap: he was blind. And when all the other children would be playing, they would always exclude him from their circle, leaving him to sit all alone. Sometimes he'd hear them laughing and would feel the strongest urge to be among them, but they wouldn't have it and would shout at him whenever he dared to join in: "Get lost! You're blind. You're not like us, you're good for nothing, and it might even be better if somebody did you in." He really was good for nothing, and they never let him forget it. Even his own mother, who had disowned him. She left him alone in a hut without a roof, so that the snow could fall in from above, and she gave him nothing to eat. Yet he didn't starve, since his sister loved him very much and would bring him food and something to drink at night.

As the men would go out on whale hunts and he wanted to join in, they'd just laugh at him. When they got back, there would be a great celebration with lots of eating and drinking and dancing. All were merry, except for him, who would just sit in a corner and gnaw on a bone somebody'd thrown him. His mother thought he should be put on an ice floe and allowed to drift out to sea, since all he did was eat without contributing anything.

One daye on the beach, a 'loon,' a sea-diving bird, set down next to him and said, "I feel sorry for you. I can help you, but you must do as I tell you. And what I tell you to do will be difficult to carry out. But if you can do it, you'll be able to see." And the blind boy nodded his head in agreement. The diving bird told him to grab on tight to his tail feathers, and then he swam out with him into the cold sea. Then he began to dive, and the blind boy dove with him. It was icy cold, and he froze mercilessly, but he stuck to the bird's instruction. His eyes were hurting as he resurfaced, and the bird told him that was enough for today. The blind boy climbed up onto shore and found that, for the first time, he could make out a few outlines as if through a veil darkly. The next day, the bird returned, and this time the diving went deeper and lasted longer. His eyes hurt terribly, but the young man would not give up. When he returned to shore, he could make out forms he had previously only heard but never seen. And so the diving down deep into the icy water went on and on, and each time it got colder and more painful, but he would not give up. Finally the day came when he could see not only outlines but colors as well, and he knew he had gained the full power of vision. Now he went along on whaling voyages, and no one was more deadly with the harpoon than he, and no one outdid him in the catch. And so he was named the head of the clan, and only the wicked mother, who had cast him out and had wished to drive him out onto the icy sea, was no longer among them. Once as he was heaving

150

the harpoon at a white whale, the line wrapped itself around her feet, she fell over and the whale pulled her with it, from ice sea to ice sea, and she was never seen again. But the man who had once been blind was deeply revered for his wisdom, and one day when he died, rich in years, many came from other clans to mourn him:

Sculpture from Aisa Amitsu

She finished and fixed me with her gaze, which now seemed to see right through me. Obviously she was sitting there on my bed, but she was also far away, there where the outcast had proven himself and had hunted the great whales that kept him and his fellow clan members alive. Then she stood up and left, turning around one last time to wave good-bye. As I drifted off contentedly to sleep, I was thinking that I too had been such an outcast, who was having a much better time of it now than earlier in life, since I was now beginning to look at everything with different eyes. Of course, that fellow wasn't blessed with a mother like mine — quite the contrary — but at least he had a "loon" to help him.

The day I was discharged from the hospital, I went straight back to work. One evening, a woman of about thirty came into the club. Her name was Inge, and she lived with a female relative right across the street. She wanted to dance, but the club prohibited dancing without a partner. We conversed for a while in German, since she had very little English. My interest in her was no doubt sparked by the fact that she was a native Berliner, from the Wedding district, who also happened to be good-looking. I took her out

151

that same weekend, and we spent a few nights in the attractive Park Hotel on 82nd,or White, Avenue. I asked her how she envisioned her life here, and she answered that she knew exactly what she wanted to do. Her mother had died within the past year, and her father, a regime-friendly general in the Third Reich, had hanged himself. Her plan was to meet a rich old man, love him to death and inherit his entire estate. She didn't need the money just for herself, she said, but also for her younger sister, whom she was now raising alone, with the death of their parents, and whom she loved dearly. She wanted her sister to have a better life than she'd had; if she (the sister) went to the university here, she'd have the opportunity to begin a new life, a better one than in Berlin. Of course, her sister was never to know where the money came from.

My first reaction to all this (which I kept to myself) was that her whole plan was highly immoral; but then I considered that even this shabby way of getting money could be viewed as having moral validity, since her primary motive was to help her sister. Was she really any different than the religious woman who'd let herself be made love to by the Russian on top of the sacks of sugar? And why exactly should a moral end not justify an immoral means? I wished her much luck with her plans, which she did in fact succeed in carrying out, as I would learn from her years later at a rendezvous in an Edmonton restaurant. It seems she had made the acquaintance of an elderly farmer in Calgary, on whose farm oil had been found. He was paid handsomely for every drill rig set up on his property. His wife had passed on and his two sons were living in another city. Inge moved in with him, and it wasn't long before he died one night of a heart attack. She was his sole heir, and although his sons contested the will, seeking to have it declared invalid, the courts sided with her and she inherited millions.

After a while, Inge's sister joined us in the restaurant, dropping a heavy textbook on the table. It was that classic by Adam Smith, *The Theory of Moral Sentiments*, which she was reading for her course in political economy at the university. She explained to us that, according to Adam Smith, the acquisition of money should always be guided by moral considerations. In answer to Inge's question whether there were any exceptions to the rule, her sister said, "Unfortunately, yes. There always are. But then they too are immoral." I looked at Inge, and I'm sure we both had the same thought, that it would be better not to enlighten her sister, but rather leave her in blissful ignorance. Inge now had plenty of money and made me the offer of buying the Park Hotel, which I would then operate with her on a fifty-fifty basis. But my inner voice said no, and we took leave of each other on friendly terms. These days she's a devoted churchgoer, donates her money to worthy causes and is highly esteemed in a society that knows nothing of her past.[55] And her sister is now a well-regarded attorney in Vancouver, British Columbia.

A few weeks later, I quit my job at Chick's Bar-B-Q. I'd heard from some diners that you could earn a lot of money "up north," i.e., in northern Canada. Since the Americans felt threatened by Russia during the Cold War, warning systems for surprise attacks were set up between 1955 and 1957. These were radar installations intended to alert the American people to an attack. There were three belts: the DEW- or Distance Early Warning Line, the Mid-Canada Line, and subsequently the Pinetree Line. All in all, 63 radar and communications systems were built, 42 of them in Canada. This defensive belt extended over 3,000 miles (ca. 5,000 kilometers) from Alaska to the Eastern coast of Baffin Island.[56] Anzac, in Alberta Province, was part of the Mid-Canada Line. John and I applied for jobs with Mannix, Ltd.; we were hired as waiters and flown to Anzac a few days later to provide service to the roughly 800 workers there.

Shortly before our departure, I went out dancing at the Trocadero Club in Edmonton with a nice woman, who had just recently emigrated to Canada. I'd picked up a small flask of whiskey ahead of time, which we surreptitiously opened under the table and used to spike our drinks. Under the circumstances, the relatively conservative attitudes that prevailed in Edmonton were the furthest thing from my mind; and I had failed to notice I was being watched by an undercover policewoman. She came over to our table, confiscated the bottle and gave me a citation. My trial was scheduled for two weeks later, which presented a problem, since I had to be in Anzac the day after tomorrow. So next day I ran over to the courthouse and implored the responsible agency to take my case up right then, on the spot. This it did, and I was ordered to pay a fine; also, a note was entered into my record stating that I had not only drunk alcohol illegally in a public place but had also provided same to a young woman. Thus I'd now been twice convicted: first in Berlin for Communist activities, and now in Canada for illegal use of alcohol.

Before setting off for the Canadian wilderness, and to shake off my current funk, I wanted to sip again from the cup of life's strongest elixir, i.e., to be with a woman. Circumstances seemed favorable, what with my dancing partner in the vicinity, whom I'd seen home the previous evening. This, of course, gave me the added advantage of knowing exactly where she lived. Besides, it was my distinct impression that she would not be entirely averse to a nocturnal tryst. So around midnight I set out on my way, and though the way was one of unrelieved snow and ice, still the flame of passion burned bright within. Since she lived in an upper story, I grabbed a ladder from a nearby shed, leaned it against her window and commenced what is known in Southern Germany and Austria as *fensterln* (lit. "windowing"), an activity entirely foreign to me as a Berliner. Just how foreign I would presently find out. After positioning the ladder firmly against the façade of the house, I began carefully climbing rung by rung. About halfway up, the ladder suddenly lost its tentative footing on the snow and ice and slid out from under me, hitting the ice with a resounding crash. I came right after, but, except for a few bruises, miraculously suffered no further injury. The noise woke up the owner of the house, who came out fuming but unable to spot me, as I'd already scooted, or rather skated, off to the shed for cover. I could hear his menacing voice booming after me that he'd empty his shotgun into me if I pulled anything like that again.

I waited until I was sure he was back in the arms of Morpheus and began again. I hoisted the ladder back up against the house, this time making sure to clear away most of the snow and ice at its base. On this try I managed to reach the top and could already see myself in the arms of my Venus, when I encountered another obstacle: I couldn't get the damned window open. Naturally, in the depths of an ice-cold Edmonton winter, with temperatures plummeting as low as forty below centigrade, it'd simply frozen shut. I shook it like mad from outside, she from inside, but it wouldn't budge. Gathering all my strength, I tried to jerk the window loose, but this heroic effort only caused the ladder to wobble, slip away again and slam against the ground with another loud bang. Again I came after, collecting another array of bruises, but lucky enough at least to land in a snowbank. No doubt the owner had managed no more than a light sleep, as he was back out again in an instant; I could see him standing in the doorway, shotgun aimed threateningly in what he took to be my general vicinity. I couldn't make out his stream of profanity this time, as his dog, a German shepherd, was standing at his side waking most of the neighborhood with his infernal barking. People were coming out into the street, sleep-drunk and bundled up in blankets and sweaters. They acted as if searching for the burglar — there was no doubt they took me to be one — but after a brief and perfunctory neighborly appearance, disappeared back inside as quickly as they'd come out.

I didn't give up. After everything calmed down, I repositioned the ladder, climbed to the top and, since my beauty had thawed the window out with a hot towel, slipped into her room. I closed the window, which unfortunately made a bit of a din, as the water had, in the intervening minutes, already begun to freeze, and turned towards my beauty. I had no trouble at all finding her in the dark; a light snoring showed me the way. She was asleep, though not at all lightly. I tried to nudge her awake, feeling my spleen rising as I did: this is not at all how I envisioned my amorous adventure. Not at all. Finally I shook her awake and asked for an explanation, which she promptly gave me. "Let me sleep, will you," she mumbled, "I only got here two days ago by ship. Don't even ask me about all I had to do on that steamer. Don't think I was just sitting around twiddling my thumbs. I'm totally wiped out and just want to recover from the stress of the voyage, so please shove off, o.k.?" Which is exactly what I wanted to do, but how? The ladder was no longer at the window, removed no doubt by the owner. The only other escape route was sealed off by the damned dog, who'd planted himself right outside the bedroom door; every move I made was answered by a threatening snarl from just outside. And from the corner of the room I could hear the deep, rhythmic breathing of my quasi-partner. All I could do was sit down in the corner and wait for morning. Early on, I heard the owner call the dog and tie him up, and then head out for work. I left the house myself right after him, but not without first giving that mutt (now neutralized by his chain) the fiercest dirty look I could muster. My sense of it was that a German shepherd should show a bit more patriotic feeling for somebody who hailed from his own homeland.

My Life Up North: Homer, Card Games and Wild Beasts

My employee badge number was 814, which I believe roughly approximated the number of employees in Anzac. As I was being flown to my destination in the small craft, a cloud hopper, I reflected on the fact that this was yet another paradox in my life: I thought I had escaped the war, yet here I was helping with the construction of a defense belt in case of war. In retrospect, however, it seems to me that money wasn't my sole, or even primary, motivation for this step, but rather the opportunity to experience the wild Canadian north.

In Anzac we were put up in wooden huts, and I was rooming with John again. We got up early and had two large tables to serve each, each table seating some thirty workers. After that there was nothing for us to do till the noon shift, and, later, the evening. We had no day off, and we worked about ten hours a day. The pay was very good: we netted up to $150 per week, roughly double the *monthly* salary we'd earned in Toronto. The food was extraordinarily good. The chef, with whom I immediately began a series of culinary discussions, was from the luxury hotel Chateau Frontenac in Quebec, and at times it felt (or tasted) as if you were dining at that hotel and not in the northern wilderness. For breakfast you could have, apart from the typical scrambled eggs with sausage, ham or bacon: soft-boiled eggs, pancakes with maple syrup, or your choice of toast or muffins, on which you could thickly spread peanut butter and strawberry marmalade. These combinations were new to me and at first I found them confusing, but with time I developed a taste for them. For lunch we served two hot meat dishes, one fish dish and cold meat and cheese platters. The same for dinner.

About a week had passed when I was summoned by the chef, who, on the basis of my experience, offered me the position of headwaiter. To my duties was now added the responsibility of training the other waiters, all untutored, in the proper way to serve. Easier said than done. We had some twenty-five waiters, most of them Greek, who spoke very little English. Not one of them had the remotest idea of correct service; when they were asked for bread, they would bring it in their hands and just lay it directly on the table. But it didn't take me long to teach them how to prepare dessert at the dining table. The chef was ecstatic over this and gave me a raise. And so, to the workers' astonishment, we began serving cherries jubilee, crêpes suzette, baked Alaska and other specialties, which we flambéed right at the table. Occasionally, on my directive, the waiters would prepare a steak tartare and serve it as tasty appetizers before dinner. Then somebody brought in candles, which we put on the tables, giving the whole hall a festive atmosphere. Everyone was pleased, and some of the workers, who for the first time in their lives weren't merely eating but "dining," went so far as to leave a tip on the table after some meals.

But the real gem of my experience there was my discovery that some of the Greeks knew Homer by heart, and it wasn't long before they found out that I too treasured this classical epic poet. Some nights after work, we'd sit around the dining room in a circle and intone those immortal hexameters from the *Iliad* or the *Odyssey* in Attic Greek. When we got to "εσσεται ημαρ," ("Soon the day will arrive . . .), I felt a deep melancholy tinged with nostalgia as I realized that I was now well on my way to that day, for I could already see the rosy-fingered dawn. It wouldn't be long now before I'd be returning to Berlin where a luxury car would be waiting for me on the wharf, at the wheel a gorgeous chauffeurette, who on even-numbered weekdays would look like Felicitas and on odd, Lore. Then we'd sail on a luxury liner to my island with the lagoon and sip our cocktails under palm trees.

I read a great deal in my free hours, especially the German classical writers. From time to time, I'd go for walks in the woods with my German shepherd, which had been left there by one of the workers upon his return to civilization and attached himself to me. The northern forests were vast and primordial and not nearly so "well-groomed" as someone from Germany would be accustomed to. Tree trunks lay all about, and fallen branches frequently blocked the path. Also, the forest teemed with life. Time and again I saw elk and bison going their way in true majesty. Once I was even chased by a grizzly bear, a loner, which was very fast and almost caught me. Lucky for me he ran off in another direction. I also crossed paths with many brown bears; you always had to be careful to avoid the vicinity of a mother bear with her cubs, an extremely dangerous situation. You could also observe the bears as they fed; at dusk they would come to the garbage dump and rifle through the heaps for edibles, which were always there in plentiful supply. Bears being nearsighted, you could approach them, but only when you were upwind of them, so that they couldn't catch your scent. We'd actually do this once in a while, and whenever we did, I'd get that giddy feeling of being in the Old Wild West. Since firearms were illegal, the Indians would lay traps, and one time it so happened that a bear stuck its head into such a snare and couldn't get it off despite great effort. It certainly would've died, had John not approached it from behind, pressed its claws hard against his own body with one hand, while lifting the snare up over its head with the other. Later, this heroic deed was appropriately feted in the dining hall.

Playing cards, specifically poker and black jack, was the main form of entertainment. I didn't know either game, but learned both quickly. The rules were Draconian: if someone made a mistake dealing out the cards, the pot would immediately be divvied up among the other players. And the pots tended to be huge. Since we were paid by check, never by cash, the pot would usually be raised by the amount of a given check, though this tended to happen much more often among the workers than the waiters. Sometimes there'd be over ten thousand dollars on the table, a considerable sum, and not only for me, who'd had to work in Toronto for a lot less. One time someone was caught dirty-dealing; he was dragged outside and hanged! Next day the RCMP came and was told the dead man was troubled by family problems and hanged himself in a bout of depression. This actually did happen often enough, since the men would be separated from their families for months at a time, and their women had little trouble finding replacements, being a minority as they were. So this explanation sufficed, and the Mounties took off.

It was always tempting to deal from the bottom of the deck, since winnings were substantial. But the pots were much too rich for my blood, so I abstained and found myself two other guys to play skat with. Our antes were only a tenth of a cent, which of course could also add up fast, but nowhere near the grandiose amounts of poker and black jack. I didn't even have the expense of purchasing decks of cards at the canteen, since the poker addicts changed decks every ten hands or so. They'd shove the old cards aside, take a new deck, pass it around and only then brake the seal on it and start the next game. We skat players would, of course, grab the discarded decks and count the cards. Sometimes we'd find the deck contained five aces or picture cards, the extra card smuggled in by a cheater. Naturally we'd keep our mouths shut about this, out of fear that they might not believe us and that we too could find ourselves at the end of a rope, just like the dirty dealer.

In the kitchen there occurred only two "catastrophes," but both in the same week. We had a dessert chef who worked nights, baking cakes, pies and, later on, even tarts. He was a former *patissier* at a good hotel on the East coast, who for some reason had given up his job and relocated here. We soon found out what his Achilles heel was. The man drank. In fact, he was an alcoholic. Sometimes he'd put too much sugar in his cakes and tarts, at other times too little, or maybe too much shortening, or the base of the cake would crumble, or turn out as hard as a board. But because he performed his duties quite conscientiously otherwise, they kept him on. In time things got worse, as virtually any confection he made was inedible. The chef wanted to give him one last chance and had all bottles containing alcohol removed from the kitchen. One morning we found him dead-drunk again in the kitchen; he'd poured the contents of all the little aromatic bottles together and mixed a cocktail. He was fired, along with a just-hired German cook, who, without any training at all, had only gotten his well-paying job through connections. His job was to make scrambled eggs in the morning. He only made them once. He took 200 eggs and threw them, still in their shells, into a large mixing machine, where they were stirred so long as to be reduced to the consistency of a large foamy mass. Then, with the big dipper, he took out portions and filled all the frying pans. As we were serving the eggs, we watched in horror as everyone spat them out onto the floor, no surprise since the granular bits of shell were still in them. The explanation offered by this wanna-be cook was that he was convinced the mixing machine had totally pulverized the shells, to the point where a diner wouldn't notice them. His theory was that the shells contained lime and that this lime-additive was conducive to health. The chef was of another opinion. Both cooks were replaced, the one by a breakfast cook from the Hilton Hotel, the other by a *patissier* from the Hotel Vancouver.

At Christmas and New Year's, most workers took off for home, leaving only a handful behind. I was among those who stayed on, each of us now earning double-time pay. Unfortunately, the chef had neglected to adjust the foodstuff orders, even though we were now reduced from over 800 to a mere 30 diners. Food was delivered every day, and soon the refrigerators were all stuffed. We were told to simply throw the food away, and so many sides of bacon, chickens and steaks could be seen inversely "littering" the garbage. One day on a walk, as I came upon an Indian youth of about sixteen, I asked him if he wanted any of the excess food. He eagerly nodded yes, and the next day we schlepped dozens of flitches of bacon and several kilos of meat to his village. The boy introduced me to his father, who thanked me for everything. I chatted with him for quite a while and told him I was extremely interested in Indians. He wanted to know why, and I told him all about Karl May and his characters: the Apache chief Winnetou, Winnetou's father Intschu and sister Nscho-Tschui. Then too about Old Shatterhand and his two trusty firearms, the legendary Henry repeating rifle and the bear-killer; not to mention his horse Hatatitla, a gift from Winnetou; as well as Old Firehand, Old Surehand and Apanatschka; finally also about Old Wobble and the two fast friends, Dick Hammerdull and Pitt Holbers. The old man listened attentively, at the end remarking only that much had changed in the intervening century but also that he found this description of the old West otherwise very interesting.

After fourteen months I'd had enough. I was now almost 26 years old and wanted to see something different. This time opportunity came as both an inward and an outward turn, such as I was later to read in Eichendorff's novella, "From the Life of a Good-for-Nothing." How beautifully that tale opens with the words, "[T]he snow quickened its dripping from the roof, the sparrows twittered and flitted in and out of the drops . . . it's time for me to make my way into the vast world and shape my destiny." I said goodbye to the chef and to my Greek waiters, emptying a few glasses of some strong Greek schnaps with them, and was driven to the airport. Already assembled there were eight other passengers, all ready to board the small craft for Edmonton. I caught myself staring at the stewardess, who struck me as exquisitely beautiful, even though she was clearly on the north side of fifty and a bit pudgy as well. But as Goethe so aptly puts it in *Faust:* "With this drink in your blood you'll pass/ Fair Helen by in every lass."[57] He might well have been versifying to me, for, although I'd only drunk a modest amount of the Greek whiskey, I had not seen a woman in over a year. We had to take our seats, the plane taxied to the runway, the pilot revved the engines and then once again brought the plane to a standstill. He turned around and said, "She's tail-heavy. All of you sitting in the back three rows, please come forward so the plane can lift off." This we did, allowing the rest of the flight to Edmonton to pass uneventfully.

Not long after landing, I began wondering why people were staring at me and laughing. It hadn't yet dawned on me that much of the veneer of civilization had, in a sense, peeled off me during these fourteen months. I was "bushed," as they say in the North. Being "bushed" meant that you did weird things, like stopping perfect strangers on the street and inviting them to dinner, or going into a store and buying great quantities of totally unnecessary items. If you'd looked up "bushed" in an edition of Webster's at that time, you might've seen my photo. I went into the Hudson Bay Company, a large department store in Edmonton, and purchased, not one, but a dozen shirts, and then invited an entire family to join me in a steak dinner. But I shook off the malaise soon enough and, a day later, resumed my old job at Chick's Bar-B-Q; somehow my boss had caught wind that I was back in town. After a week, though, I knew I'd had enough of Chick's, and I sort of fell back into contemplation of the question what I wanted to do with my life. The meaning of life, for me at least, was not to be found in the Canadian north, stunningly beautiful though it was, nor was it to be found in the supper club, as pleasant as working conditions there were. I decided to consult my friend Gerhard and ask him about his own plans and prospects.

Like me a native Berliner, Gerhard was a skilled mechanic who worked for Mercedes; he'd come to Canada to make a new life for himself. He's the opposite of me. Whereas I'm right-brained by nature, and strongly so, Gerhard is left-brained.[58] So I went to him for some advice. As we talked, I noticed that he seemed more pensive than usual, and when I asked him why, he told me that his girlfriend Ingrid in Berlin had written him that she intended to marry, not him, but someone else. It so happens I had myself just received a kind of "Dear John" letter from Felicitas, which was very much on my mind.

When I say "a kind of 'Dear John' letter," I mean to convey a sense of the anguished uncertainty of the whole situation. Actually, it was two letters that revealed unequivocally the emotional vacillation on her side. In mid-February, 1957, she wrote telling me that she had applied for employment as a stewardess and that, if accepted, she would have to move her residence to New York, where we could rendezvous easily. The response from Pan Am Airlines came the very next week, and, since it bears so directly on my own destiny, I offer here excerpts from the follow-up letter that Felicitas sent me at the end of February:

> . . . *in my last letter I told you about my idea of becoming a stewardess. I mean, as far as I'm concerned, I would've jumped at the chance, but they didn't accept me — don't know the reasons. Maybe because I'm a former* Ostsektoraler *[person from the East sector]; the Americans are so paranoid. On the other hand, I don't have any regrets either; somehow I've always believed that things happen exactly as they're supposed to. I don't know of any better way of putting this, I'm so at a loss myself—such a horrendous letter, like no other I've ever had to write. I can no longer envision having a life with you. Too much has come between us. And it would only make things worse to see each other. I think we would both be sad, and that would be all. And what would be the point of that? Just as I never again had such a feeling of happiness, of joy, such as it would sometimes come when we were still together, never was that ever there again. And today I wouldn't even want that anymore. Life now is very much about other things than being happy, for me in any case. My thoughts keep me awake and torture me. It's the war, it's the whole business of that time that bothers me . . . it would be nice to be able to write each other about these things. And as for the rest, please be content without me, make a life for yourself somehow. It'll all be fine, and somewhere there's someone who'll be fond enough of you to make everything pleasant for you. And please, please, look for a job that leaves you time and leisure and without too much stress . . . it's so important that you feel well. Then too, maybe I really am too strong a personality for you — I don't know. . . .*[59]

I was stunned to receive this letter, and, without discussion, Gerhard and I decided to fly to Germany at once. We had only two days to prepare for the trip. We flew first to Montreal and then to Shannon. After a substantial breakfast, it was off to Frankfurt, our paths separating there with Gerhard heading to Berlin and me to Munich, where Felicitas was living.

Our reunion was affectionate, though not quite in the way I'd anticipated. Though she was still very fond of me, she stood firm in her decision to remain in Germany and not to marry me. Today I realize that it must have been my lukewarmness that decided her not to come to the states. She was the kind of person who demanded an unconditional commitment, and I just wasn't mature enough for that yet. So we said good-bye and I went to Berlin, where I surprised my mother for her birthday on May 1. Then I looked up Lore, only to learn that she was now going with Crassus, who had apparently wasted no time showing up at her door after I left Berlin. But I could see that he had genuine feelings for her, and since Lore, like Felicitas, had no desire to come to the States, I discreetly withdrew. I'd always prided myself on getting along with each woman I knew well enough to marry her, and now I had to face the sobering fact that women could get along quite well entirely without me, thank you.

I stayed in Berlin for three weeks, during which time I received an announcement of Gerhard's wedding on the 18th of May in St. Matthew's church on Schloßstraße. As he related to me later on, he'd gone straight to his girlfriend's place and insisted to her that, once firmly given, one could not so easily break one's word, that he'd spent all this time in Canada preparing a life for both of them and that she couldn't simply turn around and now say, "Thanks, but no thanks." She thought it over, found herself convinced of his love, steadfastness and even his arguments, and said yes. I served as best man and gave a little homily in which I depicted the beauty of Canada in the brightest colors, to help Ingrid (the bride) over the hump of her departure from Germany.[60] I added that a life spent with another person is much more enjoyable than one spent alone.

Such a sentiment certainly spoke volumes about me, as I had neither the one nor the other. Moreover, I realized that I no longer enjoyed life in Berlin; everything seemed so small, people here lived such narrow lives, and their views were no less narrow than their living conditions. I wanted to go back, back where the land was vast, the lakes gargantuan, the mountains snow-covered, and the people as open as the world they lived in. My mother could see I didn't like being in Berlin and said to me, "I know you won't be staying here long. Soon you'll find a woman who loves you and whom you love too. Then you can bring me over there." I promised her I would and went, later that same evening, over to Resi's in Hasenheide Park, a popular dance hall with colorful fountains and table telephones. There I met Brigitte. She was sitting at the next table, young and beautiful, with luminous blond hair and milky blue eyes. She was a typical Berlin girl, scrubbed with Spree water, quick with a quip, jaunty, independent, free and uninhibited, and with just the right dash of coquetry. We talked, and she told me it was her plan to come to Canada some day. I gave her my address, and we walked the whole way to her place, since the subway didn't go past Seestraße after midnight. She lived in the Tegel section. I spent the night with her and went back to my mother's the next morning bone-tired, packed my things and flew back to Canada.

Once back in Edmonton, I immediately found work in Fort Nelson, which lay in the northern part of British Columbia. Since the Alaska Highway was still under construction, I had to be flown in. It was late summer, but the nights were already so cold that I started making use of the oil heater in my tent. I got a job as a cook, as my predecessor had, so they told me, resigned. This was not exactly true, as I later found out. He'd been living in a tent close to the radar station, whose fourteen technicians he had to serve, along with the chief cook, and one night a gray or grizzly bear slipped into his tent and clawed him. This opened up his position, and I inherited his tent, which had to be patched up. When I asked if there were any firearms around, I was told they were not permitted, but that bow and arrow were. So I made sure to have these weapons close to my bed, and although I'd always admired how Odysseus was able to span that mighty bow upon his return to Ithaca, to this day I have not learned how to do that, never mind shoot an arrow with it.

Fort Nelson is set in an exquisitely beautiful landscape. Located in the northern Rockies, at the 300th mile marker of the Alaskan Highway, it lies just north of Dawson Creek and Fort St. John. The radar station I worked at belonged, as did Anzac, to the defense belt, with the one difference that it was not presently under construction but already built and deployed. I knew my sojourn here would be brief; on the basis of my Berlin past — schooling in East Berlin, classmates like Ebert, who'd waved a red flag at a mass demonstration, participation in marches in the eastern sector, not to mention my citation in Edmonton — it wouldn't be long before I'd be removed for security reasons. So I wanted to make sure I enjoyed whatever fleeting interlude I was allowed here, and I certainly had plenty of opportunity to do this.

The chief cook was a binge drinker, though one savvy enough to know when the demon was about to overcome him. He taught me how to butcher and prepare wild game, along with myriad other things necessary to insuring the care and feeding of this team of ravenous workers. There was certainly no shortage of game meat. The technicians went hunting every week, armed with bow and arrow, usually stalking the large wild game like elk and stag. On hikes you could also see other kinds of animals, such as mountain sheep or mountain goats, and sometimes you'd hear wolves. It was an Eden for eagles, falcons and owls, and we were warned several times of a grizzly bear, a maverick, which should always be given a wide berth, assuming you have enough time to do so. Proof positive of that for me lay, of course, in the grim fate of my predecessor. Beyond all this, the fishing in the big rivers and lakes was abundant, more than enough to provide a richly varied bill of fare. And occasionally Indians would come by, wanting to trade game meat for a flitch of bacon or a bottle of whiskey.

My paradise lasted for just about half a year. My suspicions were realized when, one day, two security officials showed up; they had come from Anchorage by helicopter. They came into my tent, instantly spotted my portable radio, which I had attached to the 30-meter-high antenna of the radar station to get Germany on shortwave, and gave me a half hour to pack my things. Excepting, of course, my radio, which they obviously regarded as somehow suspect. They brought me to the airstrip, and before I knew it, I was back in Edmonton. I phoned Gerhard, who told me there was a small room open upstairs in the house whose basement flat he was renting. I checked it out and found it appealing enough, although it was quite small and unheated and had a busted window, all balanced out, however, by a wonderful comforter on the bed. I moved in and arranged to take my dinner with Gerhard and Ingrid for a modest monthly fee. I'd saved some money, but it was only enough for essentials. So I spent the evenings rifling through neighborhood garbage barrels for discarded bottles, which I would then return to some grocer for their deposit value. This provided me with cigarette money. At night in winter I'd occasionally sit in front of the house watching the northern lights in their endless flickering and flaring dance. Sometimes the heavens would be ablaze with those lights, as they slowly, subtly changed their hues and twitched here and there above the horizon. It was an enthralling spectacle that would unfold before me, one so brilliant I could easily have read a newspaper by its light. Now and then I'd notice the bizarre contrast of the regal lights up there and the garbage bottles down here next to me and shake with laughter. I especially enjoyed celebrating Christmas with Gerhard and his family, including his parents, whom he had brought to Canada:

A German Christmas in Canada

Later that winter, I nosed around for other ways to earn a little extra cash besides the deposit bottles, and a lucrative opportunity soon presented itself. An acquaintance of Gerhard's who owned a small truck asked me if I'd be interested in going into the fish business with him, and I answered with an enthusiastic yes. The deal involved driving out in winter to one of the big lakes surrounding Edmonton and purchasing fish from the Indians that they had ice-fished, i.e., pulled out of the lake through a hole in the ice. Each fish weighed around two pounds and sold easily. We paid 25 cents per fish and sold them for 50 cents, going from house to house and offering them mainly to housewives. It turned out easier than I thought: after we'd sold a few, the customers began calling friends or acquaintances and sending us to their addresses. Occasionally I'd be regaled by a housewife with coffee and snacks, and once in a while even a sexual favor would be offered, all the men being off at work and the poor "straw widows" doubtless feeling lonely, for, as Goethe has poor Martha lament in *Faust:*

> *Please God forgive my busy man,*
> *For me he's not done what he can!*
> *He plows the big world on his own,*
> *And leaves me on the straw alone.* [61]

But I stoically resisted all temptations; the only thing that interested me was unloading all my fish. We'd begun with only two crates, but as business picked up, we were soon trucking dozens into the city, and it would take some time to sell them individually. The enterprise flourished and we made out very well. Of course, that same winter our business came to an abrupt end: we had bought a load of fish, intending to unload them the next day. During the night, however, the temperature did a stunning about-face, as sometimes happens in Edmonton. The change was the result of a "chinook" or "snow eater," as the Indians so aptly named this occasional warm winter wind. I took the fish with their sad eyes out of their crates and laid them all on the flat roof of my dwelling, hoping they would have a better chance of "surviving" the night up there. In the morning the roof was swarming with cats, all feasting on the fish and meowing their bloody heads off with pleasure, as well as leaving me the miserable job of cleaning the roof. And all this happened to *moi*, who had been informed not so long ago that all Jews were good businesspeople. But then maybe I just didn't have enough Jewish blood in my veins.

Still, I didn't give up, for the New World was a world of boundless possibilities, as many believed. And besides, I was young and enterprising. When I brought up this latest business fiasco to my tablemate at the local German club, the latter suggested a fail-safe method for getting rich quickly. His job was selling Colliers encyclopedias, which meant that he was pushing close to twenty volumes per set. To be precise, "selling" is a misnomer here, since he didn't actually sell the volumes, rather he gave them away free of charge, but only, as he put it, to certain carefully selected families. Of course, these families had to sign off on buying the annual supplementary volumes, some ten of them, and *they* were anything but cheap. Many families were lured into this scheme, happy as clams to be getting something for nothing, at least at the beginning, very few of them looking ahead to the next ten years. So I tagged along with him. The very first family we called on, coincidentally a family of émigrés from Germany, showed interest, as they had a daughter who was just beginning her university studies. The handsome set of volumes filled with all that knowledge struck them as the perfect gift for her. My mentor immediately launched into his spiel, singing the praises of his wares and pointing out that these volumes were of inestimable value for their daughter, guaranteed to lift her far above the stumbling blocks of even the most difficult courses. I asked the daughter, who by the way was also very good-looking, what she had in mind to study, and she replied German and English literature. Well, now I was on my own turf, and I just chatted on and on with her, totally ignorant of the sinister glares I was getting from my mentor. When we finally left the premises, to be sure without closing the sale, he gave me a stern lecture, ending with his considered judgment that I was not cut out to be a businessman. Perhaps I should try my hand at some sort of academic study.

Since I'd already decided in any case that it was time to take on academe, I registered at the University of Alberta. The subject I'd decided to major in was hotel administration, but this area of study was not offered by the university. So I registered for the "Commerce and Business Administration" program, figuring that this was at least close to what I wanted. The very day after registration I received a phone call from the president of the university in which he inquired about my English skills. I told him they were adequate, but he seemed not to agree, as I had made some significant errors on my application. He had me come to his office, put a few questions to me, and arranged a tutorial course for me with an English professor by the name of Dr. Alice White, who sat with me twice a week and helped me improve my skills in English, for which I was extremely grateful to both of them. My curriculum consisted of economics, law, English, bookkeeping and statistics, plus extra hours in different study groups and science labs. I kept up very well, but it was a lot of work, which moved me to take a leave for the following year.

My Life on Wheels and My Job in a Vancouver Steakhouse

In the summer of the year 1959, I began work as a waiter for the Canadian National Railroad or CNR. The job required me to leave Edmonton and move to Vancouver, since that was where the trains began their journey. First I had to take part in a short unpaid training course and learn such things as how to spread a tablecloth in a moving train and where in that tiny kitchen all the different items were located. During this course I also made the acquaintance of a young Englishman named Bill, a good-looking fellow, who, on that account, was a big hit with the guests. Unfortunately, Bill didn't have a clue about serving guests, a situation only exacerbated by the fact that he absolutely detested this kind of work. He was a dyed-in-the-wool socialist who believed that the rich had nothing better to do than oppress and exploit the poor. To him the occupation of waiter, in which one did not merely submit to oppression but thanked the oppressor for it as well, was fundamentally abhorrent. Of course, neither one of us had two nickels to rub together, and there were days when there was nothing to eat. One day, however, we got lucky as we watched, from our window on Adanac St., a delivery man placing advertising sample packs of Corn Flakes at the doors of local residences. The minute he moved on, we ran over and scooped them all up, and thus were relieved, for at least a few days, of next-meal anxieties.

In an effort to keep our heads above water, I took a job with the custodial staff at city hall. My eight-hour shift started evenings at 10 p.m., and I must confess that I didn't exactly kill myself. Usually I'd finish up within four hours, sweeping all the rooms, emptying the wastebaskets and dusting a bit here and there. After that I'd just wander around and check out the different office machines, which, though they fascinated me, I generally didn't have much success trying out. One IBM calculator in particular almost did me in. It was housed in gleaming chrome and, since it was attached to a typewriter as a special feature, it hummed softly. Suddenly I was seized by the prospect of unearthing the deepest secrets of the universe. Finally I could lift the veil that had forever been draped over the mystery of infinity! Carefully I typed a "1" into the calculator, followed by the division sign, followed in turn by "0." At first nothing happened, and I merely felt disappointment. But then the carriage of the typewriter slowly began to shift, as a vast jumble of numbers, interwoven with all kinds of mysterious signs, commenced to type themselves onto the paper. Suddenly the machine began to hiss, and the carriage raced faster and faster from one side to the other, each time ringing at the end and heading straight back to the opposite side. I began to panic; after all, what would the consequences be for me, should this machine, which was not at all cheap, suddenly collapse in a heap? I went to pull the plug, but couldn't find any, as the typewriter cable was attached to a main cable inside the wall. As if all this weren't enough, just then the general alarm bell went off, causing a tremendous racket in the still of the night. The alarm didn't have any plug either, being likewise attached to the inaccessible main cable. I immediately unscrewed the top section of the alarm housing, shoved a piece of paper between the bell and the hysterical hammer, stopping the cacophony, and then screwed the upper housing back on. Next evening when I showed up for work, I was greeted by the deputy mayor who proceeded to enlighten me on what I had done: I had succeeded in blocking all incoming telephone calls, with not so much as a single call getting through to city hall. It took engineers hours to track down the cause; it was late afternoon before all damage could be repaired. I, of course, was given my walking papers and told not to let the door hit me in the arse on my way out. Still, the most momentous thing was that the mystery of the universe that I had so wanted to reveal remained as hidden as ever.

Our last money spent, we headed over to the pawnshop. Bill had two pair of pants, of which he hocked one, and I had an old Leica, which brought thirty bucks. We bought butter and cheese and thoughtlessly placed both on the window ledge. When we got home the next evening, we found the butter had totally melted and oozed down the wall. Bill took his socks off and tried to clean up the wall and the rug, which he did manage to some extent. Then he washed out his socks in the bathtub, but as the water drained down, the suction was so strong that one sock got pulled deeply into the drainpipe and, despite several heroic attempts, couldn't be rescued. The pipe was fatally stopped up and the tub no longer drained. At first we did nothing, hoping that over time the situation would somehow normalize itself. But, since the faucet continually leaked, even when tightly shut off, within a few days the tub was completely full, and the landlord was forced to call in a plumber. That evening he came over breathing fire and asked us threateningly if the sock he was holding in his hand belonged to us. We of course shook our heads vigorously, having no intention of paying for the repair; nor indeed could we have paid for it, as our finances were just about at zero. When the landlord left, Bill fished the discarded sock out of the wastebasket, washed it out and put it back on.

The worst thing was that, even though we had this intensive training course under our belts, no one called ordering us to report for work. So I went over to the Hotel Vancouver and introduced myself to the headwaiter of the dining room, a Dane or Swede, who cut a handsome figure in his tails. He put me on the midday shift as a trial and was satisfied with my work, so I was now an assistant waiter for the midday and evening shifts. I got along with him famously and dropped hints that I had a roommate who was also a waiter. Consequently, Bill was also given a job, though he only kept it for one shift. That evening, when he had to serve a party that had just come from the theater and wanted to snack on a few cold dishes, he placed the large silver platters containing the food directly before the guests. When they asked for plates, Bill asked in retort whether the silver platters for which the poor proletariat had slaved in the silver mines for dirt wages were not good enough for them. When the guests responded in chorus with an outraged "No!," he cursed them and showered them with maledictions such as "exploiters," "capitalists," "bloodsuckers," and the like. Before you knew it, the headwaiter was unceremoniously ushering Bill towards the door. The next day Bill left

Vancouver. I never saw him again, but I do hope he's learned to temper his idealism.

At that point the expected phone call came and at last I was able to begin my job with the railroad. I rode the Vancouver-Winnipeg-Vancouver stretch all summer long, sometimes for an entire month without going home once. As soon as we pulled into Winnipeg in the morning, I'd head for the local CNR hotel and work the breakfast shift as a waiter, even though at times I'd be dog-tired. In the evening we'd ride the stretch back to Vancouver. Afternoons I'd go for walks in the park with Yvonne, a divorced waitress with a little daughter, and tell them stories which they'd both listen to with rapt attention. I told them all about the ancient world, of Homer and the battle for Troy, of Penelope and Odysseus and the latter's dalliance with the "fine-assed" nymph Calypso, as Inge Merkel would later somewhat indelicately phrase it, of Antigone and Agamemnon and Achilles, the last of whom I'd always held in highest esteem, before reading Christa Wolfs novel, *Cassandra.* The little one especially was taken with the words as they flowed from my lips, as I went on to speak of Hector, Menelaos and his exquisite Helen, whose beauty had inspired an entire people to wage a war of total destruction, of the grieving parents Priam and Hecuba, one of his many wives, and I conjured all the other figures from the dog-eared pages of those epic poems and sated my imagination on them. Much later I received a letter from her mother informing me that she herself had remarried and that her daughter had just completed her studies in classical philology. The mother also mentioned that these afternoons were among the most beautiful her daughter had ever known. Sometimes I like to think that this was more than just an expression of polite gratitude on her part.

This interlude came to an end one evening in Winnipeg when I was startled by a sudden thunderstorm. The train was full and all the provisions locked up, but we couldn't depart. A clamor of frightful force was raining down upon us; several storms had come roiling together over the city, and the lightning flashes came in such rapid sequence that you could've read a newspaper by their brilliance. The track embankment was already under water, and some of the passengers fell on their knees, praying for a speedy end to the calamity. Finally, after a few hours' delay, the train lurched into motion in the direction of Vancouver. The whole absurdity of the event was the last straw for me, for, apart from the pleasant afternoons in Winnipeg, the constant riding back and forth struck me as ridiculous. You ride, you arrive and you ride back the same day, and the pay, about fifty bucks per trip, was so-so at best.

In Vancouver I'd made the acquaintance of a young German woman named Hilde, who worked for a sugar baron in the city as part of the household staff. We met often on weekends to go dancing at the Danube bar, which was located on Robson St. in the German quarter, where you could find good German food and German products like Nivea Crème, Grundig radios, and German-language books, newspapers and magazines.[62] Hilde mentioned to me that her boss was friendly with the owner of a well-known steakhouse in the city. I asked her to put in a good word for me with him, which she did, and the very next week she phoned me and said I should present myself at the steakhouse. I thought I knew where the restaurant was, i.e., opposite the Hotel Vancouver, and that's where I went. Since I happened to get there just at the rush-hour crush, they handed me a uniform, and Mario, the Italian headwaiter, gave me to understand that the job was mine, provided I proved myself here and now under fire. This I did, topping $50 in tips in a brief two hours, and the next day my job proper began, which consisted of the midday and evening shifts. But there's an odd sequel to this story. The day after my trial shift, Hilde called to say how steamed she was that I had never showed up at the steakhouse, since her boss had spoken up for me there. I was dumbfounded at the obvious fact that I'd gone to the wrong restaurant, especially since the air of confidence I'd exuded at my grand entrance there rested on the assumption that a man of influence had already paved the way for me. So it seems that there were two steakhouses in Vancouver and that my assumption had been false. My guardian angel had guided me to the other one, called Oscar's Steakhouse, which, as it turned out, had better food and earning potential than the place at which I never showed up.

In this steakhouse, not only did we serve outstanding beefsteaks, which were dry-aged for weeks, making them so tender you could cut them with a fork, but also game meat, such as buffalo and elk steaks. The spareribs were especially popular, a large rack having about eight long ribs, each one thick with succulent pork and slathered with homemade barbecue sauce. Although it was common knowledge that the meat was pork, we would occasionally tell a white lie by assuring the customer that the dish consisted exclusively of beef ribs. Our motive here was noble: it was to enable our orthodox Jewish customers to enjoy their meal without guilt. Of course, they knew very well we were flim-flamming them (you might even say they were complicit in it), but because those ribs tasted so good, they didn't want to know. These experiences only confirmed for me my long-held conviction that man is a complex, multi-layered being who has the ability to preserve his enjoyment of life by thinking in a compartmentalized or quasi-Balkanized style. You need only make sure, I reasoned, that those parts containing conflicting information have no contact with one another. Such as the parts containing, respectively, religion and pork.

I worked in this restaurant for over a year. A highpoint of my performance there occurred one evening when I was serving a party of five men, who were on their way up north to hunt big game. They were all decked out in leather, with high boots, looking just like cowboys, having probably taken those stereotyped magazine images as their models. They all ordered steaks, big as toilet seats, one rare, two medium rare, one medium well and one well done. On top of that came salads with different dressings and baked potatoes, some with sour cream only and some with sour cream and a hot cheese sauce, chives and bacon bits. Five weeks later they returned from their trip and told all about their adventures in the bush, which apparently did not include a single felled game animal. They were sitting at the same table they'd occupied before their safari. Finally, one of them said, apparently in jest, that I should bring them all exactly what they had ordered the first time. The others laughed and wagered that that would be impossible, since, in the first place, the order was much too elaborate, and in the second, too much time had passed for me to recall it in detail. I accepted the wager and brought them the very same meal as five weeks earlier, including the variety of salads and potatoes. I used the hundred bucks my achievement won me as a down payment on a used car, a 1954 Hudson Hornet, which came luxuriously equipped for those days, had a six-cylinder motor, and was one of the most coveted cars in Canada at that time.

Occasionally I'd drive it to Seattle, which wasn't all that far from Vancouver, but had the advantage that I could write my mother I'd been in America. And since it was a kind of "vintage" luxury car, I could use it to impress Brigitte, my recent Berlin friend, who in the meanwhile had completed her studies in that city for becoming a draftsman and, soldier of fortune that she was, immediately set out for Canada. She was even more beautiful than I remembered, with her mesmerizing blue eyes and perfect figure. But her outer appearance was matched by inner substance. She had a strong will; she knew exactly what she wanted, and she needed no prodding to express an opinion on things. The thing that counted most for me was that she would never marry someone who was merely a waiter; such a life would be much too insecure for her, as her father, a qualified but all-too-often unemployed mason, had clearly demonstrated. Her ultimatum to me was that I either continue my studies or we end the relationship right then and there. And since I had it in mind anyway to forge ahead academically and was really only waiting for an occasion to do so, I registered as a student at UBC, the University of British Columbia, in Vancouver for the Fall of 1960. Not surprisingly, I listed economics as my major.

Flirting with Psychology

My choice of major was a mistake, as I had little aptitude for the subject. I had no trouble with statistics and calculus, but economic theory, which we were required to take for three years, was foreign to my nature. How could it be, in analyzing something, that you must proceed on the assumption that all other things remain constant? The formula for this was *ceteris paribus* (other things being equal), and I spent many a sleepless night pondering this static absoluteness. To me it seemed obvious that everything was always in flux, and if, as in a chess game, you moved one figure, well, then that changed the whole board. My first analysis got me a low grade. I was assigned to investigate the question what would happen if the price of milk were to rise. My conclusion was that such an event might well lead to the decline of morals and, conceivably, even to an increase in population. I reasoned as follows: the price of milk goes up, and, in consequence, the price of cream. Since cream is used to make butter, people take to using margarine. In the production of margarine oils are used which also happen to be used in making plastic buttons. Ergo the textile manufacturers have to pay more for these buttons, at least in the short run, and this price increase is passed along to the consumer, who then purchases fewer textile wares, since the demand for textiles is very volatile. So, in the end, people wind up not only buying but actually even wearing fewer clothes, which can all too easily become a source of arousal and temptation to the opposite sex.[63] I could give a more detailed picture of my findings, but even the brief summary offered here should serve to point out that I had little of whatever it takes to become an economist. At times I had the impression that the same could be said of my instructors in the subject, since almost all of them drove old jalopies, unable to afford, so I assumed, anything better. I was, thankfully, quick to realize my lack of ability and switched majors to psychology, to which I later added German.

In psychology I had truly first-rate teachers. Unfortunately, however, my very first course was one in advanced statistics which gave me some trouble. I explained my problem to a certain Baron von Mach. He and his wife occupied the ground floor of the house, and occasionally we would discuss political issues and, especially, parapsychology, a field in which he claimed to be an expert. One evening there was a barely audible knock on my door. On opening, I saw standing there a frail wisp of a child who asked me if I was the one having problems with statistics. He offered me his help, so, to test his competence, I gave him a problem, the solution to which I knew, since it was given in the back of my textbook, though without the accompanying steps. Victor, as he was called, sat down and, within a quarter hour, gave me his answer, which coincided with the one in the textbook. Then he apologized and asked for my forbearance for taking so long, explaining that he hadn't cracked a statistics text in two years and was a little out of practice. He told me he was seventeen years old. When, upon Victor's departure, I went to Herr von Mach for an explanation, he said only that the boy had just yesterday been released from the local asylum following a two-year detention, that he *had* been profoundly schizophrenic and even dangerous at times, but that all of that was over now. By the same token, von Mach added, he was also a genius in mathematics (which he had certainly proven to me). Thus began my strange acquaintance with Victor.

My reaction to Victor was one of initial bewilderment followed by inspiration. Destiny had delivered a mathematical genius right to my doorstep from whom the world might yet benefit. Besides, as I reasoned from my fresh knowledge of economic principles, without direct intervention a natural resource can all too easily remain unexploited. I went to my math professor and told him about my new ward. He had me bring Victor in and gave him a long test in advanced mathematics which Victor passed with flying colors. Since Victor lacked a high school diploma, he couldn't be accepted as a matriculating student. But that meant nothing to him, as his concerns lay — I was about to learn — in another area altogether. Receiving as he did a mere pittance from social support services and with his rent more than he could afford, he accepted my invitation to move in. The next day, he showed up with his few belongings and slept on the sofa in the corner of my room.

When I got home from the hotel the day after that (I was waiting tables weekends at the Hotel Vancouver), I saw to my astonishment that the refrigerator, which stood outside the door to our room and served all lodgers on the floor, had been completely cleaned out. In place of everybody's food stood a dizzying array of bottles, dozens of them, all filled with the juice of red beets. The next morning Victor told me he was conducting an experiment, and I learned to my amazement that Victor wasn't actually Victor at all but a kind of "Victoria," or, as he called himself, "Aurora." His parents, so he claimed, were extraterrestrial beings who, several years earlier, had been compelled for some offence to abandon him on this planet; here he had been turned into a boy, though clearly his basic identity was that of a pretty girl. Several of his features supported the credibility of this view, he argued, such as his slender limbs, his delicate face, his dark, expressive eyes and even his formidable intelligence. He was, at present, a woman imprisoned in the body of a man, and it was his mission to liberate the inner woman from this prison. One means towards this liberation was the juice from red beets, he explained, which would provide him with the chemical building blocks of female attributes. And he did indeed enjoy an enormous amount of the red juice, downing perhaps one tall glass per hour, which colored all his teeth red and made him look like a pretty vampire. A few days later he proclaimed a great success, announcing that he felt on the brink of sprouting breasts, which he eagerly proceeded to show me. Of course I saw no change at all, but, not wishing to burst his balloon(s), I affected astonishment over his "metamorphosis." He wasted no time buying himself a skirt and panties and pressed me to get him some kind of bra from my landlady. Moreover, he now started putting on make-up, but only of the organic sort: for lipstick he used the juice of a red turnip, while for mascara he mixed oyster plant extract with ashes, and so on. One day my landlady took me aside and asked me what was going on in my room. She assured me she had nothing against a lodger's occasionally bringing a female student home with him, but having to watch this young man run around the place in drag (she actually said "women's garments"), that crossed the line for her. Actually, it was edging across the line for me too; in the evenings, I felt as if I were living in some weird wax-figure gallery, with Brigitte sitting on the sofa knitting and Victor in an armchair next to her, clumsily attempting to do the same.

Brigitte gave me an ultimatum: either Victor or her. The decision came a lot sooner than I thought it would. One evening, while I was working in the hotel, she called to tell me that Victor was standing outside in front of the house holding a large knife with which he intended to kill me. I called the police, who picked him up and brought him back to the asylum. I no longer know whether it was anger or curiosity that impelled me, but either way, I needed an answer to the question how such a thing could happen, especially in view of the fact that Victor was under psychiatric care. So I looked up the doctor who was treating him and asked for enlightenment. The man explained that he was treating Victor with the so-called "mirroring technique," according to which the doctor mostly listens to the patient and gives him the sense that he's being taken seriously. The psychiatrist's job here, at least in the initial stages, is to refrain from giving any advice and merely to repeat whatever the patient says. So, for example, if Victor were to say, "Schneider is robbing me of my identity, and I'm going to kill him," the psychiatrist might parrot back, "So, he's robbing you of your identity and you're going to kill him." It may be that some exchange of this sort took place between them, causing Victor to assume the doctor was sanctioning his intention. I must say I don't think much of this treatment method, since obviously this "word echo" can at times have dire unintended consequences. I only saw Victor once more after that. He was living in a shelter for abused women, sitting in a circle with all the other refugees, drinking tea with tastefully upraised pinky. His name was no longer "Victor" but "Aurora," and the other women treated him as one of them, which made him, or rather her, very happy.

The curtain may have come down on this little melodrama for Victor, but not for me. I wanted to learn something about the actual cause or causes of his behavior. I went to my psychology professor, who knew me well, and told him the whole story. He invited me to present a detailed case study to our seminar, which had the title and topic, "Dynamics of Human Behavior." Happy though I was to do this, I still couldn't give any satisfactory causal explanation of the experience. Later on my professor took me aside and told me he was well acquainted with this case and that he considered the following explanation to be at least plausible: as a boy, Victor had been raped by a male relative, not just once but repeatedly over a period of years. In the beginning, these encounters were met by resistance and rejection on Victor's part, but in time he began to take pleasure in them, while yet, as a boy, remaining inwardly unable to accept this form of love. A girl, on the other hand, could certainly accept it. And so he wrapped himself in the delusion of being, in essence, a girl, with all the feelings and sensibilities of a girl, with the charge, moreover, of restoring himself to his natural female condition. In me, of course, he saw an obstacle to his aspirations, for I treated him as a boy, thereby robbing him, as it were, of the true identity he was so valiantly struggling to reestablish. By the logic of his delusion, he had to kill me. This was, my professor hastened to emphasize, merely a theory, a possible explanation, and he was sure that a thorough investigation of the case would

176

yield other persuasive explanations. I must confess I was sorely disappointed by all this, for I had firmly believed that I knew Victor very well. I was to be reminded of this episode some years later when I came to read *Danton's Death* by Georg Büchner, a tragic drama in which the titular hero, right at the outset, asserts the impossibility of any true meeting of minds and spirits: "We know little of one another. We have the thick skin of elephants, we stretch out our hands to one another but it is a vain gesture, all we're really doing is rubbing one patch of coarse hide against another. – We are very lonely . . . . Know one another? We'd have to crack open our skulls and rip each other's very thoughts out of their synaptic fibers" (I,1). Then again, even if such a communion of thought were possible, there would still be no guarantee that one truly knew the other, since thoughts are diffusely spread out over different regions of the brain (again, "compartmentalized"), where they lead their own individual, separate existences.

The whole business led me to confront the question whether I could even say, with any assurance, that I knew myself. Psychology fascinated and inspired me, and I saw in it a possible path to self-knowledge. Besides, my experience with Victor had cut close to the bone, and I wanted to know if I was made up of as many different worlds as Victor-Aurora. I discussed the issue with my friend Stephen, a Norwegian, who was also studying at the university. His major was English and he spoke the language splendidly, although sometimes it was hard to follow his line of thought, as each and every month he would dutifully expand his vocabulary with the latest issue of *Reader's Digest*, which always contained a page-long list of arcane, rarely used words, expressions having precious little to do with the lingua franca of mere mortals. He reminded me of the old man in Peter Bichsel's short story, "A Table Is a Table," who went around renaming everything just to add a little excitement and variety to his life. Of course, Stephen didn't need to do all that; he had *Reader's Digest's* wordlists to help him with the names, but the result was the same. So for him "torment," for instance, became "excruciate" and "serenity" "equability." People had lots of trouble catching his drift. The problem was compounded by the fact that he idolized Shakespeare and introduced as much of the bard's obsolete vocabulary and syntax into his speech as he could. (This happened even in simple situations: e.g., whenever it was time to walk the dog, he would shout, "Out, out, damned Spot!") Anyway, Stephen suggested I take up the question of the inner world or worlds with Baron von Mach, who was after all a psychologist. So I called on the good Baron, who informed me that the inner world could be made at least partially conscious, and this through the power of the word. Since I had taken a course in social psychology that semester, I thought I knew what he was getting at; besides, I knew only too well from my own early experience living in the Third Reich how profoundly convincing propaganda can be. Herr von Mach hastened to assure me he meant something different.

Just how different his meaning was, I was soon to find out. He said he wanted to conduct an experiment with me, judging me to be a good subject for it. It would start off with a relaxation session. I didn't know what that meant but agreed to it anyway, as I was curious to see what he had up his sleeve. I was told to lie down on the rug and close my eyes. Then I heard his voice, as it systematically put more and more parts of my body to sleep, more or less as follows: "You're very tired. You feel no tension in your upper right arm, no tension at all, the stress is gone, and you can no longer move your arm." On it went like this, until all extremities had been addressed and relaxed. Then he went on to speak to my internal organs, stomach, liver, etc., until he got to the solar plexus, which too was to be exorcised of all its tension. And that's when it happened. I suddenly saw an immense dark cloud plunging down on me, arousing in me a profound fear. I flailed about and then folded up into the fetal position, in which I felt my legs involuntarily pressing hard against my lower body. The experience was extremely unpleasant, and Herr von Mach wasted no time bringing me back to the world of external reality.

In the post-mortem he explained, "You have some serious emotional problems anchored deep within the body. Had I not quickly jumped out of the way, you'd have laid me low with one blow." I told him I had no idea what a solar plexus was, as I'd never heard the term before. Later on, I speculated that there must be something like an internal dictionary, containing things whose existence is utterly unknown to us. Of course, he never found out what secrets lay festering inside me, notwithstanding his serious intention to do so. He had a certain inkling about me he wanted to pursue, so in the next experiment, in which I was to squeeze a rubber ball hooked up to a column containing mercury, he threw some names and expressions at me, to which I had varied reactions, as indicated by the rising and falling of the mercury column. Out of the blue, he mentioned something that instantly drained all sense of control from me. My hand locked itself in cramp around the rubber ball, as the mercury climbed threateningly towards the acme. This was proof positive to the Baron that I had problems, but my feeling was that I was much better off not confronting them at that particular time. After all, who could guarantee that I'd be able to manage them then and there? I found it wiser, for the present, not to raise my "black holes" up into the light.

Nevertheless, the experiment did intensify Baron von Mach's interest in working further with me. We repeated the relaxation phase, this time omitting mention of the solar plexus, doubtless a self-protective move of the experimenter. The result was a sense of being inwardly loose, as if I were in a vacuum. Then the second phase began. He had me take an imaginative elevator from the tenth floor to the basement, soothingly intoning words much like the following: "You're standing in an elevator that is on its way down from the tenth floor to the ninth. And as you watch the number 'ten' slip up and out of sight, you also see the number 'nine' rise up into view from below." He repeated this sequence until I reached the basement. All tension had dissolved from my body, and, although I retained my normal waking consciousness and remained, as far as I could tell, unhypnotized, still I couldn't move any part of my body. Then he instructed me to achieve this weightless condition even without all these preliminaries, simply by responding to three taps of his pen on the desk. He used this short-cut method the next time too, and I wafted like smoke straight into my inner world. As a rule, these "trips inside" left me with an enormous boost in strength and energy upon awakening. The net gain of these experiments for me was that I could now put myself in this half-waking condition whenever I chose to. I could even give myself commands while in it which I would reliably carry out afterward. The one intractable problem I had at the time was smoking. I was still a heavy smoker, and whenever I would read in the library, I'd have to go outside every half hour to light up. So I gave myself the suggestion that I'd feel like throwing up every time I lit a cigarette, and this worked like a charm. The pleasure of tobacco totally vanished, and I was able to quit smoking, at least for a few weeks. My other problem was that I wasn't getting enough sleep. Mornings I had classes at the university, afternoons I did my assignments and studying, and evenings, since I had a good relationship with the headwaiter there, I'd wait tables at the Hotel Vancouver, sometimes well into the night. Whenever I had some free time, say, between shifts at the hotel, I'd lie down and put myself through the relaxation ritual. This enabled me to get by with very little normal sleep. It also reinforced my desire to become a psychologist.

Just then, my relationship with Baron von Mach came to a quick and unexpected end. He was so enthusiastic about my hidden inner life that he wanted to write a treatise on me. Moreover, he asked me to let him hypnotize me, not simply for the purpose of taking me back to an early stage of childhood, but also to put me in position to make a leap into a state lying beyond individual experience entirely, a state in which one finds oneself far back in the chain of generations dwelling in the psyche of an ancestor. That sounded enticing, so I agreed. I would have to come to his office.

When I walked in, I saw to my astonishment that he was not alone. A journalist armed with a camera was sitting next to the couch, a few other people had notepads and pens at the ready, and a tape recorder was set up on a shelf above the couch, presumably for the purpose of transmitting a message from that other, invisible bygone world to our own skeptical world and the one to come. The whole scene gave me a feeling of confidence that Baron von Mach was convinced his experiment would turn out successfully. Under the skeptical eyes of several of those present, I lay down on the couch, closed my eyes and took the elevator down into my basement, a place I now knew well enough. After telling me I was to recall my 24th birthday, thus an event from six years earlier, Herr von Mach then slowly led me back stage by stage. I remained, as always, fully conscious and told the people there about all the things usually associated with birthdays: friends, birthday cake, alcohol and the like. The Baron was encouraged by this and proceeded to subtract another ten years from my life. This time I had to think about it. What exactly *was* I doing on my 14th birthday? The time to which the Baron was trying to bring me back was, unfortunately, 1945, and that was not a good year for me. Silently I considered what to do, finally deciding to go with Freud's technique of free association, which consisted in simply ejaculating an apparently random stream of words. Since I didn't know the English equivalents for some of the expressions, I decided to associate in German. A few people there knew German and listened to my revelations carefully, one or two even taking notes. I associated siren, airplane, cellar, bomb, explosion, Stalin organ, David and Bathsheba, Uriah and God, rain, shrinkage of the suit, merchant, paint company, hotel, kitchen, Adlon, and on and on. Then he took me back even further towards the beginning, pausing now at age three. I knew from my psychology class that, according to Freud, a young child is fully capable of experiencing sexual feelings, and, based on this knowledge, I ventured the accompanying profound verbal leap out of the anal and into the genital phase, at which all present exchanged glances and nodded knowingly, since right here before their eyes the Freudian theory of child development was being confirmed for them. Then at last, the *pièce de résistance*. The Baron intoned words calculated to lead me back into a previous existence altogether, one in which, as he hoped, I would turn out to be some kingly figure, or at least a prince. I continued to play along, but by now I was sweating blood. Upon brief reflection I slipped into the psyche of an Egyptian prince, even managing to stammer a few words I thought would be appropriate to my ancient identity. Alas, this ploy completely backfired, as one of the witnesses happened to be an Egyptian, who rubbed his hands with glee at the opportunity to converse with me in his native tongue. My swindle was exposed, sending the assembled company into a fit of rage, which was only further inflamed by my half-suppressed laughter. This concluded my relationship with Baron von Mach, who moved out of his apartment shortly thereafter, no doubt to avoid having anything further to do with me.

These experiences opened up for me into a general phase of psycho-spiritual experimentation. When I told Stephen about my abortive transcendental hoax, he responded that he was convinced that such a thing was possible. I asked him to let me put him through the relaxation procedure, and that went very well. At my suggestion, he gave himself the hypnotic command to stop smoking, which worked well enough, at least for a time. Then he took up Zen. He carried out the prescribed meditative exercises, but overdid it and almost lost his mind. He would spin out arcane theosophical dogma to me, saying things like "Man is not an individual being, but is made up of many persons, all of whom have attached themselves like shadows to a particular mind-body complex. Originating at different times in different places, all these 'shadow persons' have a need to make contact with the 'common-denominator' person who binds them all together. They make such contact through writing." As proof he showed me hundreds of pages all covered with illegible script. But these persons apparently did not remain satisfied with mere written contact; they wanted to speak with him. To this end they started "announcing" themselves, all six of them, which was the number of these phantoms then orbiting around Stephen, each one clamoring to identify itself. A typical scene would have Stephen sitting nearby quite normally. Then all at once he'd raise his hands and shout gibberish. That would be the Chinese announcing his arrival. Others made their presence known through a stamping of feet or a shaking of the head. Of course, this was all well and good at home, but if we happened to be in a restaurant and Stephen suddenly raised both hands high above his head, a waiter would come right over and ask what we wanted to order. To keep a low profile, or at least not let it get any higher than it already was, I'd usually order another round of espresso. Once it happened that we downed four or five cups of the stuff, and I found that my head was shaking beautifully all by itself, without any help from the phantoms, thank you. In time I found myself becoming anxious, and I made sure we stayed away from restaurants.

It was now the end of the semester and time for finals. I passed my exams in my two German courses and my psychology course with distinction. Stephen told me he'd written wonderful essay answers on his English finals, the more so thanks to the inspiration he was getting from his phantoms. When he got the exams back, all pages were blank — he hadn't written a single word. He dropped out of school for half a year for health reasons and was granted the option of re-taking the exams upon his return. This he did, successfully meeting all requirements. Today he's a master carpenter in Vancouver, but has broken off all contact with the other world.

My time in Vancouver was also coming to an end. I now held a B.A. degree with three majors: economics, psychology and German. My grade average in the first subject was "B" (barely), in psychology "A," and in German "A+." Now I stood like the proverbial ass before three haystacks, all equally tempting. But I knew this situation could lead to slow starvation—a decision had to be made. As I wrestled with this, rumors reached me of a teacup reader in a coffee shop on Robson St. who was supposed to be very good. People were flocking to him, hoping to get a glimpse of the future. You had to sign up at least a week in advance. I did, and went to see him at the appointed time.

Alas, the way there was an ill-omened one. On my route to this clairvoyant, who was about to reveal to me my true path, I passed by an old junk shop, in front of which a beautiful mynah bird was sitting perched in a suspended cage. The bird was sunning itself, watching the passers-by as they scurried to and fro past its cage. There was a young and very shapely woman taking a leisurely stroll in front of me, probably window-shopping. A real eye-catcher for any man! And not just for the men either, but the bird as well, which ogled her as she passed by, finally letting out a piercing whistle in her direction. And not just one whistle, but two or three. The woman stood rooted to the spot, as if bitten by a tarantula, then turned around slowly, and I could tell instantly that I had a seasoned feminist before me. Her whole body language shouted at me that we lived in different linguistic universes. She looked for the source of the whistle, but could find only me, as the bird had smartly done an about-face and pretended to be pecking at a few seeds. The woman rushed up to me and began shrieking with eyes ablaze with rage, "If you do that again, I'll slap your face and call the police! You're to stop molesting us women this way!" Shocked speechless, all I could do was point to the bird, who seemed to be eyeing me mischievously. My gesture failed, however, to persuade her to transfer her rage to its rightful target, which was now cowering anxiously in the corner of its cage. "You must be some kind of nut," she hissed, "trying to throw suspicion like that on a sweet, little bird." She did a quick 180 and stormed off. I stood there looking at the bird, which returned my gaze in all innocence and then, as I walked away, shot what can only be described as a smug bird-cackle my way, one that echoed in my ears for quite some time. My parakeet would never have done that, as good a whistler as he was, I thought.

I had no trouble finding the coffee shop; near the entrance hung a shingle advertising the great man's services. Apparently he had conferred upon himself the title "professor," though spelling it on the shingle with two "f's." This did not exactly fill me with confidence in the man's expertise or truth claims. I ordered a cup of tea, drank it down and stared at the tealeaves in the cup. After a while, I was summoned behind the Spanish partition shielding his little corner of the coffee shop from the eyes of the other patrons. A Chinese man in middle age greeted me, focused his gaze on my teacup and announced in a sing-song voice, "Your initials are . . .". Here he stopped, looking at me long and hard. Finally he concluded: "G. K. S." Then he went on, "Your full name is . . .". Again a pause, followed by his completion of the sentence with "Gerd Klaus Schneider." And so it went, he telling me what subjects I'd majored in and that I didn't know what to do with my life. Each utterance he made seemed to contain the same kind of pause or interruption, half convincing me that the man suffered from a speech-defect. The grand finale was a look into my future, which revealed to him that I would become a celebrated doctor, specializing in psychology. I liked that just fine and gave him a fairly substantial tip.

I was impressed with this fellow and told my friend, Rainer, all about my visit. Rainer was far and away the best student in our economics class, an extreme skeptic and thoroughgoing rationalist who later got his Ph.D. at Stanford. I asked him to go back with me. He agreed to, but insisted on going immediately so as to avert any unintended dropping of helpful hints to the clairvoyant during an appointment phone call. So back we went, and since there was no one else there in need of the great man's gifts, he agreed to interview Rainer. Rainer's session followed exactly the same procedure as mine, right down to the pauses. Since we still hadn't a clue as to how he was pulling this off, we went to my psychology professor, related our experiences and asked for enlightenment. The professor merely smiled and suggested we send the man a third customer, this time someone who had conjured up a fake identity in advance. We both settled on the same girl from our class and sent her over there after instructing her carefully. She made up a name for herself and gave herself a different major and minor, and, like clockwork, got that very same phony information back from the teacup reader. We were more confused than ever and went back to our professor. He explained that this Canadian 'professor' was well known throughout the city for his ability to receive or take in the alpha waves of a subject and decode them, so that, in effect, you're first thinking the answers yourself and then just hearing them "repeated" by him. The way this played out in practice was that each statement the fellow made would contain a juncture that would cause the subject involuntarily to supply a "completion" in thought. The man would then simply read off this completion, to the amazement of all present. The professor insisted, however, that he had no more ability to see into the future than we did: "His gift is limited to seeing what is, not what will be."

In 1962 I received my B.A. degree, of which I was very proud. I'd always considered it inconceivable that I would ever become a "man of learning," but I now had the proof of it. My only wish was that my mother could've been there to see her son, of whom she was always very proud. I had now reached a higher stage in my life and was in a position to determine what I wanted to become:

Another rung

However, as it turned out, my future was, shall we say, turned in a particular direction by someone else. I refer to a certain Mr. Loeb, my favorite German professor, whom I admired not only for his knowledge but for his genuine humanity as well. He had left UBC a year earlier in order to finish his doctoral dissertation on the subject of water symbolism in Goethe's works and moved on to the University of Washington, taking up a position there as Assistant Professor. He was considerably older than most students in the final stages of their dissertations. The reason for this was that he had formerly been politically active. I'd already written him from Vancouver, seeking his advice on a point of scholarship. He wrote back promptly and offered me a position as a graduate student at the university, which I accepted with gratitude and relief. I wanted to get out of Vancouver anyway, as Brigitte had recently settled on Rainer as her life's companion.

A Vacation Paradise on the Golf Islands and Flying Spaghetti

During this time I got to know Sheila, a former kindergarten teacher from London who was now working as a secretary in Vancouver. I was introduced to her by her husband, Haimi, a Jew from Breslau, who, like me, was waiting tables in the steakhouse. Haimi's parents had emigrated to Israel, and when it came time to sail there for a visit with his new wife, he suggested to her that they get divorced on the ship. His reason was that his orthodox parents would reject his marriage to a gentile. Of course, in the same breath he reassured her he would marry her again right after the visit. But he did no such thing, instead abandoning her. Sheila returned to Vancouver alone and needed quite some time to get over the emotional blow. She invited me to dinner a few times, and I must say I enjoyed these evenings a great deal, since she was not only an outstanding cook but knew her way around English literature as well.

All of this took place in 1962. We spent the summer of that year together on Saturna Island, which is one of the Gulf Islands. The approximately two hundred Gulf Islands are small and only five of them have a surface of any size: Salt Spring, Pender, Mayne, Galiano and Saturna, the last of these named for the Spanish schooner, Saturnina, whose captain, Jose Maria Navarez, discovered the island in 1791. It's hard to reach; it lies at the southern end of the Gulf Islands between Vancouver Island and the mainland of British Columbia. It's sparsely settled and, with its thirty-one square kilometers, offers everything you could wish for on an adventurous vacation:

marvelous beaches, dangerous reefs, dense forests and rich grazing land for the many sheep whose flesh is a gastronomic delicacy. We were there on July 1, Dominion Day. On this, Canada's national Independence Day, a large number of tourists came to the island to take part in the famous lamb barbecue. Many Americans reached the island on their luxurious yachts, others came in seaplanes and motorboats, the crush making it hard to find overnight accommodations. This issue didn't concern us, of course, since Sheila knew a farmer there who happened to own a major part of the island and was happy to put us up. His farm was nestled behind a chain of mountains, and everyday we would climb the 500-meter-high Warburton Mountain to get a panoramic view of the wild goats, eagles, falcons and even vultures.

It was on Saturna Island that I began to deepen my interest in English literature. As Sheila and I sat next to each other on the mountain's edge, looking down on the majestic Pacific with its frolicking seals, she would recite Shakespeare's sonnets, a few of which I was able easily to commit to memory. Then we read some plays and two novels of Thomas Hardy, *The Return of the Native* and *Tess of the d' Urbervilles.* In the evening, Sheila might cook a salmon on the beach, freshly caught from a boat the farmer gave us permission to use. She'd clean the fish, salt and pepper it, wrap it in foil and lay it on the grill where it would slowly sauté. We'd drink a bottle of white wine with our meal, usually purchased from the local vintner, who was part of the island's hearty wine culture.

We visited the farmer, Jimmy Campbell, every day to buy fresh vegetables. One morning, just after we got there, Jimmy came rushing into the house, his leg awash in blood. He'd slaughtered a cow and, while skinning it, had accidently plunged the knife deep into his own thigh. He quickly covered the open wound with sulfur powder, which slowed the bleeding a bit, long enough at least to enable him to run his motorboat over to Pender Island, which had a large hospital. As we left, he groused about the accident, not only for the injury, but also because he knew that, through his own carelessness, he'd probably wasted a good cow. When I got back, I walked over to the slaughterhouse, and, as I entered, I saw the slaughtered beast hanging from a winch. Since I'd been casting about anyway for a way to show the farmer my gratitude, I not only finished the skinning process but also fastened some cable wire around the cow's innards and pulled the whole business out with a tractor. After that I sawed the cow into two halves with a power saw. I really didn't know a thing about butchering animals, but it all turned out fine in the end. In gratitude, the farmer told us to help ourselves to as many steaks as we wanted.

Upon our return to the mainland, I went back to my job at the Hotel Vancouver. For some time already, I was no longer working in the dining room, but had been moved upstairs to the topmost floors, which were so high you could sometimes see the clouds beneath you. It was up there on every Saturday evening that a concert was given that was broadcast to all of Canada as "Music from the Top of the Town." I happened to get along very well with the headwaiter, who was quite pleased with my work, and so I was assigned the best workstation, which was the area right in front of the band. On one particular Saturday evening, I had a table with guests who showed up only a quarter hour or so before broadcast time and insisted on ordering dinner. I suggested spaghetti and meatballs, at which all four nodded. Since this dish prepared quickly, I already had the bowl with all extras arranged on a tray shortly before 8 o'clock. I was a bit nervous, as I knew the band would be starting up any minute. The ritual culminating in the downbeat always fascinated me: the bandleader would look at his watch, baton held high, the engineer would run a final check on the equipment, and the guests would wait with bated breath for the opening beats of the trombones and saxophones, played in Glen-Miller style. It was precisely at that moment that I left the kitchen with my tray, upon which sat, next to the four plates, a huge bowl brimming with spaghetti, a bowl of meatballs and a gravy bowl with extra sauce. As I kicked open the kitchen door with my foot, there directly in front of me was an assistant waiter speeding back into the kitchen; he had obviously confused the "in" door with the "out" and collided full-strength with my tray. I bounced back, but, alas, the disaster was already a *fait accompli.* My tray took off like a mini UFO, heading stage-ward, then flipped upside down, dropping the spaghetti bowl and its saucy accoutrements onto the heads of the musicians, who at just that moment were sounding the opening beats. You could scarcely hear the plates crashing down to the floor, as the deafening percussion was by then in full swing. Some might even say my crashing plates reinforced, and possibly even enhanced, the total acoustical effect. But the worst of it was the spaghetti, which dangled from the myriad tubes and slides of the trombones, looking like so much wet wash hanging on a clothesline, being tossed hither and thither as if to dry it out.

Totally fascinated by the spectacle, the audience applauded wildly. Naturally I wasn't looking for any kudos, but then, I really was blameless in the whole debacle. The applause intensified markedly, as one of the sax players turned his instrument upside down and a meatball fell out. The headwaiter dragged me into the kitchen, where he laughed until tears streamed down his face. He also took me under his wing after the show, thank God, as the musicians headed towards me looking none too happy. We served them all a free meal, and, of course, I had to wait on them. The headwaiter made a point of telling me that I was, under no circumstances, to recommend spaghetti and meatballs to them, since they'd already had that as an appetizer.

Two weeks later I left Vancouver, a city that is among the most beautiful in the world. My goal was now clear: I wanted to study German literature and culture and, to that end, I drove that weekend in my Hudson Hornet to the border town of Bellingham. There I was asked if I was interested in obtaining the precious green card,[64] coveted by so many. Eagerly I answered yes, and, within a few weeks, would have the card in hand, which felt like a kind of official welcoming gift from my new country. After a drive of four hours, I arrived in Seattle and headed straight for the institution where I was to spend the next four years: the University of Washington.

2. My Life in the United States

Sex and Romantic Irony

Everything was so different, so much more hectic, than I had imagined. I rented an apartment not far from the university, a basement flat, where I lived for the entire tenure of my study. The flat was near an apartment house Sheila had moved into, after hearing about the superior earning potential in the States. Wasting no time, I registered for the Master's program the day after my arrival. The program was structured over three academic quarters, each quarter offering four courses. In addition to that, I had to teach a beginner's course in German five times per week. My section had twenty-five students, half of them barely conscious, since class began at a, for them, ungodly 8 a.m.

The courses I took myself went beautifully, and I earned a perfect grade point average, which encouraged me in the second year to sign up for the doctoral program. The work for the Ph.D. was not at all easy, as we now had to take three courses, each of which made great demands on the students. Moreover, you always had to be well prepared, since a seminar typically had fifteen to twenty participants and involved a good deal of high-powered discussion. This motivated me to spend my evenings alone in my little room. The furnishings there were Spartan; besides a bed, table and chair, I had only a bookcase. The room was heated and cooled through a system of pipes that connected it with the neighboring room in the basement. This connection almost cost me my life.

The room next to me was occupied by a young man who was almost always at home. He was having an affair with a woman who, I was later to learn, was married to a philosophy student. His mistress would come to him every Monday, Wednesday and Friday afternoon, and, almost before you could name the first three positions of the *Kama Sutra*, they would be having at it. Nor was there anything shy or discreet about their love-making, as both were extremely passionate, and, the instant they'd had their fill of shrill and graphic descriptions of each other's ample physical assets, they would lunge at each other like starving hyenas. Naturally, I could hear every word through the pipe system, which made it hard for me to concentrate on my studies. Sometimes their erotic exchange could be intellectually suggestive, as it was, for instance, one time when I was reading Hofmannswaldau's lyric, "How He Preferred to Be Kissed," but mostly it stood in jarring contrast, particularly when it came to such classical dramas as Goethe's "diabolically humane" *Iphigenia* or *Tasso*, which latter's passionate declaration of love, "So take thou, then, my total being," could elicit from the Platonically inclined princess no more than a curt "Off with you!" (V, 4). Usually I'd go for a walk during these trysts and not return until I felt sure my neighbor had sunk down deep into the exhausted sleep of the just, or unjust, as the case may be.

After a few weeks of this, the turning point came. One evening I heard a rapping on my window, and when I opened it, I saw a young man standing outside who asked for permission to come in. Scarcely had he entered my room when he drew a pistol from his coat pocket and pointed it straight at me. Feeling more curiosity than fear, I asked him why he wanted to kill me. His explanation was astonishing, culminating as it did in his assertion that I was his wife's lover. "Three times a week," he exclaimed, "she comes to you and leaves your apartment two hours later. You're not bad looking either, and my wife has a thing for black hair and dark eyes. You don't exactly have to be a rocket scientist to find out what you two are up to. And to think, my wife told me she was taking courses during those hours. I can imagine what sort of courses she had in mind!" I assured him I was involved with another girl, to little effect. Since I'd seen him around campus a few times, I assumed he was a student, and his answer to my question confirmed it. "I'm studying philosophy in the doctoral program," he said coolly, "but don't think for a moment that would prevent me from killing you."

Just at that point, my guardian angel intervened once again. In the middle of our discussion of my alleged relationship with the man's wife, I heard my neighbor's door open and quickly close again. It wasn't long before the voluble foreplay began its usual moaning through the pipes, soon raising the curtain on the play itself. We looked at each other briefly, and he apologized. He stayed a while and we discussed Nietzsche, whose works I was just then studying in my seminar with Professor Ernst Behler. Among other things, the discussion raised the question whether it was at all possible to apprehend truth, but it all seemed so academic, given the fact that the truth was groaning so unmistakably through the pipes. Much more interesting was Nietzsche's question as to which was of greater benefit, finding out the truth or allowing oneself to be deceived, it being far easier to live with a lie than the truth. In any case, we realized that our views overlapped a great deal, and he paid me a few more visits in the course of the semester, during which we would take up profound philosophical problems over a bottle of wine. It may well be that I have him to thank for successfully completing my Nietzsche seminar with a grade of "Very good." The seminar leader, Ernst Behler, was one of my two doctoral advisors, and I have no doubt that the mingled influence of Behler and this poor cuckolded husband played a powerful role in igniting in me a love for the thought of this poet-philosopher that has endured to this day. I also learned subsequently that the husband and I shared an interest in science fiction, a genre that came alive for me after my encounter with Victor and that now gave rise to many fascinating conversations, extending well beyond the man's divorce. I was saddened to hear the news of his death from heart attack at a fairly young age.

The feverish love life of my neighbor was a symptom of the times, in which students too were deeply involved in the sexual revolution. Perhaps it had always been that way, but in earlier times we were more cautious and not so blatant about it. I remember having a young, red-haired female student of about eighteen in one of my classes, who had an eye for me. One day she came up to me after class, giving hints through both her verbal and bodily language you'd have to be brain-dead to miss. I politely declined, giving as the reason that I would never enter into such a relationship with a student, in any case not so long as she were in my class. Since we were on the quarter system, with the semester lasting only about ten weeks, she registered for the following quarter with another teaching assistant, and it didn't take long for her to show up at my office. This ploy proved fruitless, and so she came to a party in the student dormitory one evening dressed only in a sheet, with nothing underneath. We danced once, and she invited me to visit her at her parents' home the following Sunday, her parents apparently being quite affluent, what with a gorgeous house on the lake and even a stud farm. I turned this invitation down as well, thus effectively ending the relationship before it could get off the ground. I never saw her again after that.

Sex also popped up in our seminar on Romanticism, this time entirely inadvertently. This class was taught by Professor Raymond Immerwahr, a well-known expert in the field of early German Romanticism. He was a Quaker born in the States whose German was hard to understand, leading him to give his lectures in English. At first everything went quite well, since the Romantic poet, Novalis, beautifully complemented the modern novelist, Hermann Hesse, whose works we were reading in another seminar. But then the time came to take up the concept of Romantic irony. This aspect of Romanticism is based on the premise that the author creates a work, but in doing so becomes aware of its imperfection, since all created things are fragmentary and, therefore, imperfect. However mightily he may strive for perfection in his work, the author cannot overcome his awareness of human inadequacy. For this reason he distances himself from his creation and demonstrates his freedom from it by playing with his work and bursting its illusion, as is the case, for example, in Ludwig Tieck's fairytale play, *Puss in Boots*. This theory was new and, I must confess, entirely alien to me. Hoping to get a firmer grasp of the concept, I formulated a question in my best English, which at that time still had some serious lacunae: "Professor Immerwahr, do you mean to say that the Romantic poet takes pleasure to play with himself?" Scarcely had the words escaped my mouth when the entire class erupted into a roar of bestial laughter; indeed, one of the women could not regain her composure. She dashed out of class and ran straight to Professor Loeb, my esteemed adviser, reporting everything to him. I found the good professor waiting for me after class. Taking me aside, he opined with an amused smile, "Herr Schneider, what you were asking about was not Romantic irony, but rather love in, of and for itself. And that's a theme we'll take up when we get to the novella, *Cat and Mouse*, by Günter Grass, a writer who is anything but Romantic." This episode led, as you might imagine, to my being acknowledged by my classmates as an expert in this particular form of love, in which the subject and the object are identical.

At the end of my first year in the Master's program, I had an experience that was to prove significant for my future career. I'd always had a fear of speaking before a large group, probably dating back to my early youth when I was told over and over that, for me, German was a foreign language and I should not communicate in this language. But that was all I had. In any case, at the end of the academic year, we were scheduled to mount a production of a play by Gerhart Hauptmann. We selected *The Weavers*, for which I was cast in the role of the textile manufacturer, Dreißiger. Moreover, I was chosen for the coveted assignment of saying a few words to the audience before curtain about the play and its genesis. Since the prospect of speaking before so many people, including the German consul who was there by special invitation, filled me with dread, I learned my role by heart, knowing I could always count on my strong memory. There was plenty of scholarly material on Hauptmann, so I had no trouble putting together three pages, which I learned to recite in my room from memory in two days. The day of the performance arrived, and I walked out in front of the curtain slowly and deliberately, poised to deliver my bookish wisdom. I must've gotten to around (mental) page three, when I committed the lethal mistake of looking directly at the audience. Panic gripped me as I gazed into that sea of faces, and I drew a complete blank on the remainder of my well-rehearsed talk. I made several halting attempts to get back into the flow, but could do no better than a few whispered words. I fell silent. After about two minutes, which seemed an eternity to me, people began to get restless; some laughed, others giggled, and finally the chairman of the German seminar stood up to bring the introduction on stage to a successful (and merciful) end, thereby rescuing the honor of our program. I closed my eyes and waited for that big hole in the ground to appear and spirit me away to my lagoon island and my beach-chair beauty. And then something happened that defies rational explanation. All at once I felt this tsunami of inner power arise within me, paired with a sense of absolute invulnerability that I had never known before. I opened my eyes, looked slowly all around me and made a fresh start. And the talk I now gave bore little resemblance to the one I had memorized. I apologized and made reference to the fact that Hauptmann was, among other things, a poet of compassion. Spontaneously, a rich stream of ideas seemed to flow into my speech, and it must all have been well received, as the lively applause at the end would indicate. I had literally talked my way out of a crisis. And ever since, I've held the unshakable conviction that you can attain a great deal in this world, if only you can somehow manage to will it unconditionally. There is, I believe, a limitless amount of energy in each of us. You need only find access to it, and this access is gained, always and only, when you want something *no matter what*. Such was the case that evening.

Summer Schools, Eichendorff's Good-for-nothing, and My Marriage

I had to work during the summers, and right after my first year at Washington, in the summer of 1963, I had the good fortune to be assigned to teach applied linguistics at the University of Alberta in Edmonton. This was one of my minor subjects, but one I studied with great interest. I was very happy to be in Edmonton, since it gave me a chance to spend several weeks "summering" with my friends, Gerhard and Ingrid. As so often seems to happen with me, my first day of work almost turned out to be my last. In my class, which was relatively large, I had two slightly older students. As part of my run-through of the course syllabus, I announced with a mien of grave self-importance, "So, this course is an introduction to German phonetics and phonemics. Part of the course will be a laboratory for corrective phonetics. Morphology will be treated only briefly, and morphosyntactic neutralization not at all." This technical expression, which, after only a single quarter of linguistics, ended up betraying my less than firm grasp of the subject, basically meant no more than that the nominative and accusative were formally identical, as, e.g., in "*Die* Frau ist hier" (*The* woman is here) and "Ich sehe *die* Frau" (I see *the* woman). No sooner had the sentence left my mouth, when a voice resounded from the back row, where the two older students were sitting, "And just why is that?" I t turned out that both of them were from MIT, the renowned institute of technology in Boston, and already had several semesters of linguistics under their belts. What had brought them to my class was not the desire to deepen their knowledge, which was already a good deal deeper than my own, but the need to improve their somewhat shaky German. We worked out a compromise: I gave them extra instruction in pronunciation, for which they agreed to ask no further questions in class.

In the second summer, I received an appointment from Southern Illinois University in Carbondale to one of the new state-financed NDEA institutes. These institutes were established out of U.S. anxiety over the scientific advances of the Russians, whose Sputnik had set off a sort of collective American panic attack. So in 1958 the National Defense Education Act was passed, providing funds for the advanced training of teachers, who could now take courses at these summer institutes. Courses of primary focus here were those in the natural sciences, mathematics and foreign languages. I personally benefited from the law by having specialized in applied linguistics, an area containing few active experts. A further stroke of luck was that Caroll

Reed, my linguistics professor, was impressed enough with my work to recommend me for a position at the NDEA Institute at Princeton University. Needless to say, I was proud to be teaching there, the more so since NDEA institutes were given categorical rankings: the highest-ranked institute, which presumably trained the best German teachers, was at Princeton, and after number one came all the others, spread out over ranks two through four. I taught at Princeton from 1965 to 1969 and formed friendships with many of the scholarly luminaries coming from Germany, among others, with Alwin Diemer, later president of the University of Düsseldorf, and the writer, Johannes Urzidil, and his wife, whom I had as guests for frequent dinners, which were invariably occasions for stimulating conversation. Perhaps I was most impressed by Erich von Kahler, born in Prague in 1885, whom I was glad to help out as a house-sitter on many occasions, and whose knowledge and library, both, I greatly admired.

It goes without saying that it was quite an accolade to be approved to teach at such a distinguished university as Princeton without the doctoral degree. However, the other side of the coin was insecurity. After all, this was the university at which Thomas Mann and Albert Einstein had taught. Who knows but that I was now standing in the very room in which these illustrious giants had dispensed their rare wisdom to students; moreover, I was involuntarily reminded how often I'd been told in my youth that I was not an authentic German and that German could never be more than a foreign language for me. Anxiety reared its ugly head, and that head swelled menacingly the day I received a letter from the Director of the Institute informing me that I was to give a lecture on Eichendorff's tale, *From the Life of a Good-for-nothing*, to the assembled faculty and institute participants, a work scheduled to be taught in the literature courses later that term. I was familiar with this novella of the early Biedermeyer period and found it quite beautiful linguistically. So I read it through again, several times in fact, but could find nothing new or original to say about it. Then, out of the blue, an idea came to me, exactly the way Nietzsche once described it in saying that ideas come to you when *they* want to, not when *you* want them to. I had noticed that birds were frequently mentioned in Eichendorff's novella, appearing in one context or another in all ten chapters. With this in mind, I read the work through once again and, not long after, went on to deliver my first lecture to the faculty and students. I believe my *Good-for-nothing* idea had three psychic roots: first, many people regarded me as a good-for-nothing in my youth; then too, my love of birds probably played a role (one need only think of my parakeet); and, finally, longing for my old homeland. I titled my lecture, "Das Vogelbild in Eichendorffs Novelle *Aus dem Leben eines Taugenichts*" ("Bird Imagery in Eichendorff's Novella, *From the Life of a Good-for-nothing*") and became the first commentator to point out the identification of the good-for-nothing with a bird, his so-called bird's-eye-view being the main narrative perspective of the story. My lecture was well received, and I was able to shine with my new interpretation in the discussion that followed. That same year, I presented it at the Modern Language Association Conference and published it soon thereafter.[65] This was my first publication, of which I was very proud.

Princeton was an invaluable coup for me; once you've taught there, all sorts of possibilities open up for you. I worked like a man possessed, going all out for every assignment. And it didn't hurt, either, that I was a well-trained gastronome; on many an occasion I cooked tasty dishes for the faculty and participants. Once I actually grilled Porterhouse steaks for forty-four persons; with the steaks I served chanterelles that I'd browned in the pan along with some finely cut onions, splashing it all with Marsala wine and sprinkling finely chopped parsley on top. During my busy preparations for this feast, a beautiful, red-haired girl came over to me and just stood watching me closely. Then, entirely without being prompted, she simply pitched in, being rewarded in turn with the biggest steak, which she consumed with supreme delight. That was the beginning of a relationship that continued beyond the Institute and that led the following year to a wedding celebration on the family farm in her native Oregon.

She was exactly the woman I'd always wished for. Having studied in Göttingen, she spoke an outstanding German, and her father owned a pig- and sheep-breeding farm, which satisfied the wish my mother had for me. I especially liked the way she blushed when she laughed; this indicated a healthy blend of sensuality and reserve, as I knew from my reading of Gottfried Keller's novella cycle, *The Epigram*.[66] We're still together today, after more than fifty years. We complement each other perfectly: she tends to a more left-brained and I to a more right-brained orientation, so that my global ideas find their realistic grounding in her concern for detail. She is capable of hard work, and proved it the time I ran the risk of purchasing a couple of two-family houses in the same year for little down payment, with the help of the banks and the owners, of course, who granted me big second mortgages. She's bright, well-read and thoughtful, and knows her way far better than I around the Byzantine terrain of computers.

The right One

She received her Ph.D. in German and had no difficulty obtaining a position in a College where she served well-liked and highly respected by faculty and students for over thirty-five years teaching and doing administrative work. Without her I would never have been able to make such a good life for myself in this country. In addition to all this, she's an outstanding cook who was once named "Chef of the Week in the City of Syracuse," which alone guarantees us a busy social life. Being married to her is never boring; she's always bringing a swirl of new ideas into our life together.

But getting back to Princeton, my career almost came to an abrupt end during my first summer there. That came about as follows: I had a Viennese woman in my linguistics class, who had left two little daughters at home. She was married, but her husband had been declared incompetent and was institutionalized. One day she came up to me and whispered, "I've been watching you, and I've noticed that you sometimes bite your nails. I'm from Vienna, the city of Freud, and I know that this kind of behavior points to sexual frustration. I want you to know that the door to my room is always open to you, in case you should ever need a partner." At first I was dumbfounded and could only blurt out to her that I harbored no such intentions. The following week, as I was sitting with some associates at a table in a local pub, a man suddenly showed up and asked if I would please make room for him at our table. I had no reason to say no, so he sat down and introduced himself. He was from Vienna, was taking part in a physics conference on campus, and had just a few days earlier made the acquaintance of the Viennese woman, who had made me the offer, which I assume he'd accepted. The woman's husband had just now come into the bar, he said, and it sure looked as if the fellow had caught on to his wife's extracurricular activities and was looking for her lover. At first the whole business appeared to end without incident, since the poor fellow disappeared and our group too broke up and scattered. However, later that night a few women came running into my room shrieking that a man carrying a gun had broken in and was looking for his wife's lover. I called the police, and he was led away and returned to his safe haven. With that, I assumed, the matter was closed.

So you can imagine how dismayed I was to receive a letter from this man a few weeks later, just after the close of the Institute. I offer here a summary of its contents:

Dear Professor:

It is my understanding that you, sir, made a proposal of marriage to my wife, at the time she was in attendance, this past summer, at the Language Institute in Princeton.

It does not seem conceivable to me, that a man would make such a proposal to a married woman, who has two children and is living with her husband.

My reaction to this was to initiate legal proceedings against you, but then I changed my mind. In this highly scholastic and liberal atmosphere the temptation is always around the corner, and you sometimes have the inevitable.

He went on to say that I didn't resemble his wife's type, even remotely, but that this was precisely the reason she had favored me — to keep him off the trail. Finally, he mentioned that he'd sent a copy of the letter to the Director of the Institute. On reading that I felt the fear run up my spine; what would happen to me if they found this loony's story more credible than mine? I sought out a lawyer for advice, but then the very next day I received another letter from the fellow, in which he couldn't be more apologetic and even begged me to accept his apology. I did so happily and felt very relieved.

In my last year of study, I received an offer from Syracuse University. This private institution is located in New York State, about a five-hour drive from New York City. It also had the advantage of being near the Binghamton branch of the State University of New York, which housed the Arthur Schnitzler archives, which I wanted to explore. Since Sheila didn't want to go to New York with me, we went our separate ways but have remained good friends. I visit her and her husband whenever I fly to the west coast, where she lives in a beautiful house on the sea. I have much to be grateful to her for, above all that she introduced me to English literature. At my home university I received the degree of Doctor of Philosophy in the year 1968, at the age of 37.

In my doctoral dissertation, which ran nearly 400 pages, I had compared Arthur Schnitzler with Friedrich Nietzsche and, in the course of my research, had had, among other things, to read the complete works of the Austrian author and the German poet-philosopher. But the thing that particularly drew me to Schnitzler was his concern with the profound resonance of all that goes unspoken in human affairs. Schnitzler is known for works written in the style of interior monologue, such as *Fräulein Else* [67] and *Lieutenant Gustl*, but the works containing an interior monologue extend far beyond these two, notwithstanding that those works aren't usually cited in the critical literature for its use. One can, of course, read a Schnitzler text superficially and stay anchored to the written word, or one can try to sense what is hidden by the words, often cued by the numerous question marks and exclamation points that make the veil before the interior life of the characters a bit more gossamer and vouchsafe a glimpse of the mysterious. Like many others of his era, Schnitzler had a deep mistrust of the spoken and written word, which can as often conceal as reveal feeling and truth. The preverbal *basso profundo*, resonating, as it were, with the verbal treble voice, gives his literary texts an effect of depth, creating something not unlike polyphony in music, but, in literature, unique to Schnitzler. I have a feeling for this literary polyphony, which reminds me strongly of bygone days when appearances so often disguised a truly horrific reality. And how often in my life have I myself not inwardly rebelled, while outwardly wearing a friendly expression for public consumption? Unfortunately many of the themes treated by Schnitzler have lost none of their timeliness since his era, not least those of his essay of 1915, "On War and Peace," which culminates in the plea that the dictionary of war no longer be compiled by the despots but by the maimed refugees and the widows and waifs — a view that has forfeited not a jot of its truth value for today.

The Vietnam War and the Students

My last years at the University of Washington and first at Syracuse University were marked by the student revolt against the Vietnam War. The opposition movement had already gathered force in 1964, and some students made plans to evade the draft by fleeing to Canada. Aware that I had lived in Canada for years, they often invited me to their meetings, which usually had this issue on the agenda. Antiwar songs were typically sung at these rallies, most popularly "Where Have All the Flowers Gone?" by Peter, Paul and Mary, "Waist Deep in the Muddy" by Pete Seeger, and "Master of War" by Bob Dylan. Here two verses from the third of these:

> *Come you masters of war*
> *You that build all the guns*
> *You that build the death planes*
> *You that build the big bombs*
> *You that hide behind walls*
> *You that hide behind desks*
> *I just want you to know*
> *I can see through your masks*
> *You that never done nothin'*
> *But build to destroy*
> *You play with my world*
> *Like it's your little toy*
> *You put a gun in my hand*
> *And you hide from my eyes*
> *And you turn and run farther*
> *When the fast bullets fly.*

The war polarized the American people, and the majority of high school students were convinced it was a mistake.

Up to this time, I'd kept out of politics, and this for various reasons. Till then I'd never in my life taken part in an election, since in Berlin there was no enfranchisement and in Canada I wasn't a citizen. But then my attitude underwent an abrupt change. I had lived subject to many political measures which I abhorred. Also, I'd had more than *enough* of war during my life in Berlin, and I remain firmly convinced to this day that we could avoid many wars through a sufficient application of political skill and diplomacy. And so my sympathies lay with the pacifists and I endeavored to help them. The opportunity to do so came along soon enough, though in a way I could never have anticipated.

In 1966 I began my employment as an Assistant Professor of German at Syracuse University. The Syracuse campus was also weathering a revolt against the war, one that was by now becoming fierce. In front of campus buildings the students set up barricades, built with wood from snow fences, of which there were many because of the region's heavy snowfall. Many of the professors supported the protest and took part in the rallies at which the war was argued and analyzed. At the time, I was teaching a beginner's course in German and nearing the end of the second month, when a student came to my office. His problem was that he had to receive a good grade, at least a "B," in my course. Should he score a "C," he'd run the risk of being drafted. He was having trouble with German, and his grade average showed it. I thought long and hard about what, if anything, I should do. On the one hand, it was really *his* problem, since he could've studied for the course a lot harder; on the other hand, there are often cases in which the "fruit" of instruction does not blossom till much later. But time was pressing, so I decided to sit with him a few times a week and tutor him. He managed to earn a solid "B" for the course, which made him proud and kept me on good terms with my own conscience, since he'd earned the grade through his own effort. After the final exam, he took part in another demonstration in Washington, as did my wife, who flew down to D.C. one weekend after finishing her teaching at a local community college, demonstrated, and returned home that same evening.

Marriage, Burial, and the Nietzsche-Symposium

One day my wife came to me with a problem. She had a male student in her class, who had recently married a German girl. From early on the couple had determined to marry, but ended up doing so sooner than intended, in order to gain naturalization status for the girl, which would qualify her for certain tuition grants. The problem was that she hadn't said a word about it to her family in Germany. What she *had* told them was that she planned to marry that coming summer. Naturally, the entire family expressed a desire to come over from Germany to be present at the ceremony. In their perplexity, the husband asked my wife if she knew anyone who could marry them. Of course, the person wouldn't have to be a legitimate minister or official, since they were already married. The only condition was that s(he) would have to be able to conduct the ceremony in both German and English, so that all invited guests could understand it. My wife asked me if I would be willing to do it, so I made some inquiries about the legality of such a ceremony. I was assured that such an act would be legally neutral, since the two parties were already a legally married couple. Moreover, the "sham" aspect of the wedding was not a problem, and since at no time during the ceremony would I be introducing or otherwise presenting myself as a minister, I could not be accused of any abuse of authority. The "bride" took only her own sister into her confidence, who kept her mouth shut, never breathing a word of this harmless swindle to any of the family.

The wedding day was especially beautiful. It was in June, the sun was shining, and the flowers were in bloom; it was weather fit for a wedding feast, much like the one Jeremias Gotthelf describes in the opening of his novella, *The Black Spider.* "The sun rose above the mountains, shone in lucid majesty upon an amiable though narrow valley, and called to blissful life those creatures that are made to bask in its light and warmth. From gilded forest's edge the blackbird croaked its morning song, between sparkling flowers in the glistening grass sounded the lusty quail's monotonous love song, above dark fir trees rutting crows did their airy round dance or cawed tender lullabies over the thorny cradles of their unfeathered brood." The ceremony was to be held in a gazebo, open at the sides and set out on a lake. It was accessed through a narrow footbridge. At the appointed time, the formally attired guests, among them the bride's parents, the sister, and three cousins (two male and one female), walked across the bridge and took their places. Then I appeared in my doctoral robes and positioned myself in front of the guests.

As the bells began to peal, the wedding couple appeared and paced solemnly across the bridge to their seats. I greeted them and immediately proceeded with my unaccustomed official ritual, performing the ceremony partly in English and partly in German. I began with: "William, have you come here, after serious reflection and of your own free will, to enter into the bonds of matrimony with your betrothed, Heike?" I directed the same question to the bride. Then I invited the couple to exchange rings: "Please extend your right hand to each other. With this I pronounce you man and wife." The two looked at each other lovingly, and it was truly a festive moment, a sublime moment, with the mother surreptitiously wiping away her tears. Then the thought popped into my head that I had here before me a kind of captive audience, as we were on a lake and there was only a narrow bridge leading to terra firma. So I took the liberty of appending to my solemn words a quotation from Nietzsche: "In conclusion, I would like to cite the words of the great poet-philosopher, Friedrich Nietzsche, who noted that, in the selection of a life partner, it all comes down to intellectual quality: 'Upon embarking on a marriage, one should squarely face the question: are you convinced you will enjoy conversing with this woman well into old age? Everything else in marriage is transitory; the most frequent form of intercourse by far is conversational.'" The bridal couple nodded assent, and with that the official part of the ceremony was complete. We repaired to the restaurant where the wedding meal was served. After eating, the bride's father came over to me and remarked, "Reverend, those were golden words you spoke. But, you know, that was the first time I ever heard Nietzsche cited on such an occasion. I've always thought of him as the one who said, 'When you go to the woman, take the whip along.' But this quotation today I liked very much." The others apparently liked it too, since I received an invitation the following year from the bridal couple to the baptism of their first child. That ceremony, I understand, was performed by a *real* minister.

Likewise, it was a real minister who spoke the last words at my mother's burial. My mother had taken a fall while washing windows and lay unattended for several days in the cold apartment. She developed pneumonia and died two weeks after being admitted to the Virchow Hospital. Each week I flew from Syracuse to Berlin, but the third time I arrived a day too late, delayed by a dense fog that held up the landing of my connecting flight from Syracuse to JFK Airport. My mother had died during the night. Since she had meticulously arranged every detail of her own burial well in advance—so characteristic of her—there were no difficulties. A few years before her death, we went together to Lehmann Burials and Cremations, where my mother and Frau Lehmann sat down together and shared a cup of coffee. My mother expressed her concerns: she wanted to be buried, in a casket somewhere in the mid-price range. To start with, Frau Lehmann showed her some cheap plywood caskets, followed by a few made of spruce, but my mother just sniffed, "Frau Lehmann, Gerd is my only son, and I don't want people talking about him. There's already been more than enough of that in the past. And a cheap casket 'll only give rise to wagging tongues. People will say about him, 'Oh yeah, there goes the rich son, who's living it up in America these days, but doesn't even show the slightest respect to his poor dead mother, who had to go through so much for his sake. He couldn't do any better than to stick her in a wooden crate for her final journey.' So, Frau Lehmann, I'd like a casket he needn't be ashamed of." So we finally got down to business and checked out all the caskets on display in the storeroom. One was made of beech wood, of a beautiful burnished red-brown hue. This is the one my mother chose. But that was only the beginning. Then the discussion between these two women who had known each other for many years went into the finer details. The next issue was the burial shroud. There were full shrouds, i.e., those with both front and backsides, and also others that only covered the front. My mother selected a full shroud, quipping as she did, "Frau Lehmann, I've never worn anything but frocks that covered all of me, and I've no intention of making an exception for my final journey. When the time came for me to appear before my God, I'd be mortified if He asked me to turn around." The next questions had to do with candles and floral arrangements on display: how many, how much, etc. Naturally, my mother had worked all this out in her mind well in advance. She wanted the chapel ceremony to be scheduled for around 11 a.m. When I asked her why, she said, "Gerd, the chapel services and the flowery sentiments expressed by the minister — all that begins at 8 a.m. sharp and usually lasts no more than a half hour per deceased — you know very well there are only 'little corpses' buried in our *Dankesfriedhof,* since it's only the little people who get laid out here in the first place. And they leave all the floral decorations there in the chapel for a while. I'm convinced you won't have to spend any money on flowers, and the other dearly departed ones won't mind a bit." And so it was, just as my mother said: there were more than enough gorgeous flowers on hand for her ceremony, kindly left behind from the chapel services preceding hers.

The problem, to be sure, lay in finding a proper minister at all. Our own Nazareth Church had one, of course, but he was, as he put it, up to his ears in work. Strangely, though, the instant he was informed that I was from America, his face lit up and he promised — even insisted on — giving the graveside eulogy. What I didn't know at the time was that he was busily engaged in carrying out archaeological excavations for the Vatican, after having discovered some catacombs whose walls were covered with beautiful Byzantine mosaics. The talk he gave in the chapel was not exactly what I was expecting: he began by perfunctorily reading off a few dates from a scrap of notepaper and then went on to speak for almost an hour about his excavations, lauding the glories of the mosaics, which my mother certainly would've appreciated, had she only been alive to see them, etc., etc. Concluding his sermon, he gave thanks to God that the son of this woman had returned to Berlin from his beloved America and that my path had led me to him. It sounded as if my mother had had to die just so that he could make my acquaintance. And that's exactly what the man believed, asking me after the burial to invite him to America, as it had long been his dearest wish to set foot on the shores of democracy just once. The following year I did invite him; he stayed in our cellar and even gave a few lectures at the university, which people had trouble understanding, since his English was poor. One day he made himself a few sandwiches, hopped a bus and was off to Washington to see the President. Of course, that didn't happen, but he did get to take a tour of the White House, which tickled him.

What was perhaps the coup of my academic carrier also falls into this period. I had read Nietzsche very carefully, since he lay at the heart of my dissertation and had in many ways strongly influenced my own views. Also, in the Musarion edition of his works I had come across a brief remark of his, to the effect that the ideal man was a mixture of Prussian and Jew, thus a blend of corporeal strength and intellect, and I must say this gave me the feeling of being thoroughly "authenticated" in my own existence. And so I made plans to organize an elaborate Nietzsche symposium at Syracuse University. I canvassed all the relevant academic departments and won their support for the project. It wasn't long before some $15,000 was in the till. Then I submitted an application to the National Endowment for the Humanities, which promptly gave its approval. The only snag was that I had budgeted the project for $30,000, of which half was to be provided by the applicant (i.e., me). But it seems the experts in Washington misread the budget statement, granting me the entire amount. Nor were they in a position to take back any of the money, as they had all left for recess. So I really had no choice but to put on not merely an elaborate but a lavish symposium. I invited Nietzsche specialists from all over the country, such as Walter Kaufmann, who had done so much to spread the philosopher's fame throughout the United States with his translations; Rollo May, the renowned American existentialist psychologist; and Paul de Man, who enjoyed an international reputation for his deconstructionist literary criticism.[68] Judged by prevailing standards, I paid these scholars very well and spent the remaining funds for enough wine and hors d'ouvres to feed a small army. This maximized enjoyment for the almost six hundred participants and insured a Dionysian intensity to the discussions for the entire three days. It was doubtless the success of this project that moved Paul Simon, the then U.S. congressman and later senator from Illinois, to dub me a "mover" at the university in his book, *The Tongue-tied American*. In the years that followed, I continued to enjoy a lively correspondence with the symposium lecturers, often seeking their advice in matters related to my publications.

Magic Mountain Atmosphere in the German School at Middlebury College

In the summer of 1973, I began what would become a "tradition" of summer teaching at Middlebury College, nestled in the exquisite landscape of rural Vermont. I was hired primarily for my training in applied linguistics, especially phonology. All future German teachers in the program were required to take this course to maximize their competence to teach proper pronunciation of German to their own students. Upon completing the summer program, the students had the option of taking the Master's degree at the university in Mainz within one year. Through this stay abroad they typically acquired a superior command of German and, upon returning to the States, had no difficulty securing a teaching position at a high school or junior college. In my very first summer at Middlebury, I had the great good fortune to meet the writers, Martin Walser and Hellmuth Karasek. I also sat in on Walser's seminar on irony, in which he lectured on Goethe's novel, *Wilhelm Meister*, and on Kafka and generated a plethora of stimulating ideas which we would continue to discuss in small groups far into the evening. Karasek shone through his wonderful ability to turn a phrase and through the many personal experiences with which he regaled us. All in all it was a summer that made a deep impression on me, and I must confess that I always nursed the hope of repeating the experience during the subsequent seventeen summers I spent there, but that particular summer of 1973 was unique and would not happen again. It was only when Peter Bichsel and Günter Kunert, both of whom I greatly admired as writers and as men, taught there that I felt an echo of that Aha-experience of the new and the interesting.

I don't mean to say that the summers that followed were in any sense of an inferior quality, just not quite so exhilarating as that first one. My good fortune at Middlebury continued apace, as I was asked whether I'd be interested in building up the undergraduate program. That turned out to be a story in itself. Middlebury College was renowned throughout the country for its graduate school and for producing graduates with a superior mastery of German. On the very first day, all students must take a pledge to speak only German for the next six weeks. The initial reservation about expanding the undergraduate program was that the beginners would use too much English, thus gradually eroding the "German-only" tradition, which would in turn tend to undermine the school's reputation. For this reason it was decided that the undergraduate program would run for seven weeks, so that beginners would already have a week of German under their belts before the advanced students arrived. On the other hand, not having an undergraduate program at all ran the risk of serious student attrition, since even then there were dire predictions in the air of decreasing enrollments in German. Since the College was a private institution, it was completely dependent on its income. The Program for Beginners in German had started up in 1973, and the number of students in that first group was a mere seven. I saw an opportunity here to build something totally new, and, confident as I was of the administration's full support, I took over the program. My plan was to focus entirely on quality, since that is the fastest and most efficient way to become well known. As a rule, summer students came from other universities and returned to those universities, and I saw this as an ideal arrangement for promoting the quality of the program. The following summer I added a second year to the Beginners Program, then in subsequent years a third and eventually a fourth. In this way I managed to form a complete curriculum, extending from beginning German up to and including the fourth year, with qualified fourth-year students even having access to one or two graduate-level courses.

Soon I introduced so-called modules, i.e., half-courses lasting three weeks which conformed to the interests of students and in which they could study their own major subject in German, be it art history, philosophy or political science. This heightened their motivation, inspiring many to throw themselves into the work with abandon. At both the beginning and the end of the program, they had to take a test devised by the MLA (Modern Language Association) to provide an objective documentation of their progress. The results were exceptionally good, with most students scoring in the top classification, which meant that they could return to their home universities, including the Ivy League schools, and skip one or even two class-levels in German. It goes without saying that the program wouldn't have become as successful as it did, had I not hired outstanding faculty. In this regard, I would mention above all Jochen Richter of Allegheny College and Karl Obrath of the University of Cincinnati, who were quartered with the students in the dormitory and who made themselves available to them at all times to discuss any academic or personal problems that might arise. Obrath's wife, Lilian, was a painter and a highly gifted sketch artist who captured many of the scenes and events of the program in her drawings, often accompanied by her own, and sometimes her husband's, wry commentary.

In the States the program was assessed as exemplary and much written up in the press. To this day I remain in contact with many of its former participants, individuals who today occupy high places in industry and academe, and we still enjoy reminiscing about the many people and events that made life interesting in this program that was so charmingly sequestered from the outside world. Many of the students are now teachers themselves and practice in their classes many aspects of the pedagogy by which they were taught in their own classes. We always strove to deal with students on an individual basis, since each one has different interests and learns differently. This principle I inherited from a wise former teacher, Ernst Loeb. At the beginning of my career, he told me the tale of how Michelangelo is supposed to have created his famous Pietà. He went to the stone quarry where he spent days carefully examining the various blocks of marble, none of which met his expectations. Then finally coming upon a particular block that, to ordinary eyes, looked no more promising than the rest, he took it and shaped it into the Pietà, not by chiseling his idea into the stone, but by removing from the stone everything that was not part of the Pietà. For he had seen that the Pietà was already resting there inside the block; one had only to liberate it, by discarding what did not belong to it. You have to know your students in some depth, my teacher continued, in order to see what is dormant in them, and then liberate it. It doesn't always go according to plan, but when it does — and you never know this till much later — your mission as a teacher is fulfilled.

The program was cloistered from the outside world in the truest sense. This became clear to everyone in relatively short order, as the participants were forced to speak only German and watch German films (without subtitles). The advanced students even listened to lectures given in German. None of this was easy, and we lost some who were just not up to the pressure.

The well-known painter and sketch artist Lilian Obrath, wife of my colleague Karl Obrath, has sketched the developmental career, with all its attendant agonies, of a student in the seven-week program for beginners with deft humor:

It was, in the truest sense of the expression, a magic mountain atmosphere that captivated you fully and completely. The students were carefully selected and possessed that most important skill of time management; they knew how to proportion their time to achieve the optimal balance of study and relaxation. They spent their time not only at their desks and in the language lab but also playing communicative sports such as football and volleyball, in which they could "try out" the language they'd just learned.

This didn't always go as well as one might wish, but with patient correction they would stick with it and gradually improve. The advanced students, who'd already studied in Germany, would also teach the others a lot of, shall we say, questionable expressions, which, of course, were always and without exception immediately and indelibly committed to memory.

For me as a language teacher, it's a wonderful experience to observe how students learn a foreign language. The dictionary is, of course, a big help, but not always. I recall a female student who, in an essay on the disposal of nuclear waste in Germany, wrote that it was beerdigt" (interred). She'd looked up the word "bury" in her dictionary and, of course, found under it a long list of different meanings; she'd simply chosen the wrong one. In reading through their written work, it gives you pause for thought to see how students attempt to describe their most personal feelings in a language still so strange and new to them. One summer I was teaching second-year German, the level on which students are introduced to literature. I'd selected the story, *Outside at the Door*, by Wolfgang Borchert.[69] From a linguistic point of view, this text is ideal for classroom instruction, and we took our reading of it as a point of departure for our discussions of post-war Germany. Then the students were assigned to write an essay for class, in which they were to record their own thoughts, feelings and impressions. Many years later, when I ran into one of the female students from this group and reminded her of the essay she'd written on Borchert's story, she grew suddenly thoughtful and revealed to me that the assignment had virtually thrown her into an emotional crisis. She became unbearably sad at the thought that there must've been very many Germans in the post-war period who suffered the same fate as the tragic hero Beckmann.

Another experience in the summer program will suffice to illustrate the intense single-mindedness with which the students set about mastering German. It was the first week of the program and I had asked my colleagues to meet with me in my room for a conference. All of a sudden we smelled smoke coming from the stairs, which seemed to grow stronger with each breath. I stepped out of the room and saw a student rushing down the stairs holding a dictionary in his hand. I asked him in English where the smoke was coming from. He merely looked at me with astonishment and stammered "Da ist . . . " [There's . . .]. Then faltering, he paged furiously through his dictionary. Meanwhile my anxiety was going through the roof, since a fire in danger of spreading could be catastrophic, and once again I pressed him in English. He just waved me off, articulating in an even voice the words, "Wir sprechen hier nur Deutsch" [We speak only German here], a sentence I had been drumming into the heads of all program participants from day one. Then once again sticking his nose in his dictionary, he finally ended his sentence with "ein Feuer in Etage vier" [a fire on the fourth floor]. I darted upstairs and found a student asleep with an empty wine bottle at his feet. His lit cigarette had fallen onto the mattress and burnt a big hole in it. We woke him, dragged the mattress outside, where it lay smoldering for two days, and sent the student back upstairs to his room. Before leaving, he asked us how to say "upstairs" in German. We told him, and as he headed up, we could hear him murmuring, "ich gehe nach oben . . . wir gehen nach oben . . . ihr geht nach oben" [I'm going upstairs . . . we're going upstairs . . . you're going upstairs]. He was happy to have learned something new.

Then we had a student in the beginners program who lived by the reality principle that everything he learned in theory must be applicable to some practical situation. This approach to learning caused him some difficulty with certain pattern-drill sentences in our textbook which the authors had obviously included out of some misguided sense of humor or amusement. One of the sentences read: "Inge fiel aus dem Bett" [Inge fell out of bed], a patently ridiculous sentence which we always just passed over in silence in class. However, this student insisted that he had a right to every sentence in the textbook, since he'd paid a lot of money for it. So he asked his instructor for the meaning of the sentence, and was told as much. When the hour was over, the student went to his room with furrowed brow and gave the matter a great deal of thought. Finally he came up with a solution to his "reality requirement" problem.

There was a student in the program named Inge, and he took to sitting with her at lunch in the cafeteria. Soon they were studying together, and one day he came into my room beaming with joy to inform me in his best German: "Inge fiel aus dem Bett." I looked at him in astonishment and was about to question him when he cut me off, calmly adding "Aber sie ist o.k." [But she's o.k.]. My instincts told me to let the matter rest there, which I did, but I made it a point to write to the authors of the textbook, requesting that they delete that particular sentence from the next edition, since there was no way to know what further havoc it might wreak in this magic mountain atmosphere.

Living with the students within the same four walls, tooth by jowl, so to speak, is an experience that makes the teaching profession one of the most beautiful. But, of course, it also brings its own unique complications. I had structured the classes in such a way that participants' problems, whether personal or academic, could be dealt with more or less as they arose, without the necessity of waiting on a teacher or committee. Each Friday class participants were asked to write down and hand in any problems. Some of them did, and these were immediately read aloud in class and discussed, provided the participants had checked off the box labeled "Diskussion" on the form. One day I read the following note aloud, which was of course written in German: "I'm so ashamed. My room is in the basement, which has a concrete floor. Since it's so hot, and there's no air conditioning, I bought a small exhaust fan, which I've placed on the floor and which runs all night. And 'run' it does — literally! — since its rotations cause it to actually start 'wandering' around the room. It's a real *Wanderventilator.* Since my room is small, it doesn't take long for it to get stuck under my bed and start banging against the wall. What must the people in the next room think of me? I don't even have a boy friend, and I go to church every Sunday. I'm so ashamed. What can I do?" In this case the answer was simple: just placing a small rug under the fan kept it from wandering around the room.

Other problems weren't so simple. These young people were living away from home for the first time, the family home usually quite a distance away, and many of them didn't always confide in their parents in any case. One summer, just as I was moving into my room on the fourth floor of the dorm, I noticed a girl quickly disappearing into a room opposite mine. She was carrying only a small purse and a guitar. She was eighteen years old and would be entering Yale University that Fall as a freshman. She wanted to get a head start on German before beginning at Yale, so as to assure herself of a strong start when she got there. Although she was a beginner, she learned very quickly and asked excellent questions when she didn't understand something. One day she didn't show up for class, nor did I see her in the cafeteria at mealtimes. I knocked on her door and found her just sitting there on top of her table, her guitar on her lap, looking gloomily through the window at the mountains. She wouldn't answer my questions of concern, leaving me no choice but to leave her alone. When she failed to appear in either class or cafeteria the next day, I brought some dinner on a tray to her room, set it down and pressed her for an explanation. She looked at me and burst into tears. Then she showed me a letter she'd received from her boyfriend, her first boyfriend. He wrote her that he'd met someone else. I sat down and had a long talk with her, finally persuading her to come back to class. She showed up the next morning, and all the mornings thereafter, plowing through the

211

textbook in record time, so that she placed into the intermediate level at Yale. She was one of the best students I've ever taught.

At the end of the program, we said goodbye and she gave me an envelope containing a story she'd written in German and even illustrated, all on her own. It's worth noting that this girl had had no more than six weeks of German. As I read her story, which amounted to a kind of mini-autobiography, it occurred to me that young people who are just beginning to acquire a foreign language sometimes show an ability to express themselves in that language with striking guilelessness, displaying feelings with a disarming candor and vulnerability. Their expression resembles a picture that they present to you without a frame, allowing you to immerse yourself totally in the "language-picture" alone. Whereas in the advanced classes, after students have amassed a substantial vocabulary, they are in a position to hide their feelings behind the words, and the picture they now give of themselves and their feelings is neatly fitted (more or less, according to individual facility) into a beautiful frame that at times displays baroque or even rococo embellishment and that may often seduce your focus away from the picture itself to aesthetic considerations. Only much later is it possible for that inchoate immediacy of expression to manifest itself again, but even then only after a great deal of hard-won maturity and experience. Long after that time, when I came to reread Heinrich Kleist's wonderful essay, "On the Marionette Theater," I had to think back on this girl's story and so many other "beginner's pictures" like it. In his essay Kleist describes how innocence and gracefulness become lost to our conscious life, but then he considers that sometimes it's possible to reproduce this pure condition, or, as he himself says at the end, "[We'd have to] eat again from the tree of knowledge, in order to fall back into the state of innocence!" Not many manage this.

Sometimes there were also minor catastrophes. Once, at an opening ceremony, when alcohol was still permitted on campus, we popped the corks on some bottles of wine while getting to know one another. I was talking with a female student who seemed very enthusiastic as she told me how her parents, who owned an island in the Thousand Islands region of upstate New York, had had her flown to campus. Suddenly she tossed her glass into the air and collapsed. My friend Jochen and I wondered what we should be doing for her. Jochen suggested opening her blouse so that she could breathe better, but that struck me as too chancy. Then, noticing the girl was wearing a wristband, I read on it that this attack would only last a moment or two and that she would promptly regain consciousness. This she did and then told me that she suffered from a certain blood disease for which there was at that time no treatment. But she always knew precisely one second before an attack that she was about to fall down and always made sure she fell in such a way as to avoid injuring herself or anyone else. We quickly got used to these attacks, which could occur anywhere, in class or in the cafeteria, and came to regard them as routine. One time, however, while we had a visiting female dean with us whom we'd invited to the cafeteria for lunch, it transpired (inevitably!) that the girl, who happened to be sitting next to her, threw her arms up in the air and dropped down onto the floor. Naturally we all just continued eating undisturbed, while the dean jumped up in a rage and screamed that she'd never known colleagues or students who could be so inhuman as to allow such a thing to happen without so much as putting their forks down. She stormed out of the cafeteria without waiting for the girl to come to. The girl sat down again and finished her lunch.

Another time I was having dinner with a small group at a table in the cafeteria. Sitting nearby was a female student who also studied at Middlebury during the regular academic year. Not only was this girl very pretty, she was also provocatively dressed, wearing a blouse with a plunging neckline that was quite an eye-catcher for the young men at the table. Every now and then as we ate, we seemed to catch a fleeting glimpse of a rat's head in the girl's cleavage. In and out the head would go, quick as a flash. But we just kept eating, not quite believing what we were seeing. Again and again the head would pop out, only to dart back in. Finally the whole rat presented itself, crawled down the girl's arm and, perching itself at the bottom, stared at us with glinty eyes. A teacher sitting at our table jumped up and cried out, "I only had two glasses of wine before dinner, but I think they did me in. Usually you only see white mice, but this is an anomaly: I see a white rat!" And he was quite right, it was a white rat, as the others were quick to confirm. Meanwhile the girl had run off to her room, locked herself in and wouldn't open up for anyone. It wasn't until the fire department arrived and climbed up into her garret on an extension ladder that the girl and her pet rat were extricated. The bottom line was that the girl was punished and the rat taken away. The reason for the latter was that her room was so unhygienic that the SPCA ordered the rat's removal FOR ITS OWN GOOD! Besides this, college statutes prohibited students from keeping pets in their rooms.

There were two problem cases that remain especially green in my memory. One summer at the start of the term, a long limo pulled up in front of our dorm. The chauffeur got out, opened the rear door and out stepped a young girl. Since I was sitting outside on the lawn at the time, she came up to me and asked where she could find her suite. This confused me a bit, as girls usually slept in a double room. I checked my book and found that this girl had actually booked two adjacent double rooms. She asked where the elevator was. When I told her there wasn't any, she had her chauffeur carry her caravan of trunks and suitcases up to her rooms. That evening she made her debut appearance in the cafeteria wearing an expensive outfit, one she had recently picked up in Europe, as she smugly announced to anyone who asked. It was quite a show she was putting on, but one that became completely understandable to me once I had a look at her personal file in the office: her father was the CEO of a large, well-known refrigerator company, was reputed to be as rich as Midas and had numerous residences in the States and Europe. His daughter had never known anything but a life of luxury and came here expecting nothing less. Moreover, she'd always been privately schooled and it was only now, as she prepared to enter one of the elite universities, that she would finally be mingling with the great unwashed. She wanted to study German at Middlebury to give herself a head start. It took no more than two weeks of summer school for this girl to undergo a complete transformation: she sent some suitcases home, dressed like everybody else and behaved like one of the gang. Little remained of her former star allure.

The other problem was more dire, at least at the start. One summer we had a participant who was living off-campus. Her husband had booked her into a suite of rooms at the expensive Middlebury Inn, located not far from the college. She came to class faithfully, but always went straight back home afterwards, avoiding all participation in program events, which we regarded as essential, as they gave students invaluable opportunities to practice their German. I asked her to come to my office for a chat, which she did. At first she was somewhat hesitant, but it wasn't long before the floodgates opened up: her husband was very rich and was carrying on an open affair with a younger woman, with whom he was accustomed to traveling about for weeks at a time. He frequently reproached her for being too psychologically ill to care properly for their little son, whom she loved very much. She was far too browbeaten and intimidated by him to contradict him, not even when he suggested she attend the summer school — an obvious ploy on his part to clear the way for a summer of adultery. Since she had some previous German, she was placed in the upper classes, which I was teaching. I noticed almost at once an extraordinarily creative quality in her essays. She was obviously a talented writer. I had another long chat with her, in which I indicated that she might well have a fruitful writing career ahead of her, provided, that is, that she would be willing to undertake the risk of the new and strange. Her self-confidence increased markedly, and she befriended an older man who had formerly been a judge and who, with his wife, was also renting a room in the Middlebury Inn. This man had long nursed the wish to read some of the original German records of a trial of which he had been one of the judges. This was none other than the Nuremberg Trials. Two years later I received two thank-you letters in the same week: one from the wife of the former judge, in which she informed me of her husband's death, but added that, thanks mainly to the astute tutoring of my student, his dearest wish had been fulfilled: he'd been able to study the original trial proceedings, which made him very happy. The other came from the woman, who wrote that she had divorced her husband, was presently living with her son and was enrolled at a university preparing for a career as a writer of short stories.

Not only were there problems with students but, at times, with faculty as well, particularly individuals who had no experience with American students and who were, shall we say, somewhat over-committed to the principle of achievement. One summer at the beginning of school, a professor of *Germanistik*, who was highly respected in the Federal Republic, came to my office and asked for my advice. The problem was, he said, that the students were dropping his course in droves right in the first week and switching to other sections. He knew he was doing something wrong but had no idea what it could be. So I sat in on his class, which I found most informative and conducted by all the soundest pedagogical strategies, which led me to conclude that his teaching wasn't the issue. Then I asked to see the written homework he had assigned the students. The assignment was to write an approximately two-page commentary on a review article. Some students did quite well with the assignment, while others had serious difficulties. Beyond the usual grammatical mistakes the essays were weak in both style and substance. Extremely conscientious as he was, the instructor marked every mistake with thick red ink and wrote long commentaries (*auf deutsch natürlich*). One of these read as follows: "You've turned in a very defective assignment. You possess neither the grammatical foundation essential to such an assignment nor the vocabulary essential to a nuanced analysis. Your work also clearly shows that you have completely misunderstood the central idea of the article. It is also evident from your summary that it was written in haste; the numerous careless errors, which I have marked in your text, could easily have been corrected, had you bothered to proofread your work before turning it in. Please examine your text carefully and rewrite it; then submit it to me again tomorrow in class." These comments instantly revealed the problem to be one of a clash of cultures, and I explained to the astonished professor that American students, for whom German is a foreign language, have a strongly negative reaction to such blunt criticism. In response to his question as to how things were done around here, I suggested to him the following rewording: "I can see from your work that you've put a great deal of effort into it. Still, some aspects of the article under discussion did not receive the emphasis they deserved, with the result that the central idea of the article is not brought out clearly enough. I suggest that you read the article again, noting down the main thoughts as you do, and bring them to me in my office hour, so that we can discuss the structure of your essay together. It would be best if you came this afternoon, as I would like to have your final summary in hand by tomorrow afternoon at the latest." All it took was a little diplomacy. From then on his classes went swimmingly and the hemorrhaging of students was completely stanched. Moreover, over time the students' performance came closer and closer to matching his expectations.

Another highly esteemed professor, one holding a chair in *Germanistik* at a German university, had a different problem. He'd written many books, trained many doctoral candidates and was an outstanding pedagogue. He taught his classes in the morning and generally spent the afternoons working on his publications. I got to know him on the very first day of summer school, when he came to me and asked if I could help him out. The problem was that he was in the habit of taking a glass of red wine in the afternoon, since it was good for his general health and particularly for his heart. Unfortunately, however, he'd forgotten to pack a corkscrew, leaving him unable to tap into his most important "medicine bottle." To make matters worse, he'd also forgotten to bring an English dictionary along with him, so that he couldn't even go into town to pick one up, and besides, his knowledge of English was pretty much confined to literary terminology, from which the word "corkscrew" was noticeably absent. I happened to have an extra one and gave it to him. He was very grateful, and we went on to enjoy many interesting discussions that summer, sometimes with and sometimes without a glass of red wine.

This professor had no interest in sports, but he did have a hobby: he enjoyed playing the organ. He had plenty of opportunity to do so at Middlebury College, as the little cathedral nearby, built in New England style, had an excellent instrument that was played on all festive occasions. The commencement ceremony of that summer's program was just such an occasion: at it, diplomas were given out, not just to the students in the German school, but to those in all schools. The professor was entrusted with the important task of playing the organ. To start off, he sat down at the instrument and played a ceremonial march, in time with which first the faculty, then the dignitaries of the College and finally the president of the College accompanied by the speaker filed in in procession and took their places on the chairs set up for them on stage. It was very hot in the church, which had no air conditioning, and the speaker droned on and on, resulting in a significant weakening of the attention spans of all those in attendance. This included the organist, who, having of course taken his medicinal glass of wine beforehand, grew groggier by the minute, finally laying his head down on the keys of his instrument and, a moment thereafter, falling fast asleep. Nor did he even wake up when the ceremony came to an end, with everybody standing there waiting for the organ recessional, which would at last liberate them from that sacred sauna and allow the real celebration to begin outdoors. Finally the bellows treader ran up into the choir loft and shook him awake. He looked down at us absently, slowly realizing that all eyes were riveted on him, and suddenly grasped that he was supposed to be playing. Pouncing on his instrument, he began the recessional at the prescribed tempo. But then something seemed to come over him, contorting his face into a devilish smile; he hit the keys again and modulated the tempo into something resembling . . . boogie, followed in short order by a waltz. The faculty did its best to move in time with the rhythm, but was thrown into confusion by its rapid shifts, ultimately becoming caught up in a kind of St. Vitus dance as it hopped and skipped its way out of the chapel, academic caps and gowns jerked up and down as if draped over puppets. The organist looked down, regarded the spectacle he had instigated with his medley of rhythms and burst into laughter so piercing, so demonic, that it reverberated off the cathedral's high Gothic walls. And all there laughed along with him, all, that is, except the faculty, who by now were assembled outside in front of the chapel trying to catch their breath and getting wet into the bargain, as it had just begun to rain.

Then too, I had a problem of my own to struggle with, one that almost cast me in the role of a demon myself. It had to do with my eyes and started when I was working on a committee with John Rassias of Dartmouth College, a well-known pedagogue whose method of language instruction had often been featured in the press and on TV. The method, called the Dartmouth Intensive Language Model, is based on the assumption that language acquisition is not simply an intellectual process, but an emotional one as well, and that the body language of the instructor, particularly his gesticulatory behavior, which can at times be quite unusual, even provocative, contributes a great deal to the student's acquisition of the foreign language. One day Rassias gave me the following advice: "Gerd, when you're teaching and you ask someone a question, look deep into the student's eyes, so that he or she has the feeling that there's no one else in the world and that the universe consists of the two of you alone." I wasted no time testing this advice at Middlebury, putting a question to a female student as I knelt down in front of her and looked her deeply in the eyes, attempting to create a universe for the two of us. The result? The student looked back at me, her eyes glazing over as she became rooted to the spot. She'd been literally put under a spell or hypnotized by my stare, and, what was worse, she was rendered speechless. The experiment had backfired. I repeated it a few more times in Middlebury and Syracuse, usually with the same success, or should I say, pedagogical lack of success. Perhaps the worst incident of this sort occurred once during an oral exam sanctioned by the Goethe Institute, an organization I represented in those days as an official examiner for the Central New York region, an area extending roughly from Binghamton to Buffalo. A woman, whose eyes I had transfixed with my own, became unable to answer the questions put to her; the exam was stopped and then continued later without me. The same thing even happened once outside the classroom: driving back to Syracuse from Middlebury with my friend Jochen, we pulled up at a restaurant for a break. The waitress who'd taken our order couldn't move from the spot. She clung to the table for dear life and had to be pulled from it and led away by the manager. Since then I've become very cautious about looking people in the eye.

The quality of the undergraduate program attracted students. This led in the following years to an increase in the number of students from seven to over one-hundred-twenty, while the number of graduate students dropped significantly. One result of the program's success was that I became well known in the country. I was elected to the Executive Committee of the Modern Language Association and the Central Committee of NYSAFLT (New York State Association of Foreign Language Teachers), the largest association of teachers of foreign languages in the state of New York. In 1982 I was chosen by the latter organization as best teacher on the university level in the state of New York:

Honored by colleagues

Two years later another honor came my way: students at Syracuse University selected me best teacher of that year in the undergraduate program:

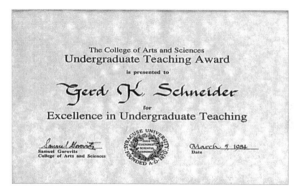

...and by students

At the award ceremony my mind went to the essay "On Language" by Hugo von Hofmannsthal, in which the author writes that there are, among foreign language teachers, some very good and bright people, his explanation being "that almost all of them used to be something else, that is to say, real people . . . . And it's almost always the case that they teach their own language in a foreign land." This certainly applies to me. That same year I also received the "Certificate of Merit," which bore the inscription: "The Goethe Institutes in the United States together with The American Association of Teachers of German (AATG) bestow this Certificate of Merit upon Gerd Schneider for outstanding achievements in furthering and encouraging the study of German language and culture in the United States of America."

The Ambassadors' Meeting

In 1987 I sat on the Executive Committee of the AATG, the largest association of German teachers in the United States, encompassing both college and high school teachers. In my very first year I was appointed secretary of the association; my signal achievement by far in the Central Committee of the AATG lay in being responsible for the organization's annual meeting, which took place from November 17th-19th, 1990, at the Opryland Hotel in Nashville, Tennessee. Since the enrollments in American *Germanistik* had been in decline for some time, I wanted to do something special for this meeting. So I wrote to all the ambassadors of the German-speaking countries asking them to come to the meeting and, as members of a panel discussion, to speak about the role of German instruction within the framework of their cultural relations, as German-speaking countries, with other countries, and to address as well pressing political problems of their own countries. Everyone I wrote to agreed to participate, so we had among us Dr. Jürgen Ruhfus from the Federal Republic of Germany, Dr. Friedrich Hoess from the Republic of Austria and General Secretary Christian Blickendorfer from the Swiss Embassy. Also participating in the discussion were Dr. Josef Joffe, the then editor for foreign policy for the *Süddeutsche Zeitung*, and other high-profile Germanists. The session was an enormous success, and the ambassadors also did their best to lend financial support to the general meeting.

I had the palpable feeling at that time of having reached a new stage in my life, for I was now in a position to deal as a virtual equal with highly placed government representatives, to discuss interesting and relevant topics with them. The best thing about it was that I was now respected (*geachtet*) by them, whereas until 1945 I'd only been disrespected (*geächtet*). I was struck at the time by the enormous significance that could accompany the dropping of an umlaut. Since it had been decided to give representatives of all the German-speaking countries an opportunity to take part in the discussion, I'd also notified Dr. Gerhard Herder, the ambassador of the German Democratic Republic in Washington. An interesting sidebar to this is that I received an anonymous letter in October warning me not to get my expectations up regarding the appearance of the GDR ambassador. And, as it turned out, Dr. Herder was indeed a no-show, since, by the time the meeting opened, the German Democratic Republic had ceased to exist.

At the meeting I also met up with the well-known German writer, Stephan Heym, whom I'd come to know in the recent past. It was in 1987, to be precise, and came about as a result of my having been sent, as a member of a delegation from the AATG Central Committee, to West Germany (to Bonn and Berlin among other places), for the purpose of interviewing government officials and reporting the results of those interviews at meetings back in the States. The East German government got wind of our visit and invited us to visit East Berlin. We were whisked through the border checkpoint at the Friedrichstraße station without even showing our papers and brought directly to the GDR Writers' Association, of which Stephan Heym was a member. We asked a lot of questions and answered all questions put to us as best we could. During a coffee break I happened to mention to Heym about my early past in Berlin; he seemed interested, so I went on to tell him my story in some detail. He listened attentively and then advised me to put everything down on paper and publish it, adding that it would be a shame if these experiences were lost to posterity. When I ran into Heym and his wife a few years later at the meeting in Nashville and joined them at their table, he could only recognize me by my voice, as his eyesight had become very weak. He repeated his advice to me to publish my experiences as soon as possible, since we were no longer spring chickens. I promised him I would.

Before returning to the States, I paid another visit to my old Berlin friends to say good-bye. I loved spending time with Felicitas and her husband, Leo Kornbrust. Leo, a former professor at the Academy of Fine Arts in Munich, had been the driving force behind a sculptors' symposium held in the summer of 1971 on the promontory between St. Wendel and Baltersweiler in the Saar region. Sculptors from many countries traveled there to take part in it; the symposium continued to meet annually until 1977. Out of it grew the project, "Street of Sculptures," which extends along the Saarland Circular Hiking Trail to the Bostalsee and took eighteen years and a total of thirty-eight artists to complete. The street is dedicated to the German-Jewish sculptor and painter, Otto Freundlich, who lived in Paris and whose dream of "une voie de la fraternité et solidarité humaine" remained for him but a dream: he was murdered in the Majdanek concentration camp in 1943.[70] Leo and I get along famously; many are the enjoyable hours we've spent discussing the role of art in our lives. This is not even to mention his most excellent wine cellar, built for him by his students on his plot of land near St. Wendel.

My visit with Crassus didn't turn out the way I expected. He had separated from Lore and was now, together with an older woman, owner of a bar on Brüsselerstraße. His father had passed on and his mother, having reached retirement age, had been allowed to leave the GDR. Crassus lived with her in a rented flat across from the bar, in which he spent his days from morning till deep into the night. He'd long since given up sports, seldom leaving the confines of the bar where he just whiled away the hours chewing the fat with his *Stammgäste* (regular customers), who were all as viscerally opposed to the GDR as he was. He condemned the wall, which had severed contact with his friends and relatives, and bemoaned the abortive escape efforts of GDR residents, including one by a close acquaintance. His opinions of the two Germanies, largely gleaned from reading and to which he clung with rock-solid conviction, were on some points at odds with reality. When I told him that maybe, just for once, he should look into conditions on the other side himself and draw his own conclusions, he just sniffed that that wasn't necessary, that he'd read all about it in the newspapers. And he was not about to subject his views to revision. Nor did he budge an inch from that stance when I tried to ply him with a quotation from the *Elegies* of Solon: "I'm getting older, but I never stop learning as much as I can."

It pained me to have to leave Middlebury, the institution to which I'd devoted the best years of my teaching career. Students there could give themselves utterly to learning German, having no other courses to worry about, and, most important, they were highly motivated to learn the language. Then too, the faculty I'd hired effectively worked around the clock, quartered as they were with the students in the dormitory. By summer's end we were always exhausted, but it was an exhaustion we endured with pride. I offer here the last photo taken of me in the German school of Middlebury College:

A last cup of coffee

Now I could devote myself more fully to my research. In addition to my papers on pedagogy, I published my longer study of the reception of Schnitzler's scenic cycle, *Round Dance*. I also wrote articles and contributions to encyclopedias on Arthur Schnitzler, Friedrich Nietzsche, Inge Merkel, Anna Mitgutsch, Tankred Dorst and Ursula Ehlers, Friedrich Dürrenmatt, Dieter Wellershoff and Peter Turrini, among others. Beyond these, for some time I'd also been exploring in some depth the work of the pacifist writer, Johannes Mario Simmel, whose biography interested me, since not only was he a half-Jew like me, but I also found the blending of exquisite menus with an espionage plot in his best-selling novel, *It Can't Always Be Caviar*, compelling. In the same way, he has done more than his share in his other novels to alert people to the covert socio-political dangers that threaten all. I wrote the entry on him for an encyclopedia and, in the course of doing so, had to consult his unpublished works, which are housed in the Boston University library. The reason they are there is that Simmel was treated less than kindly by German critics, which moved him to deposit all his writings in the USA, at Boston University. I was the first one to look through the many boxes of materials, and I still have no reason to doubt that interest in this writer remains below the radar. This is really too bad, since his work focuses on the dangers of fascism, holds Germany to account for its Nazi past and levels a blistering critique against those nations that have incited to war and destroyed human life. I believe he fully deserves the honors that are just now beginning to come his way, in the wake of so much negative criticism.

At this point I also had more time for my family. My son, Michael, did very well indeed, finishing high school as valedictorian and earning the honor of giving the farewell address before a packed auditorium, which filled me with pride. After taking his degree in mathematics and engineering at Princeton, he transferred to MIT in Boston and received from the National Science Foundation not only a tuition grant but enough money to cover his living expenses as well. He graduated as an engineer and married a former schoolmate from his high school, who succeeded him as valedictorian a year later and then graduated from MIT herself as a chemist. I hope their twins, a son and a daughter, born on February 20, 2006, will flourish as their parents have; in this country their lives will certainly be a lot less complicated than mine was.

The past was sharply brought back to me through two events in particular, events that, for all their difference, nevertheless belong together. The first was my viewing of the Spielberg film, *Schindler's List*, which was shown at a special presentation sponsored by the local Jewish community in a large theater in Syracuse. Since my wife and I had made an English translation of an article written in German by Gottfried Wagner for the head of the Jewish Studies Program at my university, we received an invitation to the showing. Sitting next to us in an overfilled theater were two young girls, perhaps twenty years old. As the film ran, the girls began to weep and to cling to each other, as if terrified that they might themselves be pulled into the events. A deafening stillness gripped the room, broken only by spasms of sobbing, as many others joined my two young neighbors in this spontaneous outburst of emotion. I wanted to say something to my wife, but thought better of it, since my English, despite the many years I'd lived in the States, still retained a strong Teutonic accent. And I did feel a sense of guilt over the events narrated in the film, even though in this story a "good" German was on display. And to this day the feeling of a personal guilt comes over me whenever I read about this period or see films portraying it. Perhaps it has to do with the fact that it was my generation that committed these atrocities and that I myself was among those who yearned for "total war." Those born after 1945 had an easier time getting over this past, one they had not personally experienced and only came to know once removed through the history books.

The second event took place some weeks later. I received a call from the university media school (which enjoys an international reputation), asking me if I'd be interested in participating in a film project. My curiosity aroused, I said yes. Some students came by and told me all about their idea. The leader of the group was a young girl of about twenty who'd been born in the States and had come across a photograph of her German grandfather in uniform, in Germany, standing in front of a fenced-in camp during the Second World War and smiling. He told her that he'd just given out cigarettes to the inmates of the camp a moment before the picture was taken, cigarettes they quickly divvied up among themselves. Ever since then the girl looked up to her grandfather as a hero and she wanted to film an enactment of this scene as the culminating project of her training. With this in mind, she and four fellow student-technicians came to us and set about preparing to shoot the scene.

It was interesting to watch them as they set it all up. One student moved all about the room with a device that supposedly registered the room's stillness. In response to my remark that there was nothing to register, he corrected me, pointing out that every room was silent in a different way and that, in the making of a film, the unique silence of a particular room played an important role. When all technical issues had been resolved, we sat down and had lunch together. I asked the girl for another look at the photo, since I was to play the grandfather who'd demonstrated his humanity in war through this generous distribution of cigarettes. As I studied the picture in detail, I noticed in it a half-hidden gate at the top of which a few words could be made out. What I believed I could accurately decode was " . . . macht frei" [will set you free], and suddenly it seemed all but certain that this was no conventional camp but rather a concentration camp, and that the grandfather was a member of its protective squadron. At once I was aware of the grotesque irony of my situation: here I was, about to play the SS man as benefactor, who once told how he'd given the inmates cigarettes, which of course could not be verified, and I was someone who could very easily have wound up on the other side of the barbed wire. I grew pensive, to the point where people were asking me if there was a problem. It took me some time to collect myself, appealing to a sudden headache as an excuse. Then, casting aside all doubts and reservations, I played my appointed role. Afterwards my wife asked me what could possibly have prompted me to take part in this fiasco. I told her the following: after my discovery, I looked into the faces of these young people who were sitting around me; what I saw in their eyes was an almost complete absence of historical understanding, a state of affairs perhaps excusable by the fact that they'd all been born long after the war. Moreover, they were all Americans, for most of whom Germany lies somewhere on the other side of the Atlantic. And finally, this was a new and fresh generation that had nothing whatever to do with the events of the Third Reich and those responsible for the atrocities. I waited till the film was wrapped up before taking the granddaughter aside and conveying to her my qualms about her grandfather. She just looked at me in wide-eyed shock and I could see that she was totally incredulous. How could her beloved grandfather ever have been a henchman of these monstrous criminals? The students went their separate ways, with only the girl hanging back a bit to turn towards me and repeat that her grandfather was a hero in her eyes and that I had to be mistaken. Maybe she was right, for it was indeed an SS man who'd saved my life, but that was a rare exception, and one that, in the judgment of history, shouldn't carry much weight, especially when balanced against the innumerable victims who died at the hands of the SS.

In May of 2004 I went into so-called "retirement." I still teach if I am asked, and I still like the contact with students. The student body had changed now; there are more international students in my class, coming from Turkey, the Arab countries, Siberia, south Siberia, Poland and also Germany. The

225

discussions are great, because of the different cultural backgrounds. And the discussions and questions are not restricted to the classroom but continued in my office:

Still in my Office as an Octogenarian

In May of 2004 I attended my final commencement, which featured former President Clinton as the speaker. The academic procession was colorful and solemn, with the faculty decked out in their medieval-ish panoply of robes, marching in step to the array of fanfares and drumbeats behind the university banner and the American flag. As I turned to go up the final steps leading to the assembly site, I was taken aback to see President Clinton extending his hand to each individual member of the faculty. I was almost speechless, since President Clinton is one of the few politicians I esteem highly. He gave me his hand and, flustered as I was, I blurted out in German, "Guten Tag, Herr Präsident." He looked at me with a smile and, without missing a beat, retorted in perfect, accent-free German, "Nein, Herr Professor! Es muss heißen: Guten Morgen" [No, professor, you should say "Good morning"]. He was right, as it was only nine o'clock. Then the procession began with all its flags, fanfares and drums, and, for just the briefest moment, I had the sense of a déjà-vu experience, but the difference between this and those processions of long ago was just too profound. The next day I cleaned out my office, turned in my office key and was officially, from then on, a Professor Emeritus, a professor without a teaching assignment. [71]

On Interior Biography

No Man Is an Island

In this effort to compose my life experiences, I've learned that not every success I've had is of my own doing, for, whenever push came to shove, and even in those few situations in which my very life hung in the balance, I was never alone. So often it is said that no man is an island, and this wisdom has certainly been borne out in my own life. Somehow, mysteriously, someone or something has always been there to help me. I could even say that this charmed quality of my life began at the very beginning, the day my father pulled my mother and me back from the edge of the bridge, being moved soon thereafter to offer us a good home. I was shot at in the war, yet no bullet ever struck me, and I managed to climb out of every mangled air raid shelter in one piece. Later on it was Hedda Adlon who smoothed the path for me into the hospitality field. Who knows what would've become of me if I hadn't gotten that apprenticeship? Where would I have wound up? And if it hadn't been for Felicitas' help, I doubt I would ever have earned my *Abitur*. Others too influenced my life and helped determine its course: the president of the University of Alberta, Ernst Loeb, and Carroll Reed. To this group also belong my colleagues in the States, who've always provided me with opportunities to become actively engaged in the different professional associations and who've helped me keep my appetite for research strong and sharp. Sometimes I imagine that all these people have been functioning together, on some vaguely covert level, on my behalf, like the members of the secret Tower Society in Goethe's *Bildungsroman, Wilhelm Meister*, whose charge it is to intervene on certain strategic occasions in the life of their ward. I shudder to think what errant paths I might've wandered down without their presence and without their aid and counsel. Certainly my guardian angel must've put in an enormous amount of overtime to protect me.

In this connection an experience comes to mind that I had only recently. Whenever I'm in Berlin, I make sure to go to the zoo, not only because in my youth we had a family tradition of going there on Whit

Sunday, but also because I like animals. And I believe the feeling is mutual, to wit: as I was strolling by the pelican preserve on my recent visit, one of these large, majestic animals spotted me. Nimbly hopping over the narrow water strip enclosing its habitat, it waddled straight towards me, giving off a few piercing croaks as it did. It was as if this bird wanted to greet me; it nodded its head a few times and then perched itself atop the fence, spreading its huge wings so far out that one of them lightly grazed me. I just stood there, returning its gaze with equal intensity, convinced beyond all doubt that this bird was one of those guardian spirits that have always protected me from the worst:

Welcome to Berlin

The Importance of Engagement

Looking back over my life, it becomes apparent to me how deep a wariness I've always nursed towards politicians and their slogans. If something strikes you as wrong, you must have the courage to say so, for as I learned only too well in school: *Qui tacet, consentire videtur* — he who remains silent gives the impression of agreement. Speaking "in" (muttering to yourself) will never wield the power of speaking out. My mother serves as a paragon here: she had the courage to take me straight to the Reich Youth Leader to get me the help I needed, refusing to be deterred from her mission by any of the great man's stooges or minions. And this in a dictatorship that had all the "rights" and "wrongs" chiseled in granite! My mother saw things differently, and she prevailed.

In this context I should also mention the intervention of the SS man and the party member, both of whom stood up for me against an angry mob. Such acts call for courage and the conviction that one is not allowed the option of passively standing by when faced with injustice. Of course, this is in no way to excuse or mitigate the countless crimes against humanity committed by the organizations of the SA and SS; it is meant only to point out a particular instance in which a child, who'd been beaten bloody, was given protection by no more than two from among the many witnesses who merely stood there gawking. On more than one occasion in my life, I've stepped in when seeing a child being mistreated, in some instances even deflecting the fury of the perpetrators towards myself.

These are all issues that affect me personally and that have moved me to become politically engaged, even if on a modest scale. I'm a Democrat, I vote, I demonstrate, I give financial support to the Democratic Party and I discuss the political (mis)steps of the government with the members of my book club.

Rejection of Stereotypes and Dogmatism

One of the things I strongly reject is stereotypical generalizing. After leaving Germany, I had to hear all manner of condemnation of "those evil Germans," the people who had wrought so much destruction in the world. While there is some justice in this, it has also led to clichéed images of the Germans, images serving to demonize them and turn them into bogeymen. All of this has been aided and abetted by the mass media and the press, although the pendulum has begun to swing the other way in recent times. Needless to say, there are good Germans, just as there are bad and good Americans or people of other races and nationalities. Such "one size fits all" characterization may make our lives simpler, relieving us as it does of the labor of thinking and differentiating, but it also robs us of the beguiling play of nuance that is part of the spice of life. With all due respect to ethics, perhaps the time has come for us to take seriously Nietzsche's withering critique of the simplistic categories of "good" and "evil."

Our endeavor must be to overcome dualistic and dogmatic thinking. At a conference not long ago, someone brought up the subject of mentally ill people who have lost the ability to think in generic or umbrella concepts: e.g., they grasp the expressions "father" and "mother," but cannot say "parents," as this idea has literally become "inconceivable" to them. But is it so difficult to think of so-called normal people in this way: many think in the categories of white and black, Jew and gentile, old and young, etc., while the umbrella term "person" is missing. Maybe it's been lost, as with the ill, or maybe it's just not there yet. Either way, as Adalbert Stifter writes in his preface to the collection, *Colored Stones*, there is, or at least should be, a law "decreeing that each person live side by side with his neighbor in mutual respect, honor and security, that he be allowed to pursue unfettered his noble human calling, gain for himself the love and admiration of his fellows, that he be cherished as a jewel, just as each of us is a jewel for all others."[72] In his *Diary* Max Frisch has put this noble thought in the following nutshell: "Make no graven image . . . . it is a sin that we commit virtually without surcease, just as it is committed against us — except when we love."[73]

As a teacher I've always made an effort to send students in my classes to Germany or Austria, not just to help them acquire a certain level of fluency in the foreign language from which to master its finer points, but also to bring them in contact with a different culture. And with the people of that culture. This can go a long way towards unearthing and, eventually, dismantling stereotypical views. By the same token, students from other countries often come into my classes. In my teaching career I've had many different nationalities sitting before me, among others from such countries as Siberia, Argentina, Israel, Lebanon, Egypt, Poland, and Turkey, as well as Germany itself. When we take up the topic of *Heimat* (homeland) in class, foreign students often describe their homes so beautifully and enticingly that many of those listening sense, perhaps for the first time, a desire to see and experience such places for themselves. Sometimes students bring dishes to class that they have prepared themselves, which we all promptly devour. Much more than mere nourishment, such food evokes intimate memories for those who've grown up with it. All of this helps to erode prejudice.

In this connection I recall an event that remains seared in my memory to this day. Some years ago, an unusual art exhibition took place in Washington, D.C. On display were the works of famous painters and, right next to each image or scene shown on canvas, a plastic, three-dimensional representation of that same painting made by artists commissioned by the museum's management. The array included pictures by van Gogh, Renoir, and Matisse, among others — landscape scenes, human figures, faces — each one next to its own lifelike effigy made of wax. Of course, everything was strictly hands-off, as a sign in bold print made clear. A young girl caught my attention; she was darting back and forth among the landscapes and carefully stroking the wax faces with her fingertips. I was incensed, as all that touching could easily cause the facial features to melt down. So I walked over to her and stood next to her mother, who was just looking on. I was about to tell the mother that touching was prohibited when she suddenly turned to me, no doubt sensing my intention. "My daughter is blind," she informed me, "she was born blind." Hearing this, the daughter turned her face to me, so that I could see her dead eyes. In my embarrassment I asked her how she liked the exhibition, and she answered gleefully, "I've heard so much about these masterworks, but today's the first time I can actually *see* them." Ever since then I've sworn off all blanket judgments; this experience was a jarring reminder that there are different truths, and that there are times when human truth exists on a higher, or deeper, plane than scientific or factual.

For many years now I've given instruction to the youth group in our local Episcopal church. One time, when I wanted to illustrate the principle of tolerance for them, I recounted the parable of the ring from Lessing's dramatic poem, *Nathan the Wise*, in which the wise Jew is asked which of the three religions dominant in Jerusalem is the true one. His oft-quoted response is that all are equally justified, that none can lay claim to exclusive authority. After that we took up each of the major religions in turn. Starting with Catholicism, we visited a Catholic church and invited the Catholic clergyman to come to our meeting and field questions. We did the same with the rabbi, visiting the synagogue (the first time for me) and inviting the rabbi to join our discussion. In this way we explored a series of religions, until one day the prelate of our church took me aside and confided to me that many of the parents were expressing serious misgivings about our project, as the children were asking them questions that revealed that they were not yet firmly committed to church dogma. Needless to say, I believe my approach is an effective one for combating stereotyping, ignorance and arrogance.

That these iniquities continue to flourish today was brought home to me in the summer of 2007 in Leipzig, where I was doing research at the German National Library. I ate at "Waldfrieden," a Bohemian-style eatery, you can eat outside in the garden. I has a few tables with tops made of large flagstones. I sat down at one of these and, a few minutes later, was joined by a family with two grown daughters and a friend. We were soon deep in conversation and, after mentioning that I lived in America, I told them something about my life, e.g., that my father had been a Jew, which made me a half-Jew. Just then the sixty-ish woman jumped up, pointed her finger at me and said, "I knew it immediately! You've got that classic Jewish nose!" All at once I felt myself transported back more than half a century. My first impulse was to explain to the woman that my nose was quite normal, thank you, that my only biological link to Jewishness was through my father and, finally, that a so-called "Jewish nose" was a trait of the Dinaric race. . She probably wouldn't have heard of the Dinaric race, and, besides, one of her daughters piped up with, "Mom, you just can't say things like that these days!" Granted, you can't say them, but thinking them is another matter entirely. Such thinking should belong by now to the dustbin of history's darkest hours, otherwise what's to become of my grandchildren, as they set out to make their way in the world with the highest hopes of full admission:

They can hardly wait to go into the ocean

It is essential that the dignity of a person not be violated. The Basic Law of the Federal Republic of Germany guarantees this in its opening paragraph. But just as vital is the inviolability of a person's dignity in his relations with others. Human beings have differing value scales, and what is important or sacred to one may be completely irrelevant to another, or even meet with his resistance. How often I've observed one person treating the views and even the dreams of another with contempt when they happened not to agree with his own. This kind of arrogance makes enemies. If there's something about another person you don't like, there are ways and means of politely distancing yourself from it. And this perspective is also a guiding principle in my behavior towards students; when they make mistakes (and who doesn't, in studying a foreign language), they must of course be corrected, but always in such a way as not to dishearten them.

Double Vision

Over the course of my life, I've also managed to acquire a kind of double vision. My experiences do not become extinguished with age, on the contrary, they remain within me, in precisely the sense Arthur Schnitzler has his character, Fedor, express in his play, *The Fairy Tale*: "What was, is! — That's the deeper sense of the 'what has happened'"; and even if I wrote earlier: the past catches up with me, here I must put it this way: the past is always already in me. And so, I will on occasion view an event from a double perspective, one that allows present and past to fold into each other, not unlike the way Robert Frost once put it: "as my two eyes make one in sight." [74] This sort of thing can happen with or without one's will; it can be a trivial matter or anything but. An instance of the former would be my recollection of the soup made from raw potato gratings in the post-war period, one that would suggest to any first-time diner a badly prepared dish. By contrast, the dish at hand tastes a good deal better; so too even a glass of water, when one recalls the boiled water we were limited to as of 1945. At the other end of the spectrum are the present-day televised encounters with maimed veterans and the gazing upon coffins containing the bodies of fallen soldiers, along with the agony of parents. Quite involuntarily, as I watch the 6 o'clock news, another memory-image intrudes on my consciousness, a composite image of the numberless maimed and fallen I saw in the war as a boy. The question burns to be asked: why must this be? Have human beings learned nothing from their past? Must we, ultimately, capitulate to the cynicism, the nihilism, expressed by Max Frisch through the character of "the Contemporary" in his play, *The Chinese Wall*: "Does history tell us / That stupidity / Forever creeps back in / And wins anew? / 'Tis like an evil dream. . . ." [75]

The Identity Question

A matter that preoccupied me for the longest time was the question of my identity: "Who am I?" The Nazis classified me as a half-Jew, since my father was a Jew, my mother not. From a cultural and religious point of view, I'm a German, since I grew up in Germany in a Christian household, went to school in that country, and consequently feel myself to be a German. This is a feeling the Nazis and their kindred spirits never succeeded in beating out of me.

Anyone born into my circumstances, raised in a working-class family, growing up in a working-class neighborhood, would've been said to have little chance of escaping that environment: in those days the *Kiez* was your destiny (cf. n. 2). You were born into it, you spent your life in it, you died in it. Nevertheless, I managed to move up from the *Volksschule* to the *Gymnasium* — not because I was especially bright, but because someone took pity on me. My problem was that my inner life was disconnected from my outer development: from kitchen apprentice, via relief worker in street construction, to apprentice waiter at the Hotel am Zoo, waiter at an old patrician country club in Toronto, followed by my job at a Toronto supper club and on the DEW line in northern Canada. The next stage was the beginning of my studies, which I gave up after a year to take a position as a waiter with the CNR. This phase ended with my job in a steakhouse and, following that, at the Hotel Vancouver. I resumed my studies in Vancouver, eventually graduating, and moved to Seattle to do graduate work at the University of Washington, which in turn gave me the opportunity to do summer teaching at the NDEA Institutes in Carbondale and Princeton, the latter venue being where I met my wife. All of this happened very fast, and my inner life simply couldn't keep up. In the first fourteen years of my life I had the problem of the "We" versus the "You"; and thereafter that of the "We" versus the "I." At this point, I believe I can say that my inner life has finally caught up with my outer, and I find myself in a condition of relative equilibrium, but it has taken a long time to achieve this balance. It goes without saying that I've been supported in this by my friends, who accepted me just as I was, and by my professional colleagues, who acknowledged and valued my efforts and accomplishments in the field of *Germanistik*. All of this strengthened my self-confidence and gave me a sense of belonging, which I suppose is what identity is.

Instead of an *Afterword*

Sometimes I ask myself what I would say if someone magically offered me the possibility of living life over again, just as it's been, without changing a jot. I would, without hesitation, say yes to such a "return of the same," for I have loved my life and continue to do so. Life for me has been nothing like the tedium it is for the protagonist of Margit Schreiner's novel, *Book of Disappointments*, in which an old woman who has passed on, speaking from the other side, narrates her life backwards from end to beginning, death to birth. For her, life has held only disappointment, one after the other, and she laments: "We get bored. We lie around, go for a walk, fulfill our obligations, read and ask ourselves what for. We live and ask ourselves what for. It is only at death that every question becomes superfluous."[76] Such an outlook is, and always has been, foreign to my nature.

Life is basically what you make of it, even allowing for the significant role of others' intervention. And if now and then things don't go according to plan, or you're weighed down by problems, you should always remember that "Things could've been a lot worse." Many years ago on a trip to New York City with my son, we visited the huge AT&T Building. At the time they had on display there a big computer that would answer all questions put to it via the keyboard. My ten-year-old son typed in: "What is the purpose of life?" In a flash the answer was spit back at him: "The purpose of life is to live." The machine seems to have got it right.

I am now at an age when one naturally begins to think about one's grand exit. Certainly I do on occasion, but then again I remember that I am not one of those who "in all their life have never bred a single butterfly," as Charles Dickens characterizes the shyster lawyer, Smallweed, in one of my favorite novels, *Bleak House*. I still have much life left in me and relish the prospect of breeding many more butterflies. And even if the writer Wilhelm Raabe insists that a man in old age is more inclined to cling to memories than nurture hope, I would aver that his insight has, at best, minimal relevance to me personally.

On some occasions, to be sure, the memories do have a way of surfacing from below. I enjoy going to the theater because New York City is rich in plays and musicals. Not too long ago I saw the *The Adding Machine* again, now an American musical. All in all, a memorable performance, but it failed to evoke the inner existential response I had when I first saw the play in 1945, surrounded by rubble, utter destruction and immense hopelessness. In 2008 the playgoers were nicely dressed and well fed, and enjoyed the musical enormously; when I struck up a conversation with a young man during intermission, he remarked that the subject matter was irrelevant today — "stuck in the past," as he put it. Of course, he was right — because *my* past came up when I watched it. I understand only too well that that young man couldn't relate very well to the subject matter of this converted play, certainly not the way I did. And it was good and fitting that he couldn't. But as for me, I'm sure I will never lose this double vision of mine as long as I live and remain capable of remembering.

Then too, as active and oriented to the present as I continue to be, I also find that I am more and more often reminded of my reduced status as a member of the supporting cast, alas, a protagonist no longer. Recently, on entering my old office at the university, I saw lying on the desk several of my publications, which had been removed from the departmental display case to make room for those of my younger colleagues. If, up to that moment, I couldn't fully admit it to myself, here was undeniable proof right in front of me: I was now officially written off. Even the social environment becomes smaller and smaller, the friends and acquaintances you have around you fewer and fewer, and the impulse to dash up a steep flight of stairs now gives you pause. Still, life goes on, albeit more slowly and cautiously. But I know full well that even the most circumspect life cannot go on forever and that I will, rather sooner than later, tread that path that leads into the Unknown. And the Unknown I picture to myself to be not unlike a scene I beheld one summer on a beach in Florida: I raise my eyes to the horizon, way off in the distance, straight into the rising sun, as it shoots its first rays down onto the restless waves of the great ocean. And on the beach sits a chair, one in which I often used to lounge and read. And when I have embarked on my final journey, the chair will still be sitting there as always, with a book opened on it — only this time without me. And I would like the following passage read at my service which I found in W. N. P. Barbellion's *credo*:

[T]o me the honour is sufficient of belonging to the universe – such a great universe, and so grand a scheme of things. Not even Death can rob me of that honour. For nothing can alter the fact that I have lived; I have been I... And when I am dead, the matter which composes my body is indestructible – and eternal, so that come what may to my 'Soul', my dust will always be going on, each separate atom of me playing its separate part – I shall still have some sort of finger in the Pie. When I am dead, you can boil me, burn me, drown me, scatter me - but you cannot destroy me: my little atoms would merely deride such heavy vengeance. Death can do no more than kill you.[77]

The end

NOTES

1. Peter Pouncey: *Rules for Old Men Waiting.* New York: Random House, Inc. 2006. First Large Print Edition, p. 54.

2. The concept of *Kiez,* as used in Berlin, refers to a small city district containing a core of old buildings and the population inhabiting them. Generally, a *Kiez* has an urban infrastructure with shops and bars.

3. Erich Kästner: "In Memoriam Memoriae." In: *Kurz und Bündig [Short and Sweet].* Epigramme. Olten 1948, p. 20.

4. Stefan Zweig: "Buchmendel." In: *Amok: Novellen einer Leidenschaft [Amok: Novellas of a Passion].* [Berlin]: S. Fischer Verlag 1946, p. 170.

5. Sten Nadolny: *Er oder Ich [He or I].* München [Munich]: Piper Verlag 1999, p. 166. For Nadolny everything "that can make me look bad [. . .] [is] hidden in a kind of balance. Memory is merely the support of forgetting. It begins with our remembering a beautiful landscape, but no longer [remembering] the blisters we had on our feet" (141-142).

6. Friedrich Nietzsche: "Jenseits von Gut und Böse" [Beyond Good and Evil], # 268. In: *Werke in drei Bänden.* Vol. 2. Darmstadt: Wissenschaftliche Buchgesellschaft 1966, p. 625.

7. Lukas B. Suter: "Erinnerung" [Memory]. In: *Kreuz und Quer [All over the Place].* Tübingen Programs 9. Playbill on the occasion of the Tübingen world premiere of *Kreuz und Quer,* April 16, 1992, p. 9.

8. On this cf. also Sherwin B. Nuland's discussion of Eric R. Kandel's book, *In Search of Memory:* "We are made of Memories. Every moment of our lives brings to a focus the totality of all the moments preceding it." *The New York Times Book Review,* April 8, 2006: 14.

9. Anna Mitgutsch's analysis of memory points to the fact that it is impossible to determine whether the images and sequences that seem real to us stem from our dreams or from our imagination: "In the best case, our memory gives us, not the reality of the uniquely lived experience, but rather a relatively accurate pictorial interpretation of our emotional reaction at the time. But presumably reality is skewed right in the very moment of our experiencing it toward the subjectivity of recollection, such that memory quickly discards what is useless and transforms what has been experienced into history." In: Anna Mitgutsch: *Erinnern und Erfinden. Grazer Poetik Vorlesungen*

[Remembering and Inventing. Graz Lectures on Poetics]. Graz: Literaturverlag Droeschel 1999, p. 7-8.

10. Johann Wolfgang von Goethe: *Faust:* part 2. In: Erich Trunz (ed.): *Goethes Werke*. Vol. 3. Hamburg: Christian Wegner Verlag 1949. Lines: 5102-5103, p. 159. Subsequent quotations from *Faust* refer to this edition.

11. A *Stammbuch* is a book containing official entries of births, marriages, baptisms and deaths. It is kept in the family for many generations, After 1933 Hitler required families to have a *Stammbuch* to prove the blood purity of family members.

12. A wooden handle with seven (or nine) leather straps fastened to it, used by parents to punish children and teenagers. Its equivalent in the schools was the cane.

13. During the period of National Socialism, the expressions "Jew sow" (*Judensau*) and "sow Jew" (*Saujude*) were used as inflammatory anti-Semitic slogans. To be sure, their origin is older. These designations reared up at least as early as the 13th century, and caricatures of Jews sitting backwards on a pig or eating its excrement were posted on church doors and city walls. Nowadays these expressions are prohibited in all German-speaking countries, and anyone who uses them can be prosecuted for libel.

14. A *Blockwart* or *Blockleiter* was a low-ranking official in the Nazi party responsible for propaganda and planning. Our *Blockwart* regularly visited 100 to 120 households in our vicinity.

15. Baldur von Schirach's image is controversial. On the one hand, he is viewed as a loyal vassal of Hitler, who had joined the Nazi party early on; on the other, as a critic of anti-Semitic hate language and of the arrest and detention of Jewish women. On this see the article by Eberhard Panitz, "Die kalte Wüste der Erinnerung" [The Cold Desert of Memory], in which he discusses Richard von Schirach's book about his father, published under the title *Der Schatten meines Vaters [My Father's Shadow]* München [Munich]: Carl Hanser 2005. This article appeared on November 24, 2005, in *Neues Deutschland:* 15.

16. A *Realschule* is a six-year course offering a more practical, scientific curriculum than the classical *Gymnasium* with its emphasis on classical languages and culture.

17. The most elite and prestigious secondary school, with a nine-year course. To get in, students had to pass an entrance exam in various subjects and, at graduation, were awarded the "Senior Matriculation" diploma, equivalent to two years of American university study.

18. The school had not always borne this name: it was first known as the *Luisenstädtische Gymnasium [Luisenstadt High School]*, then as the Heinrich Schliemann School, and, in the Third Reich, as the Horst Wessel Gymnasium.

19. Only later did I learn the likely truth about Horst Wessel. To wit: that he is supposed to have been living with a former prostitute and been shot by her ex-boyfriend, possibly even by her pimp. The Office of Nazi Propaganda under Goebbels made a martyr out of him, and every year on his death day, February 23, he would be briefly acknowledged in our school, though not by all teachers.

20. The Jewish Star was introduced in 1941; it consisted of a hand-sized, six-pointed Star of David of yellowish material, with the black inscription "Jew" in the middle. The obligation to wear it applied to all Jews who had reached the age of six.

21. Karl May was one of the most popular German writers of the day and was read by a large segment of the German population. He wrote several novels set in the American Old West.

22. The Mother's Cross also entitled the wearer to first-in-line status in bureaucratic procedures and to a seat in all public transportation. In our area there were many mothers with Mother's Crosses, which meant I usually found myself standing on busses and trains.

23. This award was given in four grades: For special bravery in the face of the enemy one received, after the Iron Cross 1st and 2nd class, the Knight's Cross of the Iron Cross; for greater bravery the Knight's Cross of the Iron Cross with oak cluster; for still greater bravery the Knight's Cross of the Iron Cross with oak cluster and sabers; and for singularly profound bravery the Knight's Cross of the Iron Cross with oak cluster and sabers and diamonds. This last and highest designation is no doubt what my mother meant by "frills and fancy stuff."

24. A *Reichsleiter* (Imperial Leader) was a high political rank within the Nazi party. These officials reported directly to Hitler.

25. Circular of *Reichsleiter* Martin Bormann to the supreme imperial authorities and party administrative agencies of September 27, 1940. Reproduction from Gerhard Dabel: *KLV: die erweiterte Kinder-Land-Verschickung: KLV-Lager 1940-1945: Dokumentation über den "größten soziologischen Versuch aller Zeiten" [KLV: The Expanded Child Land Movement: KLV Camp 1940-1945: Documentation of the "greatest sociological experiment of all time"].* Commissioned by the Documentation Syndicate KLV, inc. Freiburg im Breisgau: Schillinger 1981, p. 7.

26. The ration card, introduced during the war for the apportioning of edible and other household products, was differentiated in the final war years by item. There was, for example, a Reich's fat-card, a Reich's bread-card, a Reich's meat-card, etc. Also rationed were cigarettes, soap and shoes. Groups were a further criterion: young people were allowed more milk, and expectant mothers, those on leave from the front and manual laborers (themselves subdivided by degree of physical hardship) were allowed more of most things than average consumers, while Jews and forced laborers were limited to more modest shares. As the war dragged on, rationings got smaller. In the last months of the war, adults received weekly rationings of ca. 62.5 grams of fat, 250 grams of meat and 1700 grams of bread.

27. *Hackepeter,* also known regionally as *Mett,* is raw chopped pork that is salted and peppered, sometimes mixed with raw onions and served on rolls or bread. *Hackepeter* is illegal in the USA due to the danger of trichinosis, but is nevertheless sold on occasion in German butcher shops.

28. JWD = *janz weit draußen* (way out of town), a Berlin expression.

29. The designation goes back to Jacques Meyer, a textile manufacturer, who in 1874 built the first of these apartment blocks that warehoused many people in the smallest volume of space. Initially intended as both industrial and housing space, gradually these buildings came to be constructed exclusively as rental flats, which were more lucrative.

30. The so called aerial mine (*Luftmine*) is a high explosive bomb that was also referred to then as a *Wohnblockknacker* (apartment building cracker) for its devastating effects. This designation is particularly apropos of the destruction I am describing here.

31. The *Werwölfe* were a group of partisans made up of former SS-people and Hitler Youth. Created by Himmler towards the end of the war as part of his search for "death-defying volunteers," they were intended to "ravage the enemy like werwolves." In a similar spirit, Adolf Hitler had, in his Werwolf speech of March 23, 1945, challenged German youth to defend Germany with their last drop of blood, which is exactly what many of them did out of their misguided idealism.

32. This was one of the big propaganda blitzes of the Nazis. What actually did take place there amounted to genocide. But I didn't learn this until much later.

33. This multifaceted rocket launcher from the Stalin era was not unlike organ pipes in that the rockets were usually arranged in the shape of a ring. The launcher could fire off several salvos in a few seconds, with an ear-shattering howling of rockets that was unnerving. At this point in time, the Russians were approximately eight kilometers from Berlin, so that the artillery fire was able to reach the capital city of the Reich.

34. In the America novels of Karl May, Old Shatterhand is the invincible hero and superman who, together with his Indian friend and blood brother, Winnetou, has declared war against all evil and evildoers. A similar superman figure is Kara Ben Nemsi (= Karl, son of the Germans), who fills the same roll in May's tales of the orient.

35. Ruhnke was an optician known throughout the city. The factory is now known by the name of Ruhnke Optics, Ltd., and makes eyeglasses, watches, clocks and other optical devices.

36. This technique is also described by Hans-Werner Rückert: *Entdecke das Glück des Handelns: Überwinde, was das Leben blockiert [Discover the Joy of Action: Overcome Whatever Is Blocking Your Life].* Frankfurt am Main [u.a.]: Campus Verlag GmbH. 2004, 2. durchgesehene Auflage. By it the author means the capacity to hold in the mind two opposite ideas simultaneously, thereby giving oneself the possibility to continue living (p. 87).

37. Later I saw this film a few more times, most recently on the occasion of the DEFA retrospective at MoMa (=Museum of Modern Art) in New York City. The retrospective, which ran from October 7-23, 2005, was entitled, "Rebels with a Cause: The Cinema of East Germany." A total of 21 films from the DEFA film bank were shown.

38. Normal consumers were those who did not receive special bonuses or supplements, as did, e.g., children, heavy workers or manual laborers.

39. As of this day, no more than 40 marks could legally be exchanged daily "per head," hence the so-called "head money" (*Kopfgeld*). Savings accounts were devalued at a 10 to 1 ratio. Later on you could exchange an extra 20 marks.

40. The amount one could exchange was limited to 70 marks, and since the new currency had not yet been printed, the old bills had coupons pasted onto them, which were valid for two days. On June 25 there appeared the *Deutsche Mark der Deutschen Notenbank* (German Mark of the German Bank of Issue).

41. The town of Aue, nestled in the Ore Mountains (*Erzgebirge*), was home to the Wismut Uranium Mines Corp., which specialized in extracting from stone those metals that were strategically important for the production of atomic bombs. Since it paid well, many young women and men volunteered for this difficult and hazardous work. Other workers were recruited by force.

42. Not unlike our school, the *Lustgarten* had undergone several changes of name since first being landscaped in 1573 by the *Kurfürst* (Elector) Johann Georg. Originally laid out as a kind of kitchen garden, which makes it Berlin's oldest garden square, it became during the GDR-period a venue for mass political rallies and demonstrations. But even in spite of this radical change, a tradition was left intact, since the Nazis had already used it for such purposes, going so far as to have it paved over in the 1930's.

43. Nicotine-free *Muckefuckkaffee* was an ersatz coffee made with chicory, barley and other grains that served coffee-drinkers in the postwar period, who couldn't afford the real thing.

44. My mother had managed to salvage some collector cups with a floral pattern from the war. There was a flower at the bottom of each cup, in underglaze color. Whenever the coffee was brewed thin (more often than not), you could just make out the flower.

45. In Greek mythology the shepherd boy, Ganymede, was brought by Zeus up to Olympus to serve as cupbearer to the gods. Goethe memorialized him in his Storm-and-Stress hymn of 1774, "Ganymede."

46. Kurt Schuhmacher died in Bonn on August 20, 1952. He was well known as Chairman of the SPD (1946) and a member of parliament (1949). As leader of the opposition, he roundly rejected Konrad Adenauer's policy of *Westintegration.*

47. A pronouncement of the Roman comic dramatist, Terrence, in his *Heautontimorumenos*: "I am a human being. Nothing human is alien to me."

48. This conference took place in Berlin from January 25 to February 18, 1954. Its agenda included the *Deutschlandfrage* ("Germany" question), the establishment of free elections and the formation of a pan-German government. It had no practical outcome.

49. RCMP is the acronym for "Royal Canadian Mounted Police," informally known as "the Mounties." The RCMP is Canada's national police force.

50. This parade was the model for the famous Macy's Thanksgiving Day Parade in New York City.

51. This British specialty is usually prepared at Christmas, but can also be enjoyed on other holidays. It's a pie containing chop meat, beef fat, raisins, currants, cinnamon, cloves, sugar and apples, and is served hot.

52. Known as "the Mac," this was the largest hotel of the Canadian National Railroad (CNR) in Edmonton. Some years ago, this elegant establishment was renamed the "Fairmont Hotel MacDonald."

53. Conditions in the university clinic described here have improved considerably in recent decades. Today this hospital is among the best in Alberta Province. Alberta itself is now one of the richest provinces in Canada, a state of affairs largely brought about by its oil-rich sand.

54. There are many variants of this legend. The sculpture pictured below is in my possession.

55. The Roman emperor, Vespasian, who instituted a tax on the use of public urinals, answered those critics who charged him with sleaziness: "Pecunia non olet" ("Money doesn't stink").

56. In 1990, the U.S. turned over these Canadian installations to the Canadian government, and America contributed 100 million dollars towards the repair of environmental damages caused by PCB's (polychlorinated biphenyls). The production of PCB's had been

prohibited in the USA since 1977. The actual cost of the repair of damages came to 300 million dollars, which, for the most part, came from the pockets of Canadian taxpayers.

57. *Faust*, lines 2603-04.

58. Left-brainers take pleasure in argument; they're logical thinkers who have, or at least seek, an explanation for everything; they're self-conscious, analytical, realistic, rule-oriented; they try to maintain control, and need order and structure, which they usually have to provide for themselves, since they have difficulty accepting these from the environment. They're dominant, remember names, are consistent, rational and reasonable, and avoid mistakes. They also tend more towards introversion than right-brainers. The latter are more extraverted, communicative, and (often) eloquent; they remember faces, are sometimes illogical, inconsistent, and ruled by emotion, but are also often charismatic and witty. They prefer experience to argument, have intuition and creativity and imagination. Whereas left-brainers are detail-oriented, right-brainers see things globally. Naturally both brain hemispheres are meant to work together, but usually one side dominates.

59. Our relationship did not end with her later marriage to the sculptor, Leo Kornbrust; we've remained very good friends and intellectually kindred spirits. We've exchanged several hundred letters, and my wife and I visit her and her husband whenever we are in Germany. I can say that my friendship with her has become even firmer than it was in youth.

60. Gerhard and Ingrid celebrated their 50th anniversary on May 18, 2007, in Berlin. My wife and I, along with all surviving guests of fifty years ago, were invited to the affair. The big surprise was that, not only their son, but their daughter too, who was not expected, traveled to Berlin to be there. This was the only time I ever saw my friend and Ingrid nearly brought to tears by joy.

61. *Faust,* lines 2865-68.

62. That, to be sure, was in 1958. Today German businesses have all disappeared, replaced by innumerable Asiatic businesses and establishments, as Vancouver has experienced an enormous increase in Chinese and Korean émigrés in recent decades. The most recent

statistical survey of 2003 indicates that 10% of the population of British Columbia (some 250,000 people) is of Chinese origin and that for 72% of current immigrants Chinese is the mother tongue.

63. I subsequently learned that my reasoning here was far from the affront to logic it might appear to be. During the big power blackout in New York City some years ago, people could neither go out nor turn on their TV's. Also, the restaurants were closed. Consequently, they went to bed earlier, and several months later, New York experienced a sharp upturn in births.

64. "Green card" is the common name for "Lawful Permanent Residence." It grants the holder official immigration status in the USA, along with the all-important permission to work. The green card was preceded by the "Alien Registration Receipt Card," introduced after World War II and printed on green paper.

65. It appeared in volume 7.3 of the journal, *The University of Dayton Review*, in the Spring of 1971, pp. 47-52.

66. In this cycle of seven novellas, a young man, intent on marriage, goes out into the world to discover the truth of Friedrich von Logau's epigram, "How can you turn white lilies to crimson red, red roses?/An ivory Galatea kiss, with blushing laugh she then poses." This blushing laughter symbolizes the union of sensuality and modesty.

67. One of my first publications was an article on "Ton- und Schriftsprache in Schnitzlers *Fräulein Else* und Schumanns *Carneval*" ["Musical and Literary Language in Schnitzler's *Fräulein Else* and Schumann's *Carneval*"], published in *Modern Austrian Literature*, vol. 2, no. 3 (1969): 17-20. This short article was groundbreaking for Schnitzler research and continues to be favorably cited even today.

68. The symposium took place before it was revealed that de Man had written some 200 right-wing extremist newspaper articles, many of which were anti-Semitic.

69. In this social-critical piece, originally conceived as a *Hörspiel* or radio play, a returnee from the war named Beckmann vainly attempts to resume his life in his home town. He vacillates between hope and nihilism, between life-affirming and life-denying principles. All his efforts come to nothing, and in the end he commits suicide by plunging into the Elbe river and drowning. A differing interpretation has it that

Beckmann has already committed suicide as the story opens and that his life is narrated in a kind of retrospect.

70. Leo Kornbrust's "Europäische Straße des Friedens" (European Street of Peace) is made up of a series of sculptures on display between the Normandy coast and Moscow to make travelers mindful of the causes, forms and consequences of war and violence. L. K. suffered a stroke, so the work is unfinished. He also mourns the death of his wife, Felicitas Frischmuth, a celebrated poetess of Saarland, who passed away in August 2009 in St. Wendel.

71. This last is true only in theory, as I returned to campus in academic 2006-07 to teach, once again, language courses and seminars.

72. Adalbert Stifter: *Bunte Steine [Colored Stones]*. Frankfurt am Main and Hamburg 1960, p. 11.

73. Max Frisch: "Der andorranische Jude" [The Andorran Jew]. In: M. F. *Tagebuch 1946-1949*. Frankfurt am Main: Suhrkamp Verlag 1950, pp. 35-37; here p. 37.

74. Robert Frost: "Two Tramps in Mudtime." In: *The Poetry of Robert Frost. The Collected Poems*. New York: Henry Holt & Co. 1979, p. 277.

75. Max Frisch: *Die chinesische Mauer* [The Chinese Wall]. Frankfurt am Main: Suhrkamp Verlag, edition Suhrkamp 1965, p. 101.

76. Margit Schreiner: *Buch der Enttäuschungen* [Book of Disappointments]. Frankfurt am Main: Schöffling & Co. 2005, p. 11.

77. W[illiam] N[ero] P[ilate] Babellion. Pseudonym for Bruce Frederick Cummings. *The Journal of a Disappointed Man*. With an introduction by H. G. Wells. London: Chatto &Windus, 1931. Entry of December 22, 1912.

Back Matter

This autobiography presents the formation of a native Berliner, who grew up on the north side of the city as a first-degree *Mischling* (half-Jew) and who, upon completion of a waiter's apprenticeship in one of Berlin's best hotels, emigrated to Canada and, eventually, the United States, where he rose to the rank of university professor. This exceptional evolution from spurned *Bauchnabeljude* (belly-button Jew) to respected Professor of German studies, with all its false starts and detours, begins its course in prewar and wartime Berlin, when half-Jews were treated as outsiders, and continues through the desperate postwar period when life, reduced to the black market and foraging for food, became the simple yet horrific matter of survival at any price. The author's experiences in the New World, including life on the Canadian east coast, in Edmonton, Vancouver and the primitive northern Canadian wilderness, are described with deep discernment of human character and generous humor in the book's second part.